United States Relations with Mexico

Context and Content

Edited by Richard D. Erb and Stanley R. Ross

American Enterprise Institute for Public Policy Research
Washington and London

Richard D. Erb is the U.S. executive director at the International Monetary Fund.

Stanley R. Ross is professor of history and coordinator of the Mexico-United States Border Research Program and of the Office for Mexican Studies at the University of Texas at Austin.

ISBN 0–8447–1343–0

Printed in the United States of America

Contributors

CALVIN P. BLAIR is professor of resources and international business at the University of Texas at Austin.

FRANK J. CALL is an economist who has served as Executive Director of the Organization of U.S. Border Cities and Counties.

LEONEL CASTILLO, formerly commissioner of the Immigration and Naturalization Service, has returned to his Houston activities, which include writing a column on immigration matters.

RICHARD D. ERB is the U.S. executive director at the International Monetary Fund. At the time of preparation of this volume he was a resident fellow at the American Enterprise Institute in Washington.

RUDOLPH GOMEZ, formerly Graduate Dean at the University of Texas at El Paso, is professor of political science and Vice President for Administration at the University of Texas at San Antonio.

ROGER D. HANSEN is Jacob Blaustein Professor of International Organization at the School for Advanced International Studies of Johns Hopkins University.

MICHAEL C. MEYER is professor of history and director of the Latin American Area Center at the University of Arizona.

HENRY R. NAU is professor of political science and international affairs at George Washington University.

DAVID S. NORTH is director of the Center for Labor and Migration Studies of the New Transcentury Foundation in Washington, D.C.

REDVERS OPIE is an economic analyst and consultant resident in Mexico City.

CLARK W. REYNOLDS is professor of economics at the Food Research Institute of Stanford University.

STANLEY R. ROSS is professor of history and Coordinator of the Mexico–United States Border Research Program and of the Office for Mexican Studies at the University of Texas at Austin.

LEOPOLDO SOLIS is an economist and subdirector general of the Banco de México.

JOSEPH STALEY, former district director of the Immigration and Naturalization Service in San Antonio, Texas, specialized in immigration law in private legal practice there before his death in 1981.

REUEL A. STALLONES is dean of the School of Public Health at the University of Texas Health Science Center in Houston. LORANN STALLONES, M.P.H., his collaborator, is his daughter.

ALBERT E. UTTON is professor of law, co-director of the National Resources Center, and editor in chief of National Resources Journal at the School of Law of the University of New Mexico.

SIDNEY WEINTRAUB is Dean Rusk Professor at the Lyndon B. Johnson School of Public Affairs of the University of Texas at Austin.

Contents

PART TWO
PROBLEMS AND ISSUES: THE CONTENT

PART THREE
MEXICAN DEVELOPMENT

Preface

In his preinaugural visit with President López Portillo of Mexico, President Ronald Reagan demonstrated his intention to improve and strengthen relations between Mexico and the United States. In this regard, President Reagan is not unlike President Jimmy Carter and other presidents before him. Whether President Reagan will succeed, only time will tell.

As earlier presidents have found—in spite of the best of intentions—President Reagan's task is not an easy one. And as the papers presented in this volume indicate, the social, cultural, religious, political, and economic linkages between Mexico and the United States are too numerous to count. The difficult bilateral policy issues confronting both governments reflect the complex and often amorphous nature of those linkages.

The papers assembled in this volume represent a continuing effort by the American Enterprise Institute to bring to the attention of U.S. policy makers a range of perspectives on the more critical issues concerning U.S.-Mexican relations. Some of the papers are written by scholars, some by present and former government officials, and some by individuals whose daily lives are directly involved in some aspect of U.S.-Mexican relations. Some of the papers are written from a national perspective—others from a regional perspective. Some are focused on the past, others on the present. All of them, however, are informative and interesting.

I wish to acknowledge with gratitude the valuable contributions of my three successive research assistants Allison Golz, Peter Rashish, and Patricia Samors to the preparation of this volume. I must also express my gratitude to Lynne Balthaser and the editors Barbara Palmer, Margaret Seawell, Claire Theune, and Elizabeth Ashooh for their support and assistance.

RICHARD D. ERB

Introduction

Stanley R. Ross

A few years ago the late dedicated and talented Mexican diplomat Ambassador Vicente Sánchez Gavito and I were serving as co-coordinators of a binational border research program. On frequent occasions we would discuss the issues affecting relations between our two nations. I soon discovered that our discussion inevitably began with Vicente spending the first half hour presenting the official Mexican position on the matter. I learned to listen quietly until he had finished. Then I would ask, "Vicente, can we now discuss the issue?" He replied with a grin, "Of course, my friend."

I fear that all too often we never get beyond that first half hour in our relations with our next-door neighbor to the south. In part that may be a reflection of the impatience that tends to characterize my country-men. In part it may be due to a lack of knowledge about or sensitivity to the elements of the context of that relationship that color and con-dition responses to it. Mexican attitudes are strongly influenced by the context of that relationship and reveal a comparable lack of awareness of the elements conditioning U.S. attitudes and the characteristics of the U.S. societal and political structure, which they must comprehend if they are to understand how it functions. Both governments operate within a political and media milieu in which special interests must be weighed and public attitudes may constrain or delimit policy formula-tion. In this regard one of the great problems is the sporadic nature of the attention given the relationship. Because governmental attention and public awareness most frequently represent concern aroused by some issue of confrontation or some crisis, relations too often are con-ducted in a bristling atmosphere of resentment and distrust.

It is the purpose of this volume to look first at some of the con-ditioning elements that contribute to the context within which U.S.–Mexican relations are conducted. Essays detailing these elements compose part one of the volume. The second and largest section of the book is devoted to an examination of particular issues that constitute the substance or content of the bilateral relationship. The issues appear to divide conveniently into those of cooperation and those of disagree-

1

ment and confrontation, although there is some evidence to suggest that an issue does not necessarily and irrevocably remain in one category or the other. Finally, part three consists of several essays analyzing from divergent perspectives the whole question of Mexican development, which many Mexican policy makers and observers in the United States have regarded as the long-term solution that, in turn, might ameliorate some of the problems adversely affecting relations with Mexico's northern neighbor.

The relationship has been determined in the first instance by the geographical circumstances that, as Mexican intellectual Octavio Paz has expressed it, condemned Mexico and the United States to live together forever.[1] While Mexicans have lamented their destiny—so far from God and so close to the United States—modernist writers in Latin America hailed Mexico's divine mission as the buffer protecting spiritual Latin America from materialist, expansionist Anglo America. Granting the geographic reality, however, and adding historic, strategic, economic ties and cultural interactions, it becomes understandable that Mexico and the United States have been described as the "inescapable" or "unavoidable" couple.

The relationship could hardly be categorized as a marriage made in heaven or even one, in contemporary parlance, in which the pair just live together happily. The explanation lies in a relationship that has been colored by history, conditioned by psychology, flavored by intellectual ingredients, hardened by economic ties and economic disparity, and emotionalized by nationalism, power, and security. Furthermore, the divergent cultural and political milieus, structures, and negotiating styles of the two nations, their perceptions of the world and their place in it, the multiple pressures within each society that can affect or even delimit policy are further complicating elements in any effort to achieve a continuing and mutually satisfactory relationship in which the national interests of both parties are respected and reconciled. Those very pressures make the definition and acceptance of national interests difficult, while media sensationalism and exercises by leadership on one side or the other in political demagoguery or expediency tend to arouse emotional responses that complicate the restoration of a relationship that has been described as neglected, mismanaged, and in disarray or, alternatively, the creation of a new and meaningful relationship between equals.

The reality of geography is even more apparent today than in the past. The two nations share the second-longest—slightly over 3,000 kilometers—intercontinental boundary. The border—once remote, undeveloped, and little populated—today is growing in every sense. Though the border divides and separates, it is relatively porous, with considerable movement—both legal and illegal—of peoples and goods, not to mention significant cultural penetration in both directions. Disease and pollution do not respect international dividing lines, and natural resources are not located neatly on one side or the other.

There are both advantages and disadvantages to such proximity. Mexico benefits by its proximity to a major market for its goods and an outlet for its surplus labor supply as well as by the income from tourists, border transactions, and migrant remittances. The proximity also facilitates economic penetration by and economic dependency on the more developed of the neighbors, however. Furthermore, geography has placed Mexico directly within the strategic security zone of the United States, a major world power, and this the Mexicans perceive as a real or potential constraint on their exercise of full sovereignty and freedom of action. Despite their perception of that geopolitical reality, the Mexicans have managed in recent decades to maintain a remarkable degree of independence in their foreign policy both in the hemisphere and in world affairs. The sustaining of that independence is an important internal political consideration within Mexico and one that has been reinforced by augmented bargaining power that has come with the discovery and exploitation of vast new energy resources.

The historical relations between Mexico and the United States have been long and largely painful, beginning with the clash of two frontier societies, colored by imperial, religious, and ethnic overtones, and climaxed with the loss of half of Mexico's national territory through the independence of Texas and the war with the United States in the third and fourth decades of the last century. That experience was a national trauma, leaving an open wound to bloody relations for generations to come. The psychological impact of that defeat and territorial loss should not be underestimated, particularly when added to an earlier conquest and 300 years of domination by the Spaniards.

As Michael C. Meyer demonstrates in his essay, the Mexican War was not the only armed intrusion of Mexican territory. For every actual intervention, there were several instances of threatened intrusions or what were perceived as such by the Mexicans. It was not just a matter of armed force, however; many instances of economic penetration and diplomatic pressure have added to the scars and the resulting bitterness and resentment.

The history has not been all bad. Indeed, there have been some superb U.S. diplomatic representatives, and they have earned the respect and affection of the Mexicans; there have been periods of good feelings and of good relations; there have been spontaneous humanitarian gestures in times of natural disasters; and there has been substantial assistance from both public and private sources as Mexico has

3

sought to develop and progress. There is a human tendency to focus on the unpleasant, however, and this natural inclination toward morbidity and brooding is at times reinforced by seeming opportunities for political advantage or ideological conformity.

The contrast in culture, religion, and ethnicity has been reinforced by ideology, both political and economic. Neither society is exclusively one thing or another, but in Mexico the public sector looms much larger although there is a substantial private sector that results in the economy quite properly being described as a mixed one. In the United States, the increased role of the state has not changed the image and, to a lesser degree, the reality of a dominant private sector and a free-market capitalist economy. The economic divergence is reflected in the political arena where the United States espouses liberal democracy while Mexico does not blanch at the term "socialistic" and espouses responsiveness through a corporate-like structure with much more governmental authority under a dominant one-party arrangement.

The voguishness of Marxism in Mexican intellectual and student circles, as well as in extremist elements in labor and peasant organizations, makes criticism of the United States and its policies and of capitalism and its role almost a constant. More recently, dependency theories have been very popular with resultant critical attention to the economic dependency on the United States and to the role of transnational corporations. This has brought a sense of identity with the underdeveloped Third World nations and even some ambition for a leadership role, though Mexico contrasts with most Third World nations in degree of development and many other respects.

A very strong conditioning influence has been some of the twentieth-century development in Mexico, which is covered in the essay by Roger D. Hansen concerned with the sociopolitical context of U.S.–Mexican relations. Mexico was the first nation to experience a twentieth-century nationalist social revolution. That revolution was strongly nationalistic and aggressively antiforeign, most particularly with regard to the United States. The movement effected an agrarian reform, asserted national control of subsoil resources, and created a labor movement as leverage against a capitalism that was largely foreign and mostly American. The revolution gave Mexicans a sense of national identity and a conviction that Mexican resources should be managed by Mexicans for the benefit of Mexicans. Unfortunately, American interests were identified with the prerevolutionary dictatorship of Porfirio Díaz, and for too long American interests and their government resisted and opposed the Mexican upheaval, which adversely affected American land, mining, and petroleum holdings, not to mention the effect on those who

4

owned Mexican bonds or who sought settlement of claims against the Mexican government.

It is no wonder that friction and confrontation have come whenever the Mexican pendulum has swung to its revolutionary left and that more comfortable relations have accompanied swings to the center and right when Mexico put more emphasis on development economics, as in the decades following the Second World War. The air also was cleared when the United States demonstrated more interest and sympathy for what was occurring in Mexico and found the development of the Mexican Revolution in its later phases as more palatable than alternatives, such as the Cuban Revolution, that appeared in the hemisphere.

There is no question that the contrast between the two economies and the interaction between the two societies loom large in recent times. The disparity between the two economies, one of the most dramatic anywhere between contiguous nations, has grown even greater in recent years despite the progress Mexico has recorded. The effects can be read in the movement of capital southward and the movement of labor northward.

The Mexicans are quick to point to their economic dependency on the United States—easily demonstrable when one looks at trade relations with the northern neighbor, U.S. investments in Mexico, etc.—and on their resulting vulnerability. The issue of dependency has become almost an obsession with the Mexicans, to such an extent that only slowly have they been able to recognize emotionally what they already were aware of intellectually—namely, that appreciable changes occurring in the relationship gradually are making the two nations much more interdependent. The Mexicans tend to downgrade these changes on the grounds that the interdependence is not equal. It does exist, however, and it is growing and with time will condition the responses from both nations.

One of the most difficult things for the Mexicans to appreciate is how the U.S. system operates. They are continually being surprised—although the educated Mexican knows better—that the president does not have the final word on policy determination and may not, because of congressional opposition or a sudden wave of public sentiment, be able to carry out an intended course of action. The Mexicans have a tendency to attribute every American action directly to the president and tend to see even in the most isolated episodes a complicated plot directed against their nation. The Mexican executive is in a much stronger position both in the formulation of policy and in its implementation, although he too must take into account public reaction and the reaction of elements on the far left and the far right. It is generally recognized that, with the Vietnam war and with the debacle of the Nixon administration, the executive in the United States has been weakened appreciably.

The existence of special interest groups that exert pressure on the process of formulating policy on specific issues is another reality. The democratic process facilitates such pressure, but the end result is that it is difficult to define national interests as a basis for determining national policies. Two essays in Part 1, those by Rudolph Gomez and Leonel Castillo, focus attention on interest groups—such as ranchers and other employers of migrant labor, organized labor, and the Mexican-American groupings—affecting our policy vis-à-vis Mexico. Perhaps the most interesting is that represented by Mexican-American organizations.

As with all interest groups it is difficult to tell whether the leadership is speaking for itself or for the rank and file that the organized group is supposed to represent. In the case of some of the Mexican-American groups, there have been 180-degree changes in position, shifts that have tended to reflect more the interests of the organizations and their leaders than those of the bulk of the Mexican-American population. Whereas Mexican political leaders beginning in the 1970s established contact with Chicano leaders primarily for internal political purposes and the Chicanos sought visibility and backing from the Mexican leadership, it is conceivable that in the future Mexico will find those of Mexican origin in the United States a helpful influence on the Mexican policy of the U.S. government. Pedro Ojeda Paullada, Mexican secretary of labor, described the Mexican government as "having always been interested in the fate of our fellow nationals and their Mexican-American descendants" and urged that, in order to have permanent contacts and to undertake specific actions, an operative mechanism is needed that stresses working together in the social and cultural areas "in order to better understand each other."[2] Several Chicano scholars, Caesar Sereseres and Arturo Gándara, for example,[3] have argued that politics in the United States, and most particularly presidential politics, will assure the presence and importance of the Chicano factor in U.S.–Mexican relations. There is evidence accumulating to support that contention.

The natural growth of the population of Mexican origin with a higher fecundity than either blacks or whites is augmented by a post-1970 wave of immigrants, both legal and illegal. Mexican-American leaders sensing increased political and economic clout arising from increased numbers talk of the decade of the 1980s as the decade of the Hispanic. Some express concern about Anglo backlash, and there are evidences of outcroppings as Anglo elements become concerned about their traditional socioeconomic and political hegemony. Professor Wayne Cornelius has stressed that nativist anti-immigration sentiment, which is not new in this country, traditionally has accompanied periods of depression and high unemployment. Looking ahead at this time, he sees new elements attributable to spiraling inflation, concerns about resource limitations, and conservative backlash against welfare spending.[4]

Not unrelated has been the suit instituted by the Federation for American Immigration Reform (FAIR) to block the Census Bureau from counting illegals in the national census in 1980 because that count will be translated into legislative reapportionment and the allocations of revenue-sharing funds. In Texas the courts have been asked to decide the legality of requiring the children of illegals to pay tuition in the public schools and have responded that the districts must educate the children of the illegal aliens without special charges. That decision is being appealed. Perhaps symptomatic of nativist sentiment or perhaps only an extreme example is a letter to the editor of an Austin newspaper in which the author complained that she was "darned sick of hearing the term 'barrio' related to Austin neighborhoods. This is America. This is Texas. This is Austin. We have neighborhoods and communities, not 'barrios.' If there are persons who feel they must live in a 'barrio' to be comfortable, they know where to go—south of the border. . . . 'Barrio'-ism is not only stupid, it is unpatriotic."[5] It should be added that the letter provoked a number of critical responses from both Mexican-American and Anglo readers.

It was a fortunate combination of concern for civil rights and presidential election-year politics when Attorney General Benjamin Civiletti, in response to pressure from Chicano groups in California, directed the Immigration and Naturalization Service (INS) to halt residential "sweep" operations except in unusual circumstances. Qualifying as specifically exempted were instances where smuggling operations are centered in a residence and a government attorney has reviewed the service's basis for assuming that.[6] Responsiveness to the political clout of the Chicano voters was translated into the designation of Leonel Castillo as commissioner of the Immigration and Naturalization Service and the proposed designation of Matt García as his successor during the Carter Administration. Even more dramatic evidence was the nomination and appointment of Julian Nava as Patrick Lucey's successor as ambassador to Mexico. The latter appointment had greater significance because at the time of the Lucey appointment the State Department had opposed the appointment of a Chicano to this post, it being felt that the Mexicans would view such an appointment as aimed at a domestic political situation and that there might be conflict of interest on bilateral issues that involve or affect the Mexican-American population. In less than four years the attitude had changed, partly in response to a presidential election year and partly because of the attractiveness of Professor Nava who, a product of a poor environment, earned an education at Harvard, holds a doctorate in Latin American history, and speaks Spanish. The Mexicans found the new ambassador very simpatico, but did regard his appointment as a product of domestic politics.

The new ambassador soon discovered that there are a number of problems standing in the way of better relations between the two countries. These difficulties become clearer in the reading of the essay by Sidney Weintraub on organizing the U.S.-Mexican relationship and that by Frank J. Call on problems of cooperation at the local level. It is quickly apparent that, while the United States has been preoccupied with developing global policies to meet global responsibilities, developing Mexico has tended to concentrate on regional and hemispheric interests, excepting, of course, the Third Worldism of President Echeverría in the first half of the 1970s. Furthermore, there are the competing negotiating styles, to which Weintraub refers at the outset of his essay, including the American tendency toward a more compartmentalized approach to issues contrasted with the Mexican tendency to join a whole series of issues into an overall, integrated policy.

One of the complicating aspects is that there are so many points of contact between the two countries: individuals, organizations, border cities, border universities, and border states, to mention just a few. Equally important is the division between federal and local initiative. Governor William D. Clements of Texas commendably meets with his four Mexican counterparts from the border states and talks of the key issues that need to be resolved by the states that are most affected by them. Governor Jerry Brown of California talks of his state providing capital for Mexican development—which the Mexicans neither need nor want—in exchange for meeting the energy needs of California. Borderlands scholar Ellwyn Stoddard argues that borderlands relations ought to be left, to the maximum extent possible, to the local people and institutions.

This kind of argument is appealing but unrealistic. Though these are two federal systems, both—and most particularly the Mexican—are highly centralized. The major issues will be ameliorated or resolved—if they are to be dealt with at all—at the national level.[7] Once policy has been determined in such areas as health or law enforcement, local cooperation is essential and should be encouraged. Indeed, local input in policy determination before the fact also is highly desirable, indeed essential, if such policy is both to have some connection with reality and to enjoy any degree of local support.

On the national level there are too many facets and too many interacting surfaces. Today we have so many departments, consultative mechanisms, and other bodies talking and negotiating with the Mexicans that often no one knows fully what is happening. There is genuine need for coordination, but coordination should not mean multiplication of levels that can only bemuse, confuse, and upset the other side. The creation of the position of coordinator of Mexican affairs to which former Texas congressman Bob Krueger was appointed was intended to respond to the need for internal coordination within the U.S. government of Mexican relations as well as to be a gesture to the Mexicans of the importance with which relations with that country are viewed. These laudable aims were obscured by the ambassadorial title assigned to Mr. Krueger and his assumption of an external role, leading to confusion and the Mexican jest that "two ambassadors are less than one." The original need—the development of a recognizable and consistent Mexican policy—remains to be achieved as a new administration assumes responsibility for the nation's foreign relations.

In 1979 Presidents Carter and López Portillo, in an effort to remedy the drift, if not the decay, of the bilateral relationship, created a new consultative mechanism composed of seven working groups on such issues as trade, finance, energy, border cooperation, immigration, tourism, industry, and legal affairs. The arrangement, coordinated by Ambassador Krueger on the U.S. side, has brought together concerned experts in each area who have established personal contact and had an opportunity for an exchange of views. The working groups are intended to provide background papers for policy discussions at the highest level. The question that remains is whether one can be translated into the other. If not, the arrangement will be merely another in a series of interfaces that are complicating the relationship. As one high Mexican foreign relations official complained, the relationship is being conducted in so many different ways that neither the Department of State nor the secretary of foreign relations can control the process. He contended that both were forced to assume the role of putting out brush fires wherever they might erupt.

It is to be feared that the differing organizational and negotiating styles of the two governments seem better suited to preserving the status quo on specific issues than to managing a complex relationship of interdependence. A complicating conditioning element, which unfortunately has been little studied or even considered in regard to Mexican–U.S. relations, is the communications media. It was our hope to have a suggestive pilot essay on the role of the media for this volume. Although our commissioned essayist disappointed us, it may be useful to summarize the projected study. Though time and resources precluded an exhaustive study of the role of the press, radio, and television or even study in depth of one medium, it was felt that examining the coverage of the press and periodical literature in both countries of three marker events would be illuminating. Initially selected were the following events: the Carter visit to López Portillo in February 1979, the Mexican executive's return visit in August, and the Ixtoc I spill in the Bay of Campeche. Interestingly enough, our researcher soon discovered that the Washington visit was essentially a "nonevent" as far as the U.S. press was concerned. The absence of any substantive results, with even the matter of an agreement on gas pricing announced the week before the presidents met, and other seemingly more newsworthy distractions resulted in minimal coverage. Consequently, it was decided to substitute an analysis of the press coverage of the "tortilla curtain," the proposal to replace twelve miles of fence along two sections of the border in place of the Washington visit

The media, despite their potential to produce an informed and interested public opinion, by their tendency to emphasize the confrontation, the sensational, and the catastrophic, by their frequent failure to provide perspective and appreciation of the other nation's perception of the issue despite claims of reporting in depth, and by their lack of sustained coverage, contribute to inadequately informed, emotionally aroused public opinion, which encourages demagoguery and handicaps the rational development of mutually advantageous policies. There is a real need for serious study of the communications media's role in molding popular perceptions of the questions at issue between the two nations, of the people and government of the neighboring country, and of the policy that nation is pursuing.

Part two of the volume is devoted to an examination of the specific problems and issues involved in and affecting the relations between the two nations. One characteristic of the issues is that they are not static but rather changing and evolving. As circumstances change with the resulting shift of national interests, one notes shifts in national priorities and in the national attention given to a particular issue. In 1976, for example, a group of scholars from both countries came together to discuss themes for binational research priorities. The Mexicans at that time indicated that because the border region was better endowed in regard to health than the rest of Mexico, excepting the Federal District, they could not contemplate devoting additional human and financial resources to that area. On the U.S. side there was no question that the health situation of the poverty-stricken border region and its population would be a priority item. In a few short years the demographic explosion in the border region, with some of the urban centers showing annual growth rates as high as 12 percent, brought a shift of Mexican priorities as Mexican officials recognized that now their national interest required further attention to the health problems of their border region. Similarly, Mexico was persuaded, not merely by U.S. pressure but by the growing evidence that it too had a national drug problem, to undertake a cooperative effort with the United States to try to stop the production of and traffic in drugs.

Turning to the specific issues or problems, we find—as noted earlier—that these divide into issues of cooperation and issues of difference or confrontation. In the latter category, one might make a further division among those issues of difference or confrontation today and those that may be expected to be sources of difficulty in the future, say, within the final two decades of the century. Remembering the experience with the health issue, one may assume that categories do not have an absolute character but rather will shift depending on the circumstances at a given time and depending on the resulting perceptions of national interests.

Among the areas of cooperation there should be listed boundaries, health, environment, and crime, including drugs and other contraband. The two nations have found it in their respective national interests to reach agreements on resource zones, particularly as these apply to shellfish banks, airline routes, and communications channels and broadcast rights. The binational International Boundary and Water Commission is one of the most effective examples of bilateral cooperation one could find anywhere. I suspect that part of its extraordinary success has been the fact that the commission has the responsibility for the technical implementation of decisions taken elsewhere—principally in the political arena. This is not to minimize both the technical competence and the impressive record this body has achieved. It suggests that, once issues are removed from the political arena with its pressures by special interests and extremist elements, and with the tendency to score points by appeal to the gallery, there is both the will and the competence to carry out cooperative ventures.

The record of the commission has been so impressive that recently there have been moves to expand the area of its responsibility. Most significantly, the commission has been directed to concern itself with the pollution of the waters shared by the two countries. For a long time the two nations floundered in this area because of the basic conflict between the goals of the developed and the developing nations. As one source put it, the developed nations can afford the luxury of concern about contamination of the environment. The developing nation is concerned with what it views as its survival—development at any cost. Fortunately, Mexico has shown a trend in the past decade to be concerned about both its development and the conservation of its resources.

It has adopted one of the strongest environmental protection measures and has been actively cooperating with its northern neighbor in the Ciudad Juárez–El Paso airshed.

Oil spills threaten beaches and fishing zones without discrimination. After some particularly maladroit diplomacy regarding the spill from Ixtoc I, the two nations appear to be on their way to designing effective means for coping with future spills. The issue of responsibility and accountability is much more sensitive but also needs attention if it is not to become an issue of confrontation. Waste water as a contaminant source is increasingly a matter of concern as population grows all along the border and particularly on the Mexican side. Antiquated sewage systems resulting in contamination like that in the New River in Southern California and inadequate processing capacity are potential health hazards threatening the population in both countries. These problems will require bilateral cooperation and a readiness on the part of the United States to carry more than its share of the burden in its own interest.

With the dramatic change in Mexico's sense of priorities regarding health care in her northern border region, there has been a flurry of cooperation in this area that is truly impressive. The effort has been a joint one of international bodies such as the Pan American Health Organization (PAHO), the national health coordinating agencies in both Mexico and the United States, the state departments of health and the schools of public health in the border states, and local health delivery agencies. What has been true in regard to physical health also is true of cooperation in the field of mental health, including alcoholism and drug abuse. Here is an excellent example of how, once national policy is established, there is ample opportunity for state and local entities to play a role in cooperative binational undertakings. There are two selections detailing cooperation in the health area, one by Reuel A. and Lorann Stallones and the other a Health, Education, and Welfare Department (HEW) report excerpted for this volume. The report grew out of the surgeon general's conviction, in mid-1978, that there was an urgent need to confront the growing health problem along the border. Accordingly, he recommended to the secretary of HEW that there be developed a U.S.–Mexican border health initiative and that the resources of the department be mobilized behind it.

In the physical health field, the department's document was circulated among federal, state, and local health agencies on both sides of the border. Taking into account the substantial constructive and cooperative responses, the problem areas were consolidated into eleven program areas grouped into four main clusters. Working groups have been organized with the participation of experts in each field from both sides of the border and from PAHO. The programs are as follows:

immunization activities; treatment of tuberculosis; emergency services for accident victims; fluoride programs; maternal and child care; occupational health, planning, and evaluation; use and comparability of officially collected statistics; economic analysis of the border, focusing on current utilization of existing health resources; epidemiological surveillance programs; and the development and/or exchange of Spanish-language health education materials.

A reference to a few of the program statements should be illustrative of the nature and the spirit of the enterprise. The immunization program is directed to reduce disease preventable through vaccination, improve immunization services and records, ensure an adequate supply of vaccines, and, if needed, improve the availability of immunization services. To improve significantly the emergency services for accident victims, it is proposed to plan and implement an emergency medical service with all essential components soundly integrated. Regarding the fluoride programs, a collaborative effort was recommended to increase the population served by fluoridated water along the 3,100-kilometer border, to be initiated in 1979, the International Year of the Child.

Concern for health is not easily transmuted into transcendent policy; the hazards are often occult and the problems so diverse that they do not yield easily to generalized solutions. Thus, policy is likely to represent the summation of specific program activities, the result of actions rather than their determinant.

One could cite other cooperative efforts to control plant and animal diseases, from the binational campaign against *aftosa* (hoof-and-mouth disease) to the more recent efforts to control equine encephalitis and the fruit fly and screwworm infestations. Cooperation turns up as well for localized specific problems, such as the effort to control the outbreak of rabies in several border towns.

For the present discussion I will limit myself to one further example of cooperation—that related to crime and contraband, especially drugs. There are a whole range of problems and issues related to law enforcement affecting Mexican–U.S. relations. Major attention has been given to those arising out of the movement of peoples and the enforcement of immigration law. That topic, however, is being reserved for the following discussion of confrontation. There also has been considerable publicity attendant on the famous prisoner-exchange treaty and its subsequent implementation. The Mexicans were never happy with the arrangement, having yielded to U.S. pressure and embarrassing publicity regarding Mexican detention institutions and having viewed the pressure for such an agreement as one more example of American inconsistency, as most of the offenders were in prison on narcotics charges and the United States had pressured Mexico into a campaign against drug pro-

13

duction and trafficking. The Mexicans now are threatening not to renew the agreement unless a legal decision that they regard as inconsistent with the spirit and letter of the treaty is reversed on appeal.

Any international border creates conditions that are conducive to crimes because the proximity of sanctuary in the other country affords the possibility of the criminal's escaping detection or prosecution. The growth of population and the tremendous movement of people at the border are further compounding factors. As the late Joseph Staley reported in his review of border law enforcement, there are problems related to general crime, juvenile delinquency, drug traffic, arms smuggling, automobile theft, and contraband in addition to those related to illegal migration. To varying degrees these problems affect both nations and have evoked national responses varying in intensity. Drug production and trafficking in Mexico for shipment to the United States has been and continues to be a substantial problem. The drug culture of the 1960s and the 1972 severance of the "French connection" brought the "Mexican connection" to full flower. Amphetamines, marijuana, and Mexican "brown" heroin flowed across the border in response to a large and profitable market. Finally, in response to inordinate pressure applied by the United States and recognition both that Mexico too was experiencing a growing drug problem and that there was a link between some of the drug traffic and arms for rebel groups, the Mexican government energetically responded beginning in 1976 with a campaign called Operation Condor that involved the locating and spraying of marijuana pastures and opium fields and the seizure of drugs in transit. The success of these efforts, combined with a preference for Colombian "gold," led to Colombia's supplanting Mexico as the major supplier for the American drug market. Drug smuggling from Mexico remains a problem of important dimensions. It is estimated that in 1979 half of the illegal heroin entering the United States did so through Mexico. Even some of the Colombian drug production finds its transit through Mexico en route to the United States.[8]

Smuggling is a lucrative business whether the contraband is drugs, pre-Colombian artifacts, and parrots into the United States or stolen vehicles and electronic items into Mexico. Clearly here is a problem that cuts both ways. The principal difficulty is that where the export of an item is not illegal, as in the case of tropical birds from Mexico or electronic equipment from the United States, responsiveness to the other nation's law enforcement problems is difficult. In the area of law enforcement there is evidence of cooperation and progress but also of the persistence of problem areas. Clearly there is need for better communication and improvement of law enforcement cooperation effected on an equal-partner basis. The problems must be dealt with through mutual efforts.

The essays in this collection have focused on a number of present or prospective issues of difference or confrontation. In some instances, two studies of a problem have been included to provide more than one perspective: migration (Weintraub and Ross and David S. North) and trade (Clark W. Reynolds and Weintraub). In other instances, a single essay provides an understanding of the problem: energy (Henry R. Nau), and water (Albert E. Utton).

One must begin with migration because, regardless of the problem or issue one may be discussing, this source of difficulty inevitably arises. Furthermore, of all the current issues of difference or confrontation, this writer believes that it is the one most likely to persist because it is an intractable problem if not an insoluble one. Mexican migration to the United States is not a new phenomenon, but it has grown steadily in recent years, most particularly in the past decade, and shows no sign of abatement.

Despite increasing bilateral awareness of the problem, it is shocking how little solid information we actually have about this issue. We do not even know how many undocumented workers are here or how many are entering each year. We do know that the number detained has risen sharply, suggestive of a rapidly increasing flow even if one makes allowance for multiple detentions. Even knowledge that has been taken for granted, such as evidence of the length of stay of such migrants, is subject to reexamination as there is growing evidence that the traditional sources of migration in Mexico are giving way to new sources, especially urban, and that the patterns of stay similarly are showing changes. Estimates vary widely, but it is generally assumed that there are presently at least 6 million illegals in the country, 60 percent of whom are Mexican. That number is growing at an estimated half to three quarters of a million a year.

It is generally accepted that Mexico's burgeoning population and the inability of the Mexican economy to absorb that population, resulting in high unemployment and underemployment, are push factors and that the disparity between the Mexican economy and that of its northern neighbor provides the pull. Those who prefer to place the blame north of the dividing line stress that the push in part results from the kind of development that U.S. interests have encouraged and assisted and that the pull consists of job inducements offered by employers who are eager to obtain low-cost, tractable labor. A most debated aspect is the impact of this labor force on the American society. There are those who argue that the migrants take jobs that no one else wants and that they contribute more in taxes than they take out in services. The latter is undoubtedly true, because only emergency hospital services and the schools experience significant use by illegals. This view ignores the impact on the secondary labor market, however, the element of our society least able to defend itself. It also adversely affects unionization to have a large, tractable work force available, lowering wages and conditions of labor and ready to serve as strikebreakers.

There are strong social and humanitarian grounds for doing something about this problem. Secretary of Labor F. Ray Marshall added another consideration when he cautioned,

> I believe that the existence of an underclass of undocumented workers represents a serious civil liberties problem. No democracy can flourish with an underclass outside of its basic laws. If history is any guide, perhaps the first generation of undocumented workers will endure their privations in relative silence. But you can rest assured that the children of these undocumented workers will be the focus of a civil rights movement in the 1980s.[9]

The illegal status of the undocumented workers makes them particularly vulnerable to exploitation—by the *coyote* who arranges for their entry into the United States; by their employers, be they ranchers, restaurant owners, construction bosses, or factory owners; by the juvenile delinquents who attack them with impunity; by the Chicano host population that provides them with housing or other services; or by law enforcement authorities. This is not to condemn everyone in any of these categories but simply to identify the categories in which there is evidence of some who take advantage of the undocumented workers' illegal status. Humanitarian grounds alone would justify an effort to regularize the flow in the interest of both nations because the Mexicans always have been sensitive to the treatment their nationals receive in this country.

There are other persuasive reasons for seeking a way out of this dilemma. Whereas Mexico's population growth rate is reportedly declining—the most recent government figures show it below 3 percent—its population is still growing. With almost half of its population fourteen years of age and under, Mexico needs to create 800,000 new jobs annually to accommodate those entering the labor force—and by the end of this decade that requirement will have risen to a million new jobs annually. Mexico has yet to demonstrate an ability to create that number of jobs for new workers, let alone reduce its 40 to 45 percent unemployment and underemployment. Thus, the number of Mexicans seeking work in the United States will not abate but rather will increase in the foreseeable future.

16

On the Mexican side, this human movement represents a safety valve against social discontent and political disaffection. A major Mexican newspaper has estimated that one quarter of Mexico's work force is laboring in the United States and that migrant remittances exceed the income from tourism. These claims may be exaggerated, but a figure of one-fifth or one-sixth would still be impressive. Certainly any sharp curtailment of this human flow could create an explosive situation in Mexico. Some advocates of a more restrictive immigration policy point out that the existence of this safety valve puts off the necessity of Mexico's facing the tragic inequalities in its society. Continued stability in Mexico is in the national interests of the United States, however, and this country could ill afford to contribute to the destabilization of its neighbor.

Mexico's foreign trade is heavily oriented toward the United States with more than 60 percent of its imports and exports coming from and going to its northern neighbor. Mexico is the leading U.S. trading partner in Latin America and places fifth in this country's global trade. Though Mexico represented only 5 percent of U.S. exports in 1978 and provided only 4 percent of this nation's imports, it is one of the countries with which the United States has enjoyed perennially a favorable balance of trade.

Mexico has been concerned with its heavy trade dependence on the United States and what it regards as its resulting vulnerability. There have been strenuous efforts at diversification of trading partners, especially in the early 1970s, but the results have been disappointing, and Mexico entered the late 1970s even more dependent economically and financially on the United States. It is likely that Mexican–U.S. trade in both directions will continue to grow even more rapidly in the future as Mexican petroleum exports make possible increased exports within a favorable balance and without excessive increases in the external debt. It is also predictable that Mexico will be seeking a market for more and more sophisticated high-technology goods.

As Reynolds and Weintraub, our two essayists on the topic of trade, show, Mexican–U.S. trade already is growing significantly, jumping 34 percent, from 9.5 billion to 12.7 billion, between 1977 and 1978. Furthermore, with the United States granting special trade preferences to less developed countries as a class and Mexico being accorded most-favored-nation treatment, the average U.S. duty on Mexican goods has fallen from 12 percent to 6 percent and is expected to decline still further. More than a thousand Mexican products benefit under the U.S. version of the Generalized System of Preferences with $370 million in Mexican goods entering the United States in 1978. An additional $1.5 billion entered under the special sections of the U.S. tariff schedule whereby manufactured goods finished abroad pay duty only on the value added.

Under the circumstances, one might not anticipate that trade would be an issue between the two nations. Despite the impressive figures cited above, Mexican officials complain about U.S. protectionism—even blaming it for Mexico's unfavorable balance of trade—and call for greater access to the U.S. market. Why? Though U.S. tariffs have declined, they are higher on finished than on intermediate goods. They have been significant in limiting Mexican textiles and apparel. They also are potentially important in limiting Mexican exports of tomatoes and other winter vegetables, although there is no present quantitative limit. The Mexicans have had to contend with complicated government regulations on marketing, costly border-crossing arrangements, and an antidumping petition by Florida growers. Despite these obstacles, Mexico's trade in these products has grown significantly, and the raising of tomatoes has ceased in some areas of the United States, including South Texas.

The Mexicans have seen the antidumping campaign; they have seen farmers man Texas bridges to block shipments of Mexican produce; they have seen quotas on ladies' shoes reduced to protect domestic industry; and they realize that there will be more resistance—as labor joins manufacturers—as Mexico produces more sophisticated manufactured goods. So, although the current situation is remarkably favorable—in fact, Mexico is enjoying the preference situation while not being a member of the General Agreement on Tariffs and Trade (GATT)—the Mexicans are concerned about the future. The matter of whether or not to join GATT became the subject of national debate, with strong vocal opposition from a coalition of the left concerned with increased dependency on the United States and of businessmen on the right fearing the loss of protective walls behind which they have flourished for years.

Obviously energy looms increasingly large in Mexico's foreign trade figures and promises to reverse its unfavorable balance of trade and to make its external debt appear less overwhelming and more manageable. It should not have been surprising that the Mexicans would evidence distrust of the suddenly increased interest of the United States in its neighbor with the discovery of huge proven deposits and massive potential reserves of oil and natural gas. Obviously the United States needs oil and the Mexicans have oil, but there has not developed and there is not a strong likelihood of there developing an energy market between the two nations. The explanation lies in history, dependency, and conflict of national interests.

Mexico's perception of its historical relations with the United States is laced with resentment. In the twentieth century, Mexico experienced the first nationalist social revolution that was strongly xenophobic. If

18

the revolution was nationalistic, petroleum policy is particularly sensitive from the nationalist point of view. The expropriation of foreign petroleum holdings in 1938 is viewed as the nation's declaration of economic independence and is celebrated as a national holiday on March 18. Almost obsessively conscious of its economic dependence on the United States, Mexico is concerned that the development of an energy market with the United States would mean increased dependency on its powerful northern neighbor. Finally, Mexican officials frequently have declared that it is not in Mexico's interests to expand production to meet excessive U.S. consumption demands; rather, energy resources are to be exploited at a pace that will permit the conversion of a nonreplaceable resource to a more permanent and solid development. Thoughtful Mexicans are concerned as well about producing petropesos faster than their economy can absorb them. As Mexico moved into 1980 and in response to continued high trade imbalances and the need to increase food importations, the Mexican government announced its goal of doubling production by the end of the current presidential term in 1982.

Dr. Luigi Einaudi of the State Department has pointed out that, whereas the United States regards Mexico's petroleum potential as an energy issue, Mexico views its oil and gas reserves as a matter of national development. He does not foresee Mexico's energy resources as a solution either to the declining hydrocarbon resources in the United States or to the dilemma of substantial energy imports at high prices. On the other hand, it is likely that as Mexico expands its own production the United States will receive an increased amount of Mexican oil and natural gas even if its share of the total produced and exported declines, as appears likely. Dr. Einaudi does not anticipate energy as a likely basic point of contention between the two countries in the long run.[10]

Two energy episodes have attracted considerable attention—the matter of a gas agreement and the oil spill from Ixtoc I in the Bay of Campeche. Both are examples par excellence of diplomatic maladroitness on the part of the United States. Though both sides could make a case for their respective positions on natural gas pricing, President López Portillo was furious to be caught short by Energy Secretary Schlesinger's veto of the agreement the Mexican president thought he had. American negotiators had warned their Mexican counterparts that there were unacceptable elements in the agreement. Whether those warnings were not taken seriously or not communicated to top officials is not known, but the Mexican president felt that he had been placed in an impossible position. He had arranged for the construction of a pipeline from the Reforma Trend field to Matamoros but ordered that it be diverted when the agreement was rejected by the U.S. government. The Mexican president had ordered construction over leftist opposition that raised such anti-Yankee shibboleths as increased dependency, U.S. pressure on Mexican production, and finally, the threat of armed intervention to protect and maintain the flow of precious energy requirements. During 1979, agreement finally was reached on the pricing of natural gas with the quantity, at least initially, considerably less than earlier discussed and the price considerably higher, although less than what Mexico asked.

In the case of Ixtoc I, whose sticky flow was not to be stopped until the spring of 1980, the publicity given the U.S. diplomatic note demanding compensation for damages resulting from the spill before Mexico had a chance to consider and respond to it was inexcusable. The Mexicans denied liability under international law and rejected compensation demands. They even added unkind references to the salinity-damaged Mexicali Valley. When this writer discussed the problem with an official of the Mexican foreign office, he agreed with my view that nations, like individuals and corporations, must be responsible and accountable for the consequences of their actions. After all, I noted, if a U.S. satellite had crashed in Mexico and caused property damage or injury or loss of life to Mexican nationals, the Mexican government would have been screaming for indemnification. My friend remarked, "You are right, but when are your people going to learn how to conduct diplomacy?" The two nations apparently have been making progress on an agreement for joint action to deal with future spills. The more sensitive issue of accountability needs to be addressed in an atmosphere uncomplicated by some new spill or other source of environmental damage.

The border, with its invisible extension into the sea as far as the two nations claim resource control, offers another complex situation and a source of future difficulties in energy-related matters. Preliminary efforts are under way to achieve a protocol on the joint use of oil, natural gas, and thermal water deposits that transcend the international boundary. It should be fairly easy to reach an agreement on offshore binational exploitation because in that area the two federal governments exercise jurisdiction. Inland, however, is another story, with state jurisdictions and individual rights on the U.S. side making agreement and control of exploitation both difficult and problematic. The difficulty may be upon us sooner than we expect because there is increased interest in the energy potential of thermal waters, and elevated prices and new technology—gaseous explosive fracturing—make possible the exploitation of the so-called Austin Chalk formation, which previously has not been economical to work.

Of all the issues likely to cause future differences and confrontation between the two nations, water, right after migration, looms as the most probable source of friction in the next decade. Whether one talks about population growth, irrigated agriculture, or industrial development, more water will be required. Population and economic growth, as Albert Utton notes in his essay, are catalytic forces that can be expected to raise significant water issues affecting Mexican–U.S. relations. On the U.S. side there have been the Sunbelt growth and plans to develop the border region so as to improve conditions for one of the poorest sections of our nation. On the Mexican side there has been a population growth much more rapid than in the country as a whole. In addition, as one essayist stresses, substantial energy resources have been discovered in the Colorado River basin, and their exploitation will place substantial demands on water resources there.

As Professor Utton details, most of the quantitative issues of sharing the water have been resolved with the sole potential source of difficulty being the proviso affecting both the Colorado and Rio Grande agreements whereby, in the event of drought or serious accident, the United States could reduce proportionately the quantity of water supplied to Mexico. In such an eventuality, there are certain to be differences and difficulties, particularly in the light of the vagueness of the language of the proviso. Even more irritating has been the issue of quality and, most specifically, the whole question of the salinity of the Colorado waters delivered to Mexico.

Although the United States has been delivering water of appropriate quality since 1974, there remains the irritant of the previously damaged lands in the Mexicali Valley and the future need for the reverse osmosis desalinization plant at Yuma awaiting congressional authorization of the requisite funding. Under the 1973 agreement, the United States agreed to support Mexican efforts to obtain appropriate financing on favorable terms for the improvement and rehabilitation of the affected area. Mexico has not come forth with the amount needed but rather complains that the United States has not provided compensation for the damages done. The United States also is committed to build the desalinization plant, but the Congress has not seen fit to act on the expensive project.

The use of groundwater is complicated and is potentially a very dangerous issue. Though the border states of the American Southwest are the heaviest users of groundwater in the country, neither their laws nor their institutions are adequate to control and protect their groundwater resources. Only one state has a public control system. Elsewhere there are few constraints to discourage excessive pumping and waste. In the El Paso–Ciudad Juárez area the aquifer is being exploited at twenty times the natural rate of replacement. In Mexico the federal government does have legal authority to control groundwater withdrawals, but there is no similar authority on the U.S. side, and international competence over aquifers that transcend a frontier is largely undefined. One cannot help but agree with Professor Utton that the combination of a near legal vacuum and projected further population increases on both sides of the border will mean accelerating demand on groundwater resources and likely confrontation between the two countries.

Since finance is more a sensitive matter than an issue between the two countries it is not treated separately in this volume. With the substantial increase in U.S. private investment to a total doubling prerevolutionary American investment and with an external debt close to $30 billion by the end of the 1970s, the sensitivity is intensified. The Mexicans have preferred financing through international agencies rather than from private sources or from another government. With the substantiation of extensive energy resources, Mexico will not lack for capital or for the basis on which to negotiate for such international financing as may be required by its development needs.

Two episodes underscore the sensitivity of the finance issue. When, in 1976, Mexico found itself in the midst of a severe economic crisis, the United States came through with an interim loan until international financing could be arranged. Mexican officials remarked on the responsiveness of both American officials and American bankers. When international financial institutions imposed austerity conditions on Mexico that included the first devaluation of the peso in twenty-two years, however, the popular media placed the blame on the United States. More recently, when the Export-Import Bank, bending to pressure in the Congress, delayed a loan for the *gasoducto* being constructed to carry gas to the border, Mexico sought and obtained substitute financing in Great Britain.

The energy boom in Mexico has freed the Mexicans from dependence on anyone as far as capital for development is concerned. Mexico should have no trouble reaching its production goal of 2.25 million barrels per day of crude oil with 1.5 million available for export in 1980. It also should have no difficulty in doubling these quantities by the end of López Portillo's term late in 1982. The resulting export earnings should greatly reduce any foreign exchange constraints on development and augment Mexico's capacity for servicing its foreign debt. As President López Portillo has noted, "For the first time in our history, we shall have the opportunity to enjoy financial self-determination."[11] What Mexico will or should do with its newfound oil wealth is the object of public debate and public pronouncements.

Economic development is not new in Mexico. In fact, Mexico's overall economic development has been impressive over the past half century. During the 1950s, gross domestic product per capita increased at an annual average rate of 2.5 percent. This growth rate increased during the 1960s to more than 3 percent a year, a most impressive accomplishment in view of the population growth rate of close to 3.5 percent. Total growth in domestic product, therefore, averaged better than 6.5 percent during that decade. The growth rate slowed to about 1 percent per capita in the 1970s, although since 1977 earlier growth rates have been restored. This is an accomplishment of overall growth achieved by few countries over such a protracted period at any time since recorded figures have been kept.

There is a dark side to this achievement, however. The fruits of this growth have been very unequally distributed. Close to half the Mexican population is either unemployed or works at jobs that occupy only part of a worker's time. Poverty is extensive in those rural areas of Mexico where population concentrations number less than 2,500. The distribution of irrigation services has benefited mainly the wealthiest group of farmers. Illiteracy is much more serious in rural than in urban areas. Health facilities are inadequate in rural areas. In 1977, the 10 percent of Mexican families with highest incomes received 38 percent of total income, whereas those in the bottom 10 percent received 1 percent. The 40 percent of families with the lowest income received only 11 percent of total income in 1977. It is this disparity between overall accomplishment and distributional failure that underlies concern about the end results of the new period of development that Mexico is entering.

In 1979 Mexico initiated a National Plan for Industrial Development that projects the country's course not only through the end of López Portillo's term in 1982 but also through the end of the decade. Mexico is faced with a complicated problem and the avowed desire to avoid some of the experiences of other developing nations that suddenly found themselves oil rich. It must manage the production and sale of its energy resources so as to promote rapid development and yet avoid flagrant waste, corruption, and strong inflationary pressures. It must balance the growth of capital-intensive activities as it broadens the infrastructure of its economy with the need to create additional jobs; industrial growth must be accompanied by rural development.

The final section of this volume is devoted to an examination of Mexican development from three differing perspectives. Offering their perceptions of what Mexican development is or ought to be are a Keynesian state interventionist economist (Calvin P. Blair); a free-market economist resident in Mexico (Redvers Opie); and a distinguished Mexican economist who is an advocate of integral development (Leopoldo Solís).

Obviously, we have a fairly extensive list of issues that affect our two nations and the relations between them. Just as obviously, it is in

23

the national interests of both nations to achieve a better relationship. I am tempted to say "restore" because observers have been using terms like "neglected," "deteriorated," and "in disarray" to describe the present state of our relationship. The Mexicans argue that the old special relationship, which had its roots in the good-neighbor policy and in cooperation during the Second World War and flourished in the Era of Good Feelings following the war, is gone, *if it ever existed;* it is essential to find a new formula based on equity and mutual respect and a meeting of national interests.

We already have discussed the need for coordination and better organization of the relationship, for awareness of and sensitivity to the conditioning factors on both sides, and for appreciation of how our respective systems operate and function. One should add that both Mexican and U.S. politicians must learn that consultation or, at least, timely prior notification of actions affecting the neighbor's interests would reduce tensions and resentment provoked by unilateral actions. They must also be aware that playing internal politics with international relations can only lead to misunderstanding and difficulties.

Mr. Carter did not give Mexico advance warning of his plan to deal with the undocumented workers problem, nor did López Portillo feel that he had been prepared for Secretary Schlesinger's rejection of the natural gas pricing agreement. Similarly, U.S. officials were upset at the abrupt decision of the Mexicans not to readmit the shah of Iran. There is no question of the sovereign right of either nation to take such measures as are deemed appropriate in their perception of their national interests. Good neighborliness, however, requires at the minimum that prior warning of intentions be given.

As the full impact of their good fortune in terms of energy resources began to dawn on the Mexicans, there was an obvious tendency to evidence the brusqueness and abrasive assertiveness of the nouveaux riches and the nouveaux powerful. Where formerly it was customary and fashionable for Mexican intellectuals to tweak Uncle Sam's nose, now high Mexican officials engage in the game. A foreign office official explains that a balanced, fair, respectful, and dignified relationship means recognition of Mexico's "new stature as a determining factor in international affairs" because of its oil and geopolitical position. In view of the past sense of weakness and wounded pride and more recent irritating episodes, one may understand, if not applaud, the Mexican president's greeting his American counterpart in February 1979 with a toast that inveighed against surprise moves and sudden deceit.[12] The media in the United States blew the episode out of all proportion.

In regard to the Iranian situation, the Mexican executive condemned the taking of the hostages at the U.S embassy but also called it a conflict that is not "ours" and "an alien process." He went even further in remarks to reporters, calling the freezing of Iranian assets by the United States "precipitous" and "aggressive" and went so far as to suggest that the dollar was proving a "precarious money symbol." Many public figures and editorial commentators reacted strongly. Senator Lloyd Bentsen of Texas, long a friend of Mexico, spoke critically of Mexican actions and statements. Though conceding the Mexicans' sovereign right to do and say what they pleased, he did suggest that friendship carries with it responsibilities as well as advantages. He expressed his profound disappointment.[13] Mexico's able ambassador to the United States, Hugo Margáin, responded to critics in both the press and the public forum by saying that this was just honest talk and that sovereign countries have the right to express their thoughts.[14]

Speaking in brutally frank terms and responding aggressively may have satisfied personal and national frustrations and may have demagogic appeal at home, but such actions are not likely to advance the cause of better relations. The Mexicans have to become accustomed to their new circumstances and the opportunity these circumstances afford for a new relationship on a healthier basis. There is no question that their bargaining position has improved. In the United States it is essential, too, that it be recognized that in a number of significant ways the conditions of the relationship either have changed or are in the process of change and that this will require sensitivity and a willingness to work bilaterally toward a new relationship.

In terms of negotiation between the two countries, inevitably there is a discussion of the single issue of negotiation versus linkage. Though top Mexican officials have referred to linkage, implicitly or explicitly, Mexican intellectuals, conditioned by the fact and their perception of dependency, have expressed concern about linkage that they feel will facilitate U.S. pressure on a whole series of issues. On the other hand, the Mexicans contend that they have seen very little interest in linkage on the part of the U.S. officials. One must bear in mind, however, the complex interest groups in our society that would make difficult any effort at direct trade-offs involving energy, trade, and migration.

Though direct linkage between or among issues appears unlikely, it is inevitable that each issue will be influenced by decisions in the other areas. Progress in ameliorating one problem inevitably should help to create an *ambiente* in which it will be easier to discuss other issues.

Regardless of the manner in which problems or issues are addressed, I believe that it is vitally important to both nations that they be addressed and that they be addressed bilaterally. Too often benign neglect and a policy of drift and inaction appear politically attractive or less threatening than unpleasant alternatives. Granting the ticking-time-bomb character of some of the issues, however, inaction now can only lead to arbitrary and damaging unilateral action when crises strike. Unilateral actions tend to be ineffective and to provoke resentment, and they can produce unanticipated and dire consequences for both nations.

I am one of those who are impressed by the growing interdependence of the two nations. I use the term without condescension and with full awareness that it is a growing interdependence but one lacking in true equality. Despite our global responsibilities and the need for world and hemispheric policies, I believe that many issues with Mexico are bilateral issues that must be dealt with bilaterally. We need a new "special relationship" with Mexico, one based on equality, mutual respect, and mutual understanding.

Notes

[1] Cited by James Reston, *New York Times,* February 1, 1979. The statement was originally made in Paz's speech at the Mexico Today symposium in Washington, D.C., September 29, 1978.

[2] *El nacional,* February 19, 1980.

[3] Arturo Gándara and Caesar Sereseres, *U.S.–Mexico Relations: Too Important to Be Left to Presidents?* (Santa Monica, Calif: Rand Corporation, 1979).

[4] U.S., Congress, *Congressional Record,* December 5, 1979, H 11591–93.

[5] *Austin American-Statesman,* March 15, 1980.

[6] Ibid., March 11, 1980.

[7] Letter, E. V. Niemeyer, Jr., ibid., February 7, 1980.

[8] Ibid., February 3, 1980.

[9] As cited in Environment Fund, "Special Report: Illegal Migration," November 1978 as cited in Paul R. Ehrlich et al., *The Golden Door, International Migration, Mexico, and the United States* (New York: Ballantine Books, 1979), p. 190.

[10] David Meissner, ed., *Mexico–United States Relations: Report of a Wingspread Symposium* (Racine, Wisc.: Johnson Foundation, March 1979), p. 9.

[11] José López Portillo, "Segundo informe del gobierno, September 1, 1978," as cited in *Comercio exterior de México* 24, no. 9 (September 1978), pp. 366–85.

[12] From President José López Portillo's discourse as reproduced by the Mexican embassy in Washington, D.C. His actual words were as follows: "Between permanent, not casual, neighbors, deceit or sudden abuse are poisonous fruits which sooner or later have a reverse effect."

[13] Remarks by Senator Lloyd Bentsen before the U.S. Senate, December 17, 1979, as reported in a press release by his office.

[14] Ambassador Hugo Margáin to Professor Sidney Weintraub, January 18, 1980; Margáin to Senator Lloyd Bentsen, December 26, 1979; and Margáin to James Reston, January 3, 1980.

Part One

Conditioning Factors: the Context

Roots and Realities of Mexican Attitudes toward the United States: A Background Paper

Michael C. Meyer

Mexico is a country incredibly rich in proverbs, adages, and mottoes. One that crosses all class lines, and is often repeated, laments: "Poor Mexico! So far from God and so close to the United States!" This refrain capsulizes the ironies of a Catholic country in which anticlericalism has reigned supreme and the frustrations of a poor country on the border of a superpower. Without question, geographical proximity has produced many important Mexican perceptions of the United States. It has certainly been a major determinant in the economic and political relations between the two countries. These, in turn, condition many of the attitudes that Mexicans harbor about their more powerful neighbor to the north.

U.S.–Mexican Relations: A Brief Historical Sketch

The United States was the first country in the world formally to recognize Mexico's independence from Spain in the early nineteenth century. Having only recently emerged from a similar anticolonial experience, statesmen in Washington, D.C., realized that diplomatic recognition was important to Mexico City if independence were to flourish and a healthy nation-state emerge. Recognition was extended and diplomats exchanged in December 1822. Within a year, however, the administration in Washington had issued a new, wide-reaching proclamation that theoretically would be the cornerstone of U.S. relations with the newly emerging republics of Latin America. The Monroe Doctrine (1823) stated that monarchy as a form of government was not compatible with the freedoms recently won by the new nations of the Western Hemisphere. Therefore, the great monarchies of Europe were warned that the United States would consider any attempt on their part to extend their systems to the Western Hemisphere as dangerous to our peace and safety. Should Mexico and the remainder of Latin America not have been delighted? Was not the Monroe Doctrine a tacit promise of alliance should Spain try to reconquer her lost territories in America? The Mexican view was not that positive. The Monroe Doctrine obviously affected

29

the future of all Latin America, yet not one Latin American country had been consulted prior to its proclamation.

The Monroe Doctrine resulted in the birth of two Mexican attitudes toward the United States. First, if a partnership were to be established in the nineteenth century, it was not to be an even affair. The United States planned to be the dominant partner. More important, when the monarchies of Europe began to violate the terms of the Monroe Doctrine the United States showed no inclination to back up its haughty words with action. Spain invaded Mexico in 1829 in an attempt to reconquer the lost Mexican province. The United States did nothing. Nine years later France invaded the port of Veracruz to collect past debts. Again the United States stood mute. Mexicans began to wonder if the words of the United States as enunciated from Washington, D.C., were to be trusted.

By far the most important event in the nineteenth-century relations between the United States and Mexico was the war fought between the two countries from 1846 to 1848. Without the need here to delve into the intricacies of causation, suffice it to say that the most careful scholars of the conflict, in both the United States and Mexico, have labeled it a U.S. war of aggression, at the end of which the United States appropriated almost half of Mexico's national territory. The early fears of Mexican skeptics now seemed well founded. Since the sixteenth century Mexico had been searching in the north for the elusive El Dorado, an alluring source of great wealth. Almost as if to rub salt in the wound of Mexico's defeat, it was found at Sutter's Fort in California just a year after the Mexican War ended. The tremendous mineral wealth uncovered on the heels of the California gold rush would finance much of the United States's industrial revolution—not Mexico's. It is not surprising then that the Marine Corps hymn, which extols U.S. heroics at the "Halls of Montezuma," has never been used to inculcate pride in young generations of Mexicans. To the extent that historical legacies precipitated a Yankee-phobia in Mexico, the Mexican War must be held largely accountable.

Relations between the United States and Mexico improved markedly during the last quarter of the nineteenth century and the first decade of the twentieth. Porfirio Díaz, during a regime that lasted thirty-four years, stabilized the country, put Mexico's economic house in order, and set Mexico on the path of modernization. To accomplish the latter he invited in foreign capital and offered protections and guarantees sufficiently inviting to attract millions of dollars of American investment. This investment made a major contribution to building the vast Mexican railroad network and reviving the nation's economy, but some Mexicans began to argue that their country was becoming too lucrative as an investment field. They saw the absurdities of the Spanish colonial period repeating themselves. Few of the profits from investment were being redirected into the Mexican economy. The Spanish treasure ships, the famous galleons, were again departing Mexican shores laden with the country's wealth and leaving behind an impoverished populace.

It was not surprising then that when the great Mexican Revolution erupted in 1910 the issue of foreign investment figured prominently in revolutionary rhetoric. Díaz, another oft-repeated adage intones, had allowed his country to become the "mother of foreigners and the step-mother of Mexicans." And when the revolutionaries began to consolidate their victory, they provided that in the future foreign investment must always be kept within the framework of national interests. Most important, in the new Mexican Constitution promulagted in 1917, the state was given the expressed right to expropriate property (including but not limited to that owned by foreigners) if a different ownership pattern better suited the social needs of the Mexican community.

The chaos of the early revolutionary period (1910–1920) severely tested the diplomatic relations between the United States and Mexico. The harmonious relationship fostered by Díaz fell easy victim to the rancor of the day. On two occasions the United States intervened in Mexico with military force: once in Veracruz in 1914 and again in northern Mexico following Pancho Villa's attack on Columbus, New Mexico, in 1916. Tensions remained high in the 1920s as U.S. investors, especially the oil interests, were threatened by the implementation of the Constitution of 1917 and sought to garner promises of protection from the White House and Congress. When the long-awaited oil nationalization did come in 1938, the reaction in the United States was expectedly tumultuous. The nationalization decree of President Lázaro Cárdenas threatened to set the two countries on a collision course. That it did not do so was a tribute to Franklin D. Roosevelt's good-neighbor policy and the good-faith negotiations of the Mexican government and the oil companies concerning the issue of equitable compensation. Ironically, the nationalization of the oil companies in the last analysis fostered better, not worse, relations. Mexicans expected another military intervention. When it did not come they were relieved.

The cleared diplomatic atmosphere reflected itself graphically during World War II. It was never the intention of the United States that Mexico should make a major military contribution to the Allied war effort. Mexico was assigned a supporting role, and it performed that role admirably. Mexican strategic raw materials, kept by the government at reasonable prices, were directed to war-related industries in the United States. Mexican agricultural products helped feed the Allied armies, and Mexican workers (the beginning of the bracero program)

31

came to the United States to help fill the labor shortage occasioned in this country by the draft.

The cordial relationship carried over into the postwar era. Most outstanding issues were resolved amicably, even a century-old boundary dispute known as the Chamizal controversy. The one problem that defied easy solution and, in fact, grew in intensity throughout the 1960s and 1970s was that of the undocumented worker. Countervailing pressures in both Washington and Mexico City worked against the resolution of this issue.

The historical realities synopsized in the preceding paragraphs have conditioned the Mexican view of the United States. As one begins to probe in greater depth, however, it becomes readily apparent that there really is no Mexican view of the United States—there are a number of different worlds in the Mexican universe of views.

The Government View

In many ways the Mexican government finds itself in the position of any government living in the shadow of a much more powerful neighbor. It is careful not to overtly offend but must be mindful of various domestic constituencies. Although Mexico is governed by a single political party, and policy decisions are in no way dependent upon election results, nevertheless the press is relatively free and does not hesitate to assail those officials with whose policies it disagrees.

It is in the best Mexican political tradition that the most specific of policies can be wrapped within an all-encompassing philosophical cloak. The revolution in general, and Mexico's relations with the United States in particular, provided the successive governments of the twentieth century with one such philosophical stance. On the heels of the U.S. interventions of 1914 and 1916 Venustiano Carranza proclaimed a nonintervention doctrine. Mexico would not countenance any foreign intervention in her own domestic affairs and would not support the policies of other governments that intervened in the internal affairs of any other country.

Within the cloak of nonintervention, Mexico could oppose the efforts of the United States to unseat Fidel Castro in the early 1960s and to wage war in Vietnam in the late 1960s and early 1970s. In the latter case, when U.S. policy was criticized it was not from the perspective of devastating Southeast Asia and, in the process, claiming many innocent lives but rather from the view of nonintervention in the internal affairs of a sovereign country. (It is interesting, and perhaps instructive, that little is said about Cuban intervention in Africa.) The United States thus is viewed as a country that will withstand criticism if some moral

32

or philosophical justification can be mustered in support of such criticism.

In its international pronouncements, especially those that concern the United States, the Mexican government is sensitive to public stances that might seem to compromise the country's sense of independence and national dignity. As a logical corollary, those issues that tend to enhance independence and national dignity are given extensive coverage in the press. Thus when Presidents Lyndon B. Johnson and Adolfo López Mateos signed the Chamizal Treaty, resolving the boundary dispute in the El Paso–Ciudad Juárez area, the approach taken by the Mexican president and the press was that Mexico's honor had been redeemed as a powerful country admitted a past wrong. Similarly, when Presidents Luis Echeverría and Gerald Ford met on the Sonora-Arizona border a decade later, the Mexican president announced that his country's sense of national independence would not permit it to sell its newly discovered petroleum to the United States at anything resembling a special price.

Because of the history of U.S.–Mexican relations and the type of nationalism that grew out of the Mexican Revolution, government officials, no matter what personal views they might hold, cannot appear to be overly friendly to the United States. To do so is to lose credibility within the Mexican political community.

The Intellectual's View

Many Mexican intellectuals are eminently reasonable in their considered view of the United States, but no matter how distinguished they may be in their own fields of endeavor, they find themselves in a minority among their colleagues. The more common pattern is for the intelligentsia to be vituperative and rather conspiratorial with respect to the United States, the country they most love to hate. The Mexican Left (and most intellectuals are found somewhere within the Left) traditionally has been critical not only of U.S. foreign policy but also of the consensus of values the U.S. public holds dear.

Throughout most of the twentieth century, U.S. treatment of ethnic minorities, especially Mexican Americans, has been fertile ground on which to attack; but as undeniable progress was made in the areas of civil rights and equal opportunity, the focus shifted. The watchwords of the intellectual assault now encompass dependency, multinational corporations, and the Central Intelligence Agency (CIA). The world is composed of independent and dependent states; it serves the interests of the strong to keep the weak countries, such as Mexico, in a perpetual state of dependence. The institutions assuming this responsibility are, from the private sector, the multinational corporations and, from the public sector, the CIA. Possibly by accident, but probably by design, they work together in Latin America to foster dependence upon the United States.

Dependency theory stated in these terms sounds unbelievably crude, but just like its Marxist progenitor, the doctrine has been developed with amazing sophistication. It has no doubt been nurtured, given strength, and made palatable to many by recent revelations of covert CIA activity in Chile and Cuba and multinational bribery of officials in half a dozen Latin American countries.

The roots of intellectual Yankee-phobia, if not its passion, can be partially explained in terms of the stark contrasts between the two countries. Whereas the United States is sufficiently affluent to place men on the moon, millions of Mexicans live in abject poverty. Whereas U.S. scholars win Nobel prizes, the Mexican school system cannot educate all of the country's children. Whereas U.S. physicians regularly record startling medical breakthroughs, even including prenatal blood tests, tens of thousands of Mexican babies die at birth for want of elementary medical care.

In addition, the pervasive cultural presence of the United States appears at times to overwhelm Mexican society. This phenomenon is called, somewhat theatrically, cultural imperialism, but whatever the name, it is real. Thousands of anglicisms invade the Spanish language. Billboards advertise U.S. products. Newspapers rely on the wire services of the Associated Press and United Press International. Programs produced in the United States dominate the television screens, and motion pictures made in Hollywood draw long lines at the movie houses. American-style restaurants cater to the tourists, and loud American music blares from bars and discothèques. Certainly it can be argued that none of these phenomena is intended. Yet the cumulative impact is to produce a resentment that, when mixed with other ingredients, easily transmutes into overt hostility.

The Businessman's View

Of all groups in Mexican society, the well-educated business community undoubtedly holds the most favorable view of the United States. Leading Mexican businessmen, Roman Catholics for the most part, have even been known to praise openly the hard work, discipline, and thrift so often associated with the Protestant ethic. Often they send their children to the United States for higher education and come themselves, combining business and pleasure.

These businessmen have a positive view of U.S. society in general, but they most admire their North American counterparts. Interestingly, American businessmen are viewed less as competitors than as examples. Whenever practical, the Mexican business community emulates the latest merchandising, packaging, and advertising practices that have been successful north of the Rio Grande. Religious holidays in Mexico, as in the United States, have been commercialized to the extent of children sitting on Santa Claus's lap in Mexican department stores each December.

Because the Mexican economy is so closely tied to the United States, Mexican government policies considered unfavorable toward the United States, or those that might dampen the highly important tourist trade, encounter the opposition of an increasingly strong business lobby. The businessman sees clearly that the economic wealth generated by the U.S. business community has brought it not only comfort but also power and influence and, if this can be accomplished in the United States, it might well be accomplished in Mexico also. In short, unlike the Mexican intellectual, the Mexican businessman does not view U.S. society as crassly materialistic.

The Popular View

Because of the relative absence of careful social science research on mass attitudes toward the United States, assessment must be more impressionistic than empirical. It is obvious that millions of uneducated and unskilled Mexican workers view the United States as a country that affords them hope for a better future. Were this not true the influx of undocumented workers into the United States would not be a problem of such far-reaching proportions. At the same time, however, they come to the United States with mixed emotions. Not only is the fear of apprehension very real, but they have learned in various ways that once in the United States they will likely suffer the humiliations of exploitation and racial prejudice.

Mass views of the United States are conditioned by whatever exposure to the educational system the population may have received and by the bombardment of popular culture. In 1959 the Mexican government passed legislation making primary-school textbooks uniform, free, and obligatory throughout the country. As a result the same texts are used in every Mexican school for grades one through six. For the many Mexicans whose education does not go beyond the sixth grade, concepts of nationalism and views of the United States are constructed, in part, on the foundations of these *textos gratuitos*.[1]

The volume used in the fourth grade for history and civics is especially important as a contributor to the development of Mexican nationalism. As is true in the case of all countries, Mexican nationalism is partially rooted in its views of the outside world. Xenophobia—and, in this particular case, Yankee-phobia—is definitely one of the glues used to bind the country together. The volume used in the second grade teaches children the national anthem, and below a picture of civilians defending the country against the U.S. invasion the students are asked to fill in the missing lines from the anthem. With the missing lines filled in, the stanza reads:

> But if a foreign enemy dares
> To profane with his footprint your soil
> Just remember, Beloved Fatherland, that the heavens
> Have given you a soldier in each of your sons.

In the fourth-grade volume, the Mexican War is used to teach a basic lesson in patriotism: "It is an experience that we should never forget. The unity of all Mexicans is essential because with internal harmony comes progress and with progress comes the ability to put an end to such deceptions and injustices." It is obvious that the United States does not emerge in a favorable light in the primary texts. What comes through clearly is the picture of a bully and an aggressor.

The views of the United States presented in the *textos gratuitos* are reinforced by other elements of popular culture. The Mexican *corrido,* the folksong of the masses, theoretically incorporates lessons of "history" but in practice often misrepresents historical reality to reinforce many negative stereotypes about the United States. These folk ballads, depicting dislike of the United States at best and hatred at worst, are sung in cantinas and fiestas, are played on the radio, and are reproduced for mass distribution on record albums and eight-track tapes.

Corridos in translation cannot convey the intensity of meaning and sentimentality they have in the original Spanish. The few examples cited, therefore, are left untranslated with only brief introductory remarks.[2]

Not surprisingly, numerous corridos damn the United States for the Mexican War, especially the opinion voiced in Washington shortly after its conclusion that the United States should have taken all of Mexico, rather than only half.

> Los yankis malvados
> No cesan de hablar
> Que habrían de acabar
> Con esta nación.

The North American invasion of Veracruz, and the accompanying loss of life, provoked a plethora of condemnations of the United States.

One of the most popular is entitled "La heróica acción del Capitán Azueta."

En una Guerra Espantosa
El gran Puerto se envolvió
Por los Yankis maldecidos
Que han traído la invasión

Hubo muertos y hubo heridos
Grandes prejuicios y horrores
Han causado en Veracruz
Los bandidos invasores.

Most common in the corridos is the treatment Mexican workers receive at the hands of North Americans, whether they are working for them in Mexico or in the United States.

Insultan a los Mexicanos
Y los corren de los campos
Para ocupar a sus paisanos
Que llegan como logartos.

But the special plight of the undocumented worker in the United States prompts indignation and compassion.

Mas hoy con la nueva ley
Del Gobierno Americano
Por donde quiera es malvisto
Todo pobre Mexicano

Porque los Americanos
No nos tienen compasión
Y hombres, niños y mujeres
Los llevan a la prisión.

The picture of the United States that emerges from the corridos and other elements of popular culture (such as the murals that adorn public buildings throughout Mexico) is so unfavorable as to constitute a caricature. But its impact on the popular imagination is telling.

Synopsis of the Mexican View

Dissected into its constituent parts the Mexican view of the United States emerges as rather more negative than it actually is. It does not take into account, for example, that in each representative group there are many who deviate from the norm. In addition, in each group one can detect an ambivalent attitude that in effect constitutes a love-hate perspective. Even the most strident Mexican Yankee-phobe often finds certain things to admire in U.S. society.

Policy decisions concerning relations between the two countries should take into account that the United States is not universally esteemed in Mexico. Criticisms of the United States are often exaggerated and distorted, but many are rooted in readily understandable historical fact. Educated Mexicans are more historically oriented than their North American counterparts and not infrequently point out that we in the United States find it convenient to have short memories.

Mexican policy makers, though not concerned about being turned out of office at the next election, are nevertheless mindful of constituent interests and must be guided by the nationalistic ideology that grew out of the Mexican Revolution. U.S. policy decisions and initiatives from the private sector that fail to accommodate these considerations ipso facto diminish their chances for success.

[1] The following discussion of Mexican textbooks is based on Josefina Vázquez de Knauth, *Nacionalismo y educación en México* (Mexico: El Colegio de México, 1975).

[2] The *corrido* extracts reproduced here are taken from Merle E. Simmons, *The Mexican Corrido as a Source for Interpretive Study of Modern Mexico, 1870–1950* (Bloomington: Indiana University Press, 1957).

The Evolution of U.S.-Mexican Relations: A Sociopolitical Perspective

Roger D. Hansen

It is quite plausible to imagine that, until the mid-1970s, an analysis of the future of U.S.–Mexican relations might have entirely deleted any detailed examination of what will be called the socioeconomic perspective. If one made the following aggregate assumptions concerning Mexico, such an analysis might well have seemed of marginal significance: (1) continued political stability under the regime (the Revolutionary Coalition, the Partido Revolucionario Institucional (PRI), or whatever one wishes to call it) that has governed Mexico with such skill since the end of the 1930s; (2) continued rapid economic growth rates, with limited but growing attention being paid to the problems of income distribution and underemployment; and (3) no predictable international or domestic events likely to introduce any significant discontinuities into this picture of Mexico's "straight-line" projection into the upper ranks of the world's developing countries.

Events of the mid-1970s no longer permit any serious examination of the future of U.S.–Mexican relations the luxury of avoiding an analysis of the sociopolitical problems likely to influence that future quite strongly. This is true for two reasons. In the first place, the sanguine picture presented above is clearly one that, focusing as it might have five years ago on superficial trends, would have ignored some fundamental problems that were already recognized by some to be sizable. In the second place, unpredictable events of the intervening years have magnified many of those problems far beyond what reasonable projections might have suggested. As one surveys the same terrain in the late 1970s, the following questions arise to shake the comfortable assumptions of the earlier period.

1. Although the Mexican political regime survived the six years of Echeverría's presidency and the advent of the López Portillo administration, it is no longer possible to project continued political stability in that country with anywhere near the degree of probability that would still have been assigned a half decade ago. Indeed, the intervening years, though they demonstrate the regime's capabilities for governance quite possibly at their best, also illuminate a series of fundamental challenges

39

to its continued capacity to hold the middle ground between a potentially dramatic shift to either the right or the left in Mexico.

2. Depending on one's analytical premises, these political problems have been eased or aggravated by two unpredictable economic events: the international economic stagnation whose proximate cause was the quadrupling of oil prices by the Organization of Petroleum Exporting Countries (OPEC) in the years 1973–1975; and the later discovery in Mexico of some extraordinarily rich hydrocarbon deposits. The international economic stagnation following the oil price increase added to the major economic difficulties of the Echeverría administration and hastened the decision to float the peso. The Mexican oil discoveries appear to be an enormous boon to future development prospects in a country that has for years faced a serious foreign exchange problem; the longer-term sociopolitical implications of the hydrocarbon discoveries are far more difficult to estimate but clearly contain as much potential for exaggerating Mexican political and economic problems as they do for overcoming hurdles to rapid economic development.

3. Finally, the magnitude of the Mexican underemployment problem has lent itself to better approximation, and in the process the magnitude of the "illegal migration" problem—the movement of undocumented Mexicans into the United States—has begun to be measured. As it is measured and its causes examined, it is gradually becoming a disturbingly profound political issue for U.S.–Mexican relations.

Mexico: The Sociopolitical Parameters of Evolving U.S.–Mexican Relations

Although more and more writings appear to help us interpret the Mexican political system and its interaction with Mexican society, those writings continue to present two rather starkly opposing viewpoints. One emphasizes the continued strength and cohesion of the present Mexican regime, which has governed the country for forty years, and often suggests that the strength of the political system is actually *growing,* relative to the problems of socioeconomic evolution with which it must cope. In the 1977 view of one widely respected analyst, José Luis Reyna, "The Mexican state is well established and still retaining a monopoly on power in spite of popular pressures. That monopoly is legitimate and I do not believe that it will be threatened in the near future. The Mexican state will continue to have the capacity to bargain and to impose its rule."[1]

The other interpretation, though cautious in its general conclusions, is far more impressed with the growing magnitude of the *problems* that the Mexican governing elite must manage than it is with any growing *capacity* to manage them. Even the most deliberate and knowledgeable experts within the latter group now freely speculate on the possibility that a failure of the present regime to manage Mexico's growing problems may result in a military takeover in the coming decade.

Given the range of opinion—opinion among experts, it must be emphasized—it would be fruitless to tackle the subject in this short paper. Nevertheless, a series of observations must be made, even if they raise far more questions than they answer. The reason is simple. No other issue in the sociopolitical realm is potentially as important for the evolution of U.S.–Mexican relations as the capacity of the present Mexican political regime to govern the country in a manner that avoids a sharp and discontinuous movement toward either extreme of the political spectrum. The capacity of the United States to deal constructively with Mexico at both the formal interstate diplomatic level and at the legion of less formal levels where the two societies interact due to sheer territorial propinquity will be sharply curtailed should the present Mexican regime (or one that might replace it) move significantly rightward or leftward. Therefore, a paper analyzing the sociopolitical parameters of evolving U.S.–Mexican relations must raise the following points.

The problems faced by the present political regime are growing rapidly. Nowhere is this contention better illustrated than with regard to the Mexican development dilemma. At present it is estimated that some 40 percent of Mexico's potential labor force is unemployed or underemployed. Land for redistribution purposes is practically exhausted, leading to two migration patterns—to Mexican cities and to the United States.

It is presently estimated that 60 percent of the 3 million to 6 million "illegals" in the United States are of Mexican origin and that 500,000 to 800,000 new illegals cross the border each year in search of employment. Though perhaps two-thirds of these new migrants return to Mexico after varying periods of employment, another one-third choose to remain in the United States.

Even if U.S. policy does not limit the flow of immigrants, the problem created for the Mexican political system remains enormous. Presently there are 650,000 new entrants into the Mexican labor force each year; by the early 1980s the figure will reach 800,000. Yet Mexican growth rates are currently creating at best about 400,000 new jobs per year. No matter how strong and how well-conceived and well-financed the efforts, it would seem close to impossible for the Mexican economy to produce enough jobs to absorb all the new entrants into the labor force each year before the end of the 1980s.

The magnitude of Mexico's underemployment problem and the consequent migration to urban Mexico to avoid the worst aspects of rural poverty place an enormous burden on urban infrastructure facilities in Mexico. In the short term, there are no answers. In the long term, altered development strategies designed to absorb more labor, potentially financed with proceeds from petroleum sales, may begin to resolve the problem of underemployment.

But can the political system reach the long term? This raises a second major point. Extreme poverty and underemployment are age-old problems in Mexico, and therefore one might suggest that the situation described above represents nothing new. This reasoning would be wrong on two counts. First, the sheer magnitude of the problem makes it quite different, as the numbers (and the flow of illegals to the United States) suggest. More importantly, it would be wrong in failing to recognize that the context of this massive problem is quite different today than it was in any previous period. As the years (close to seventy) since the Mexican Revolution pass and the years of revolutionary promises by the present political regime grow (now about forty), the continued joblessness and poverty take on a different political meaning. All too bluntly, the numbers represent rapidly growing targets of opportunity for other Mexicans who are disillusioned with the achievements and the direction of the present political elite and who use rural (and increasingly urban) discontent to create various forms of opposition.

In short, the myth of the revolution tarnishes, and the joblessness and inegalitarian extremes of Mexican income distribution create growing potential for political instability.

This situation raises the two most fundamental (and most controversial) points relating to the capacity for continued governance on the part of the present political regime. The first concerns the *capacity* of that political leadership to make enough significant policy adjustments to manage the short-term difficulties; the second concerns the very *coherence* of that leadership in the face of the problems now confronting Mexico. Each point deserves a brief comment.

The present regime has for forty years successfully managed short-term problems of demands on the part of the poorer strata of Mexican society in four ways. First, it has limited the formation of demands by incorporating labor and peasant movements into the official party—the Partido Revolucionario Institucional (PRI)—where leaders could be co-opted or retired in one form or another. Second, it has appealed to the myth of the revolution and its increasingly symbolic (rather than economically meaningful) land redistribution measures to keep the hopes of the *campesino* alive. Third, it has controlled almost all efforts among the political elite to bid for dissident support by suppressing any open political contests: governing elite solidarity when facing potentially destabilizing sociopolitical situations has severely limited the opportunity for serious challenge to the PRI regime despite the potential in the Mexican socioeconomic setting for the mobilization of serious challenges to the regime. Fourth, the political regime has demonstrated the capacity to make modest policy alterations where they seemed warranted by domestic political, social, and economic pressures and problems. This well-known phenomenon is captured by analysts who emphasize the cyclical pattern in Mexican politics alternately representing leftist, centrist, and rightist tendencies.

The crucial question for the coming decade involves the continued capacity of the Mexican system to make the needed changes in policy direction—real and symbolic—to contain substantially the rapidly growing potential for serious political instability resulting from the worrisome demographic, underemployment, and poverty trends.

All that can be said in this short paper is that optimists and pessimists are in complete disagreement on this point. Optimists maintain that the state (that is, the Mexican political regime) retains much—if not an increasing degree of—autonomy from Mexican society (and individual social forces) and retains the capacity to make significant policy adjustments to ease present socioeconomic problems. This group would argue, for example, that the very modest initiatives to tackle the problems of tax reform and rural poverty begun under President Echeverría will be carried forward more forcefully by the López Portillo administration.

The pessimists demur. To them the Echeverría years suggest that whatever degree of autonomy the political system once had from Mexican social forces is diminishing rapidly and that major segments of the Mexican private sector have demonstrated a near veto power over the capacity of the governing elite to alter economic policies without their approval. All too briefly, the pessimists read into the Echeverría years the signs of a corporate authoritarian political regime finally stymied in its capacity to retain autonomy by one of the very social forces it did so much to create—a small but powerful domestic private sector. The opposition of this group to tax reform and to the restructuring of government expenditures in favor of labor-intensive rural development so limited the capacity of the Echeverría administration to introduce policy changes, it is argued, that it turned a frustrated and defeated Mexican president to Third World leadership efforts in a search for symbolic "revolutionary" victories that could not be achieved in the domestic arena.

A close examination suggests that the pessimists make the more convincing case. It would appear that the trend most important to note for this paper is a *weakening* in the capacity of the Mexican political system to escape the constraints placed on it by the highly conservative private sector. The greater this constraint, the less able will be the political regime to respond to the problems of mass underemployment, rural poverty, and the legion of difficulties resulting from a development strategy that has paid so little attention to labor absorption, income distribution, and other aspects of balanced growth that could quite plausibly ease many of the socioeconomic problems that presently produce so much potential for growing political instability.

Can this political trend be altered, or will it be strengthened in the 1980s, adding to the potential for serious political instability in Mexico? Much will depend upon the second crucial issue noted above—the capacity of the PRI regime to maintain the degree of coherence necessary to prevent an open split in the ranks of Mexico's governing elite group, a resurrection of a system of sharp and public contests for political power through appeals to an increasingly disillusioned and increasingly mobilizable public, and most probably the rapid return of the Mexican military to the cockpit of a Mexican political situation reminiscent of the 1920s and the 1930s.

If the PRI regime can retain enough cohesion in the face of present pressures to avoid any fundamental change in the manner in which bids for power at the highest levels of the political system are made, then political stability may be the hallmark of the coming decade despite the growing veto power by the Mexican private sector on Mexican economic policy changes. In considering this crucial issue, however, one must reflect upon the potential impact on present Mexican political norms of behavior of the enormous oil wealth that will alter so many of the familiar parameters of the Mexican social, economic, and political terrain within the next three to five years. Once again, the workings of the Mexican political system remain so obscure that two polar interpretations now exist regarding the impact of the very large oil revenues on the political balance in Mexico. Again we find optimists who suggest that this new wealth will provide the financial foundations for a successful attack on the economic problems presently gripping Mexico. It is argued that there will be more than enough money to finance major new rural labor-absorption projects throughout Mexico, breathing hope back into the body politic and the myth of the revolution. Refurbished political legitimacy will attend this turnabout, stabilizing the control of the PRI regime even if it takes two decades to overcome the worst aspects of underemployment and absolute poverty.

Pessimists, however, insist on raising two troubling questions about this scenario. First, is there enough support for such a program—within or without the Mexican political system—to assure that major shares of oil revenues are allocated to such novel sectors and enterprises, all implying a significant shift in the goals of Mexican development strategy? Will labor-intensive rural projects be given significant priority, or will one of industry's most capital-intensive sectors—the petrochemical field—receive priority? Much that is known about Petróleos Mexicanos (PEMEX), the Mexican government petroleum agency, and the Mexican private sector suggests that the struggle over expenditure priorities will continue despite the enormous increase in funds and that much of the increase could be consumed in the oil industry's own financing and expansion plans.

Second, what will be the effects of this very large increase in public-sector revenues on political elite cohesion? The success of the political system over the past forty years has rested in great part on the fact that in a setting of economic scarcity absolute loyalty to the PRI regime was a vital ingredient in socioeconomic mobility within the public sector. Pessimists are quick to point out that a sudden (relative) abundance of wealth may sharply alter the norms of the political game in Mexico and fragment elite cohesion in the process. Once again the final product could well be an end to the political regime that has existed for the past forty years.

Space does not permit further analysis of the Mexican situation in the 1980s. In conclusion, however, a word is in order concerning the rationale for what may appear to be unnecessary degrees of speculation in this section. The issues analyzed—or questions raised—clearly merit fundamental consideration in any serious exercise examining the evolution of U.S.–Mexican relations in the coming decade. It is all too easy to become engrossed in the study of such specific issues as energy, migration, narcotics, and trade. Each has a sweet concreteness about it that obviates the necessity to deal with the less measurable elements noted in this paper. But in the long run it will be the nature and orientation of the two political systems—Mexican and American—that are by far the most significant determinants of the evolving relationship between the two countries. Therefore, when this exercise moves from background considerations to policy considerations, it must do so with the best possible understanding of the strengths and weaknesses of the political regimes involved.

As the preceding discussion suggests, a great deal of uncertainty attends all analyses of the stability of the Mexican political regime and its likely evolution. To conclude from that uncertainty that the issue of Mexican political stability should not be factored into more concrete policy analysis would greatly simplify the problem of policy discussion, but at a cost far too great to accept.

The United States: The Sociopolitical Parameters of Evolving
U.S.–Mexican Relations

In examining Mexican sociopolitical parameters the analysis focused less on questions of *policy* change than on *regime* change. Because a change of the latter type would be far more momentous for the evolution of U.S.–Mexican relations, it received major attention even though the probabilities of such change do not appear to be high over the next four years.

A brief analysis of the United States will focus on potential *policy* changes, for there is literally no possibility that the regime change issue will arise. Nevertheless, the potential for policy change in directions inimical to friendly and constructive U.S.–Mexican relations would appear to be fairly significant. The potential for these changes is rooted in economic difficulties, a political process that presently negates U.S. policy coherence vis-à-vis Mexico and advances the primacy of domestic over foreign policy issues and a closure of U.S. society (which may be more cyclical than secular in nature).

The separation of powers in the American political system has, for better or worse, proven to be a structural element through which private interest groups have successfully pleaded their case for economic protection from varying forms of foreign competition in recent years. The present period of neomercantilist responses on the part of the executive branch to foreign competition—orderly marketing arrangements, more escape-clause actions, lower (if any) growth quotas within the multifiber agreement—is a reflection of the effectiveness of those private interest pressures. And in most instances the administration has acted because it feared that more protectionist results would be legislated by Congress if the executive branch did not take more informal actions.

The crucial question is whether this neomercantilist behavior is simply a short-term response to some quite novel international economic problems or is a rather more significant portent of longer-term trends. Both cases are argued, and all would agree that the present levels of unemployment may exacerbate the problem. Nevertheless, it would appear for several reasons—among them the inability thus far successfully to construct post–Bretton Woods regimes in the areas of trade and monetary relations, the prospects for slower global growth rates in the 1980s, and the prospects for enhanced domestic and international conflict over distributional questions—that U.S. international economic policies are slowly shifting in a decidedly protectionist direction. In the case of Mexico, of course, the shift to protectionism in the United States is likely to include a growing pressure to cut severely the flow of undocumented immigrants.

46

Together, these potential policy trends have serious economic and sociopolitical implications for U.S.–Mexican relations that are too obvious to require recitation. One might add the observation that any abrupt (and successful) effort to cut back drastically on the flow of illegals could entail serious consequences for political stability in Mexico, particularly over the next decade, by magnifying all of Mexico's major economic problems.

A coherent U.S. foreign policy toward Mexico would be one that incorporated informed calculations about such linkages as (1) migration and Mexican political stability and (2) U.S. trade and other international economic policies that might encourage more labor-intensive growth patterns in Mexico. But U.S. policy vis-à-vis Mexico is totally incoherent, because of the continued issue-by-issue approach to items that should be joined if possible in a coherent approach to U.S. relations with Mexico. What argues so overwhelmingly for a more coherent approach is the very degree of interdependence, which cannot help but characterize U.S.–Mexican relations—a degree that, by any empirical measurement, will overwhelm that of almost all, if not all, other sets of bilateral relations in which the United States is engaged.

Nevertheless, it remains very unclear whether or not the U.S. government has the will or the capacity to move in this direction. And unless and until it does, private U.S. domestic interests and interest groups will be very influential actors in U.S. policy making as it affects Mexico.

Finally, there remains the troubling issue of the ethnic aspect of U.S.–Mexican relations and the evolution of U.S. concerns and policies regarding the "Hispanic question." If the migration issue were perceived within U.S. society as a jobs problem alone, it might well prove subject to constructive bilateral diplomacy over the coming years. However, the issue is apparently being interpreted by a growing number of U.S. interest groups as far more than an employment problem. The increasing number of Mexicans in the United States is being portrayed—whether out of conviction or for more concrete, unarticulated reasons—as a danger to the American social fabric. Should this portrayal win general acceptance, then an attempted closure of American society could create very serious problems for U.S.–Mexican relations unless a coherent and comprehensive U.S. foreign policy toward Mexico proves capable of compensating in other areas of U.S.–Mexican interdependence for a severely restrictive immigration policy.

Conclusion

Two highly speculative predictions combine with one unassailable projection to suggest considerable difficulties to be overcome in evolving

47

a constructive bilateral relationship between the United States and Mexico in the coming decade.

The unassailable projection concerns the inevitable rapid growth in U.S.–Mexican interconnectedness—in commodity, capital, technology, and population flows—all familiar aspects of what we now call interdependence. The impact of each society upon the other can do nothing but grow, even if the results of that mutual impact are extraordinarily difficult to predict.

The first speculative prediction concerns the degree of sociopolitical uncertainty likely to exist in Mexico and the narrow and potentially treacherous policy space left to the PRI regime. The coming decade could see a further weakening of the political regime relative to private social forces in Mexico, less capacity to restructure economic policies to overcome Mexico's major developmental problems, increased "extra-regime" political mobilization, and a growing role for the army in Mexican politics. The second speculative prediction concerns the growing difficulties of the U.S. executive branch in developing a coordinated and comprehensive foreign policy to guide its relations with Mexico in a manner that is at all congruent with Mexico's economic and political needs.

These three fundamental ingredients of the U.S.–Mexican sociopolitical scene are not conducive to the evolution of constructive relations. Perhaps all that can be done is to hope that the two more speculative ingredients in this picture are greatly misinformed.

Notes

[1] José Luis Reyna, "Redefining the Authoritarian Regime," in José Luis Reyna and Richard S. Weinert, eds., *Authoritarianism in Mexico* (Philadelphia: Institute for the Study of Human Issues, 1977), p. 167.

Interest Groups and Selected Foreign Policies: Mexico and the United States

Rudolph Gomez

The purpose of this paper is to examine, very briefly, the influence exerted by U.S. interest groups upon the formulation and conduct of the foreign policy between the United States and Mexico. Several caveats must be noted before proceeding further: first, though there is agreement among political scientists about probable or assumed relationships between interest groups and the formulation and conduct of public policies, there is less agreement upon how, where, and what should be studied empirically to support hypotheses concerning such relationships.[1] Second, much of what has been written about American interest groups and their influence on U.S.–Mexican foreign policy has been episodic and unsystematic. Necessarily, then, the observations made herein about American interest groups and U.S.–Mexican foreign policy should be evaluated with these caveats in mind.

A nation's foreign policy can be defined "as the principles and practices used by that nation to govern its relations with the world outside its borders, especially other nations."[2] Interest groups are considered to be "organized associations which engage in activity relative to government decisions."[3] Although it may be assumed that interest group activity can occur at any stage of governmental decision making, the presumption is that "interest groups are assigned roles of some significance with regard to all the input functions of a political system."[4] As used in this paper, "interest groups" will refer almost exclusively to American interest groups. When a group is from Mexico it will be so identified. If we employ the definitions just listed we can discern some areas of foreign policy between the United States and Mexico wherein there has been perceptible interest group activity. Probably the most comprehensively documented study on the relationships of American interest groups to a specific foreign policy between Mexico and the United States relates to the bracero program.[5] Very briefly, this policy/agreement called for the employment of Mexican nationals as temporary farm workers in the United States. The program operated, under various authorizing provisions, from August 1942 until December 1964.[6]

The interest groups that aligned themselves in support of or in opposition to the bracero program during the twenty-two-year period of its existence represented, among others, agribusiness, labor, religious, and ethnic interests. A total of sixty-nine groups, for example, were identified by name as supporting or opposing the bracero program during the period 1953–1958. Table 1 contains a selected listing of the groups by name.[7]

The names of the groups listed in table 1 reveal something of their orientation to the bracero program. The groups supporting the program were the agribusiness interests, which were concerned with maintaining a large pool of manual laborers who were relatively inexpensive, relatively skilled, and relatively willing to work under onerous conditions. The groups opposing the bracero program were composed of Mexican-American, labor, and allied interests, which concerned with the impact that the cheap Mexican labor was having in keeping down the wages paid to American agricultural workers. It is not surprising, therefore, that the lineup appearing in table 1 divided as it did over the bracero program. Although the antibracero groups eventually carried the day, it is difficult to conclude from the evidence presented whether

TABLE 1

SELECTED GROUPS THAT SUPPORTED OR OPPOSED THE BRACERO
PROGRAM, 1953–1958

Supported	*Opposed*
National Canners Association	National Farmers Union
National Cotton Council of America	AFL-CIO
National Council of Farm Cooperatives	International Brotherhood of Teamsters
Western Growers Association	National Agricultural Workers Union
U.S. Beet Sugar Association	United Packinghouse Workers of America
National Mexican Users Committee	National Catholic Rural Life Conference
United Fresh Fruit and Vegetable Association	American G.I. Forum of Texas
Holly Sugar Company	National Sharecroppers Fund
Amalgamated Sugar Company	National Catholic Welfare Committee
Northwest Farm Labor Association	American Friends Service Committee

SOURCE: Richard B. Craig, *The Bracero Program: Interest Groups and Foreign Policy* (Austin: University of Texas Press, 1971), pp. 139–43.

these interest groups were of decisive influence in bringing about the program's end or whether they were just another contributory factor.

The termination of the bracero program did not eliminate the movement of Mexican nationals seeking work in the United States. Vernon Briggs, Jr., has noted that the Immigration and Naturalization Service (INS) estimated that 3 million illegal aliens "entered the United States undetected in 1973 . . . [and] it can be said that Mexicans are the majority of each category of illegal aliens . . . who have gone undetected."[8] Both the Mexican and U.S. governments have formally acknowledged the problem of illegal immigration, but to date no policy has been agreed upon.[9] Mexican-American interest groups have insisted that the immigration problem be addressed, not only by the enactment of new policies but by the more effective administration of existing ones and by eliminating the enforcement of INS immigration regulations by local law enforcement agencies, which, it is claimed, exacerbate tensions between Mexican Americans and the INS. The National Council of La Raza and the Washington office of the Mexican-American Legal Defense and Educational Fund (MALDEF) recently argued both these viewpoints before the U.S. Civil Rights Commission.[10]

On the other hand, there appear to be groups in the United States that give tacit support to the illegal aliens by encouraging them to enter the country. Professor Briggs has noted that

> the Immigration and Nationality Act of 1952 made the importation and harboring of illegal aliens a felony. *As a concession to Texas agricultural interests*, however, the Act contains a section stating that employment and the related services provided by employers to employees (i.e., transportation, housing, or feeding) do not constitute an illegal act of harboring. The effect of this proviso is to make employers largely immune from prosecution if they hire alien workers. Thus, one of the most important barriers to effective control of illegal entrants is the fact that the act of employment of an illegal alien is not itself illegal. Since an employer incurs no risk, he is free to hire illegal aliens, which encourages a continuation of the human flow across the border.[11]

Perhaps it is needless to observe that any resolution of the illegal alien problem between Mexico and the United States is undoubtedly rendered more difficult as a result of the positions taken on it by American interest groups espousing diametrically opposed views.

A recent proposal by the INS to construct a steel-plated chain link fence on the El Paso–Ciudad Juárez border precipitated the formation of a coalition of interest groups opposing the construction. The announced purpose for the proposed fence is to help retard the flow of illegal immigrants from Mexico into the United States. Representatives from seventeen organizations met in El Paso during the week of November 6, 1978, to protest the construction of the fence, which has been called, popularly, the "tortilla curtain."[12] Some of the protesting groups were identified as the Diocese of El Paso, Office of Church and Society; Texas Farm Workers Union; La Raza Legal Assistance, Texas Region; La Raza Unida party; and Equal Rights Council of El Paso.[13]

The undocumented worker problem, as it is called by the Mexicans, or the illegal alien problem, as it is called by the North Americans, will probably continue to remain the most vexing foreign relations problem confronting both countries. The fact that it is of such long duration probably offers little consolation to policy makers in both countries.[14] Nor, probably, is there much solace for the interest groups that have sprung up to assist the policy makers in resolving this problem.

U.S. foreign policy on investment by American firms abroad has been characterized by the Brookings Institution in the following manner: "Official postwar U.S. policy . . . promotes foreign direct investment as a major aspect of its foreign assistance program. The program's most straightforward tool is government insurance and guarantees for foreign direct investment."[15] The policy objectives of the "host countries," including Mexico, relative to foreign investment have been grouped into three categories: (1) to secure domestic economic goals such as reducing employment and expanding domestic research and development; (2) to secure external economic goals, "primarily improving the balance of payments"; and (3) to assure that foreign investors "will respond effectively to host country policies by localizing management control over the [investors]."[16]

The authors of the Brookings study observed that the role of American interest groups relative to their investments abroad is that "no one represents American interests broader than those of the firms themselves."[17] The consequences of such private interest activity by American groups/firms abroad might very well be beneficial for themselves but may prove to have unanticipated and, perhaps, undesirable consequences for general American foreign policy vis-à-vis the host countries.

Although Mexican interest activity in the United States is probably modest to date, we do have an example of such an interest operating in the Congress of the United States to assure itself a favorable outcome in a foreign policy field. In 1971 the "extension of the 1948 Sugar Act touched off some of the hottest lobbying" seen in Washington during that session of Congress.[18] Mexico's basic quota allotment was 229,862 short tons with its total quota and proration reaching 476,527 short tons.[19] Mexico's quota allotment was the second-highest amount granted a foreign producer, with only the Philippines receiving a larger quota.[20] It may have been purely coincidental that Mexican sugar producers retained Dennis O'Rourke, of the firm of Sutton and O'Rourke, to represent them for the fee of $4,000 per month.[21]

The example of Mexican sugar producers operating to obtain favorable sugar quotas in the United States was provided to indicate their presence in foreign policy related activities. Care should be taken, however, to distinguish them from North American interest group activities. It is likely that the example cited above illustrates an activity that was sponsored directly through a formal agency of the Mexican national government. Mexico's national government is more centralized than the American; therefore there are fewer opportunities for Mexican interest groups to operate, and they probably have fewer access points toward which their activities can be directed. It is likely that to the extent that Mexican interest groups exist they find that the avenues available for the expression of their interests are restricted to the mediums provided by the dominant, controlling political party (Partido Revolucionario Institucional) or one of its government institutions, namely, the presidency, Congress, and/or the bureaucracy.

Space requires that we turn from the consideration of examples of interest group activity relating to U.S.–Mexican foreign policies to what the theoretical relationship appears to be and what it might become, both for interest groups and for foreign policy of the two countries.

Irving Louis Horowitz, though addressing himself to the subject of *ethnic* interest groups and U.S. foreign policy, provides an insight that places the relationships of most interest groups to foreign policy in a useful context. He writes: "the consensus among researchers seems to be that the actual amount of impact [of ethnic groups on U.S. foreign policy] has been minimal; . . . A number of papers come perilously close to suggesting that the independent and dependent variables should be reversed: that U.S. foreign policy serves to galvanize ethnic sentiments as much, if not more, than the other way around."[22] It may be that if we substitute the words "agribusiness," "labor," "religious," "business," etc., for "ethnic" in the Horowitz quotation we may be expressing reasonably accurately the relationship between interest groups and foreign policy(-ies) between the United States and Mexico. The examples provided herein to illustrate the workings of interest groups vis-à-vis specific policies between the two countries suggest that the groups have functioned more in a reactive fashion than in an initiating fashion. If that is so then it might be that the statesmanship required to improve the foreign policies of both countries will have to come from elected representatives and/or their appointed administrative officers—whence conventional public opinion presumes that most, if not all, government policies do emerge.

If foreign policy initiatives do emerge primarily from formal governmental decision-making bodies it might be worthwhile for them to consider the following suggestions relative to our foreign investment policy:

> American government pressure on behalf of American companies has been, if anything, counterproductive. Simple repeal of the Hickenlooper and Gonzalez amendments would be responsive to the demands of the developing countries [including Mexico] that the United States end its "economic aggression." And it would be consistent with our principle that the foreign operations of American companies not be given favored treatment by the U.S. Government.
>
> . . . In terms of political relations, the end of direct foreign ownership in natural resources, by removing American companies from the sensitive position of exercising property rights over the national patrimony in foreign countries, would resolve for the U.S. Government the dilemma of defending or abandoning them as they become increasingly vulnerable. It would eliminate the main course of investment disputes in Latin America. . . . Hence the economic and foreign policy interests of the United States require discouragement of equity investment in the extractive industries. . . . Differences between the United States and those countries would clearly remain but would be much more manageable.[23]

The policy regarding the Mexican immigration into the United States is so fraught with emotional considerations, as well as with economic, social, and political ones, that it is much more difficult to address prescriptively. A suggestion that appears to be relevant was made by Jorge Bustamante recently when he wrote:

> Restrictive measures such as reinforcing police actions and/or launching mass deportations have failed several times in the past. This has its basic weakness in the fact that a phenomenon which responds to the interactions of factors operating at the two sides of the border, basically, U.S. demands for cheap labor and unemployment in Mexico, cannot be solved by unilateral measures. . . .
>
> This being the case, the following is a suggestion to focus on a program for *employment in Mexico* based on concerted actions from the two sides of the border.[24]

The program that Bustamante proposed to address the unemployment problem in Mexico relies heavily upon aid in the form of loans and the importation into the United States of foodstuffs grown by Mexican agricultural producers.[25] There are, probably, reservations that should be held about much, or all, of what Professor Bustamante proposes. The suggestions do have the merit, however, of diverting attention from the more conventional ways of thinking about the Mexican immigration problems, which, for the most part, have neither resolved nor ameliorated the problem.

What the policy should be toward the operations of interest groups in the United States relative to foreign policy cannot differ, save possibly in degree, from what it is presently, because all groups enjoy the rights enumerated in the First Amendment to the U.S. Constitution: "Congress shall make no law . . . abridging the freedom of speech, or of the press, or the right of the people peaceably to assemble, and to petition the Government for a redress of grievances." Because interest groups enjoy the constitutionally protected freedoms of assembly, of expression, and of petitioning government, it need not come as a surprise to us that they will probably continue to exercise those freedoms in accord with their perceptions of what is appropriate for their interests, which they probably associate with being the appropriate foreign policy between the United States and Mexico. It is difficult to imagine what sorts of changes would have to occur in the United States and in Mexico to alter the interest group relationships in both countries relative to foreign policy. Suffice it to say that they would have to be extraordinary. Perhaps the most that can be hoped for is that interest groups on both sides of the border will begin to perceive their interests in foreign policy in a broader, more statesmanlike perspective. Given the record of interest group activity on both sides of the border, however, there appears to be little reason to expect such statesmanlike attitudes to develop, much less to prevail.

Notes

[1] For examples, see F. G. Castles, *Pressure Groups and Political Culture: A Comparative Study* (London: Routledge and Kegan Paul, 1967); H. W. Ehrmann, ed., *Interest Groups on Four Continents* (Pittsburgh: University of Pittsburgh Press, 1958); R. H. Salisbury, "Interest Groups," in F. I. Greenstein and N. W. Polsby, eds., *Nongovernmental Politics: Handbook of Political Science,* vol. 4 (Reading, Mass.: Addison-Wesley, 1975).

[2] Morton Berkowitz, P. G. Bock, and V. J. Fucillo, *The Politics of American Foreign Policy* (Englewood Cliffs, N.J.: Prentice-Hall 1977), p. 2.

[3] Salisbury, "Interest Groups," p. 175.

[4] Ibid., p. 179.

[5] Richard B. Craig, *The Bracero Program: Interest Groups and Foreign Policy* (Austin: University of Texas Press, 1971).

[6] Ibid., p. 4.

[7] For a complete listing of the sixty-nine groups, see ibid., pp. 139–43.

[8] Vernon M. Briggs, Jr., "Labor Market Aspects of Mexican Migration to the United States in the 1970s," in Stanley R. Ross, ed., *Views across the Border: The United States and Mexico* (Albuquerque: University of New Mexico Press, 1978), p. 205.

[9] Tad Szulc, "Foreign Policy Aspects of the Border," in Ross, *Views*, pp. 236–38.

[10] "Immigration Laws Abused, Hispanics Say," *El Paso Times*, November 15, 1978, p. 3B.

[11] Briggs, "Labor Market," pp. 210–11 (emphasis added).

[12] The "tortilla curtain" was the name reputedly given the proposed fence by a person with the Catholic diocese in El Paso who is reported to have observed that "that fence is just like a tortilla—it is flexible and those Mexicans will eat it up."

[13] "Coalition Denounces the 'Tortilla Curtain.' " *Prospector* (University of Texas at El Paso), November 14, 1978, p. 2.

[14] Samuel Gompers, president of the American Federation of Labor, spoke out against the importation of Mexican workers in 1910. See Julian Samora, "Mexican Immigration," in Gus Tyler, ed., *Mexican Americans Tomorrow: Education and Economic Perspectives* (Albuquerque: University of New Mexico Press, 1975), p. 66.

[15] C. F. Bergsten, T. Horst, and T. H. Moran, *American Multinationals and American Interests* (Washington, D.C.: Brookings Institution, 1978), p. 356.

[16] Ibid., p. 342.

[17] Ibid., p. 350.

[18] *The Washington Lobby,* Congressional Quarterly, 1971, p. 89.

[19] Ibid., p. 90.

[20] Ibid.

[21] Ibid., p. 91. Original source: Foreign agents' registrations, U.S. Department of Justice.

[22] Irving Louis Horowitz, "Ethnic Politics and U.S. Foreign Policy," in Abdul Aziz Said, ed., *Ethnicity and U.S. Foreign Policy* (New York: Praeger, 1977), p. 175.

[23] Bergsten, Horst, and Moran, *American Multinationals,* pp. 397–98. The Hickenlooper amendment (76 Stat. 260–61) denies the president the right to waive the requirements to cut off aid to countries that expropriate U.S. companies, even if the cutoff adversely affects the national interest. The Gonzalez amendment (86 Stat. 59) requires the American representative in the Inter-American Development Bank to vote against loans to countries that expropriate American property (ibid., pp. 389–90).

[24] Jorge Bustamante, "Impact of Undocumented Immigration from Mexico on the U.S.–Mexican Economies," in *Fronteras 1976: San Diego/Tijuana,* Conference proceedings, San Diego, November 19–20, 1976, p. 37 (emphasis added).

[25] Ibid., pp. 37–38.

What Hispanic Groups Think about Immigration

Leonel Castillo

Introduction

For some years many persons have looked for a "Hispanic view" on immigration. During the two and a half years that I served as commissioner of the Immigration and Naturalization Service (INS) I was often asked for the Hispanic view on immigration. Occasionally I would read articles, some in major publications, stating that the Latino position on immigration was the creation of an open border between the United States and Mexico. Sometimes I would read articles or hear speeches that indicated complete unanimity among Hispanics in the United States of America on all immigration issues.

I knew, however, that major differences existed among leaders on key issues and that many Latino groups were unaware of the major concerns and issues. Immigration was not the top item on anyone's list of priorities. Discussions with Chicanos in border areas, elected officials, and trade unionists usually centered on the need for controlling and regulating entries. The leaders of national civil liberties, church, and service organizations, however, usually focused their attention on the need for much more generous quotas and on the necessity for a more "open" border.

It was obvious that the unanimity that did not exist on all issues did exist on most of the basic ones. Unfortunately, many of the groups and their leaders were operating from different definitions of the same concept; for example, the phrase "open border" meant something very different to business leaders from what it meant to political leaders. People who lived away from the border were astounded to learn that the Immigration and Naturalization Service was planning to construct twenty miles of border fence. People along the border knew that border fence had existed for many years and that fencing of property is very common along the border, some opulent homes being enclosed by six-foot walls with shards of cut glass on the top. Amnesty, temporary worker, quotas—all were terms without commonly held meanings.

In late November 1977 a national conference on immigration took place in San Antonio. Present at this conference were leaders of many national groups from throughout the country. Unfortunately, the leadership of the conference came primarily from the Socialist Workers party and from several Texas leaders of the Raza Unida party. The guest speakers included the 1976 candidate of the Socialist Workers party, the president of the U.S. National League of the United Latin American Citizen (LULAC), Leroi Jones (or Imaru Baraka), the president of the Mexican-American Legal Defense and Educational Fund, the executive director of the National Council of La Raza, and approximately 1,500 persons from various ideological persuasions. The group adopted positions that called for a completely open border and denounced President Carter's compromise proposals for dealing with the immigration issue. The San Antonio proposals never reached anyone in government but did receive some press for a short period of time in Texas and in the country. Unfortunately, they created a national perception that the Latino position on immigration was one of total amnesty, no temporary workers, open borders, higher quotas for Mexico, and no sanctions on employers of undocumented aliens.

One prominent Mexican-American leader, however, César Chávez, had been urging the Immigration Service to take more vigorous steps to deport more undocumented Mexican nationals when they were being used to break strikes. And the Comité en Defensa de los Inmigrantes (CODI), a New York City coalition of approximately forty Latino groups, supported the Carter package.

In this article I will try to outline those areas in which there is general agreement among the Latino groups and those areas in which there seems to be serious disagreement among these groups. In my conclusion I will try to show the areas of disagreement where I think compromise is possible and the areas where compromise will be a difficult goal.

Latino Views

There are some basic issues on which almost all of the Hispanic groups are in agreement. The groups agree, for example, that all immigrants should be treated in a humane fashion. They agree that a liberal program to allow persons already here to adjust their status (an amnesty program) is essential. They agree that an employer sanction proposal would be a mistake, and they believe that some increase in the quotas for Mexico would be in order. There are slight differences in the degree to which the various groups accept these proposals.

The position often expressed by Congressman Edward Roybal from California is that all persons currently here without papers should be given legal status effective as of the date of signing of any legislation on amnesty. Most of the other groups, such as the National Council of La Raza, have argued for an amnesty date of roughly three to five years before the effective date of any legislation. One coalition of Latino groups, CODI, took the position that they supported the proposal of President Carter that amnesty be effective roughly seven years before legislation became effective. All groups believe that the current 1948 date is unrealistic and cruel.

Perhaps the major differences among the Latino groups can be attributed to their own national origin. For Mexicans any date that would require them to have resided here for more than one or two years would result in making adjustment extremely difficult. The law requires continuous physical presence in the United States. Mexicans, because of the nearness of their homeland, rarely reside in the United States continuously for more than a few years. Viewed in this light, it is not surprising that the New York City–based Latino groups would be more amenable to the adoption of an adjustment date that is five to seven years old. In fact, one Mexican authority on immigration, Dr. Jorge Bustamante, argued that enactment by Congress of President Carter's 1977 proposals would enable a relatively small number of Mexicans to change their status from that of undocumented alien to permanent resident. I argued that roughly 25 percent of those people are eligible for conversion. Professor Bustamante and other noted authorities opined, however, that the correct figure would be closer to 10 percent. The only thing certain is that Mexicans will not benefit in large numbers unless a rather recent amnesty date is selected or some other changes are made. The Carter proposal took the middle position on this matter and created a class of immigrants to be known as temporary resident aliens.

The temporary-resident-alien status was to have been available to persons who resided as undocumented workers in the United States and who would, in effect, receive work permits to remain here for an additional five years. The individuals would not have the right to receive public services such as welfare benefits and would not be made permanent resident aliens. They would be given legal status as workers. Practically every Latino group in the country attacked this proposal as being too harsh. The groups argued that the proposal would classify too many persons working in the United States as truly second-class citizens.

Not surprisingly, the same proposal was attacked from more restrictionist groups because it was too generous. Thousands of letters denounced the plan for "legalizing an illegal activity."

With the exception of the Labor Council of Latin Advancement and CODI, practically every major Latino group in the country opposed the concept of placing penalties on employers who knowingly hire undocumented aliens. All of the groups cited concern for the civil liberties of Mexican Americans and other U.S. citizens who looked foreign. These groups expressed strongly felt doubts that the law could be administered in a nondiscriminatory way.

It remains unclear as to whether the community position on this matter is reflected by the views of the leadership, and it is also uncertain that the Latino leadership groups are expressing the views of the undocumented workers themselves. In 1978, for example, I commissioned a statewide survey in Texas on attitudes of Texans toward immigration issues. The survey was conducted by Telesurveys of Texas, acknowledged experts in polling, under the general direction of Dr. Guillermina Jasso. One part of the survey sought to determine attitudes of Mexican Americans in Texas. The findings were surprising. One consistent finding was that Mexican Americans from all points of the state and all income groups supported by an overwhelming margin the concept of employer sanctions. Mexican Americans and Mexicans living in areas along the border endorsed the idea of employer sanctions by a margin of more than 60 percent. The survey also indicated that Mexican Americans and Mexican nationals away from the border had no great difficulty in accepting the concept of employer sanctions. It may be that Mexicans familiar with Mexico's rather tough position on foreigners who work in Mexico without authorization simply accepted employer sanctions as a way of life. It could well be that the leadership of the national Latino groups simply did not accurately reflect the views of the Latino community. It may be simply that the leadership was more informed and more sensitive to possible civil rights abuses and was being cautious. It could be that the national press managed to convince the general Mexican-American population of Texas that sanctions were a good idea. In my opinion an employer sanction proposal would be met with great opposition from the organized national Latino groups and would be viewed as a major issue in most local communities. Those groups that did not oppose it in 1977 would oppose it now because their local economies are more dependent now on undocumented workers.

There are some major differences of opinion among Latino groups on the question of an open border. The labor groups and border groups, as indicated earlier, have been strong proponents of the need for increased vigilance at the border. César Chávez, for example, testified before the Labor Committee of the U.S. Senate that he favors hiring additional border patrolmen and wants much stricter measures taken to effect deportation of certain undocumented workers. Other Chicano groups, however, have either remained silent on the question of border patrols or asked for no additional support for enforcement until the service aspects of INS are given more attention, or they have concentrated their attention on efforts to make the border patrol more humane.

There is an interesting difference of opinion between Mexicans and Mexican Americans on the subject of immigration. At one point I jokingly accused the leadership of a major Mexican-American organization of being anti-Mexican. I argued that the Mexicans did not want complete amnesty, did not want U.S. aid, and were not in favor of making it extremely easy for Mexicans to become U.S. citizens. Although the long-range political and social interests of Mexican-American groups favor the rapid creation of a large Spanish-speaking population in the United States, many Mexicans argue that they want "trade, not aid," and that their national pride impels them to oppose any massive effort to help Mexicans become U.S. citizens. In short, the Mexicans want to remain Mexicans but would like an opportunity to work in the United States for temporary periods, whereas the Latino groups would prefer that the Mexicans in the United States have all the rights and benefits of U.S. citizens.

Local Latino groups have ambivalent views on immigrants. At earlier points in the history of the GI Forum (Latino Veterans Organization) and LULAC, it was argued that the "wetbacks" and later the braceros were a tremendous drain and strain on the economy. Even now, if one were to spend time in the predominantly Mexican-American barrios of Houston, Dallas, or many other cities, one would hear complaints made by the local Mexican-American population that the undocumented Mexican nationals were causing trouble, were taking jobs away from U.S. citizens, and were weakening the character of neighborhoods. One would also hear that the undocumented Mexicans are hard workers, that they are exploited, that they pay their debts, and that they are making some persons rich. In many parts of the Latino world one would hear of a growing network of services and information for these newest arrivals.

While this ambivalence continues both in the Mexican-American community and in the community at large, the de facto national policy continues to allow a tremendous wave of workers to enter the United States and live here in close proximity to the Spanish-speaking community of the country.

A Growing Consensus

All of the above is not to suggest that a national consensus on immigration policy is impossible. In fact, one is emerging. As an example of this trend, it would be useful to review briefly the recommendations of the national conference on Jobs for Hispanic Americans held at Albuquerque, New Mexico, July 30 through August 2, 1979, under the auspices of the Labor Council for Latin American Advancement (LCLAA), the Latino arm of AFL-CIO. The conference included representatives of over seventy-five national, regional, and local organizations.

They recommended that the number of legal immigrants from Mexico be increased from an annual rate of 20,000 to "at least 50,000 or 60,000" persons, that special impact aid be given to the areas in the United States where legal immigrants concentrate, that the INS receive more funding and staffing, that stronger efforts be made to stop noncitizen strikebreakers from coming into the United States, that more foreign aid be given to Latin America, and that future twin plants be built in the interior of Mexico. The delegates then made several significant policy statements.

The conference delegates endorsed the proposal that "the government of the United States should extend general amnesty to all undocumented workers now present in this country." This is much more generous than the position of the AFL-CIO and is an important move toward building a Latino position.

The LCLAA conference made two other important recommendations. It said that the "federal government should *not* include any type of 'Bracero' program, or foreign labor importation, as a solution to the current problem of undocumented workers." Then, in a significant concession, the recommendation goes on to state that "the experience of other nations . . . should be examined before any temporary or guest worker program is considered." The fact that LCLAA is willing to examine other programs is a softening of their previously unalterable opposition. The LCLAA conference did not mention the subject of employer sanctions, a basic tenet of trade unionists for years. This, of course, also enabled it to avoid the question of universal identification cards.

Conclusion

It now appears that with the recent statement of the Latino labor unionists the national leadership of the Spanish-speaking community is closer together on immigration issues than ever before. If a program of community information and education can be launched it is quite clear that a view can be sold to the Congress and the press as the Latino view. The view calls for more humane treatment of immigrants, increased quotas for Mexico, a broad amnesty for undocumented workers, a crackdown on exploiters of immigrants, study of temporary worker programs in other countries, and more resources for the Immigration and Naturalization Service.

Given the increasing political power of the Hispanic population of the United States and the growing affluence of Mexico, I feel confident that a program with these elements will eventually be adopted by the U.S. Congress.

Organizing the U.S.-Mexican Relationship

Sidney Weintraub

Competing Styles of Negotiation

When the two presidents, Jimmy Carter and José López Portillo, came to power at about the same time in the United States and Mexico, the auguries were favorable for improvement in the cool relationship between the two countries. President López Portillo was the first foreign leader invited to the United States, a symbolic step deliberately taken. In May 1977 a new U.S.–Mexican consultative mechanism was created to add negotiating content to the symbolism. None of this succeeded.[1] The relationship is still cool, as was evident from the reception President Carter received when he visited Mexico in February 1979. Why?

In part, the failure stems from real differences between the two countries. President Carter wished to curtail drastically the number of illegal immigrants entering the United States, and President López Portillo has no interest in closing this escape valve for unemployed and underemployed Mexicans. The disagreement between the two countries on the price of natural gas that could be exported to the United States was based on different national priorities. The trade conflicts are classic. The United States seeks to protect its farmers (high seasonal duties on tomatoes and other winter vegetables flow from this) and workers in labor-intensive industries (such as in the textile and clothing industries) by high tariffs and nontariff restrictions.

The failures also are the result of competing habits of action. The natural gas price decision is almost too perfect an illustration of this. The decision was made by the U.S. government to reject the arrangement worked out between private U.S. companies and the Mexican petroleum industry (PEMEX) because it did not mesh with the existing domestic U.S. gas price policy.[2] The wider Mexican–U.S. relationship was a peripheral issue. From the Mexican vantage, this occurred in a sector replete with past conflict with the United States, which the Mexican president was trying to overcome and on which rest many of Mexico's hopes for financing future development. It was a price issue for Mexico, but it was also much more than that. It was a price issue for the United States—period.

In its way, the president's proposed legislation to the Congress on illegal immigration followed a similar stylistic pattern. The U.S. government, concerned over its perception that illegal immigrants were having an adverse impact on the U.S. labor market, consulted with the Mexican government on this issue, did not get very far, and then acted (proposed legislation) unilaterally. The Mexican reaction was predictably angry. There is a quotation from López Portillo that expresses his view of this issue:

> There are no isolated problems; everything is part of everything else.
>   If, for example, we want to solve the problem of undocumented workers, we must understand that the problem lies in Mexico's economic situation. This will improve if we achieve a better balance in our very unfavorable trade relations with the United States.[3]

The U.S. governmental ideal is to decentralize and compartmentalize decision making, as in the checks and balances among the branches at the federal level. This style is carried over into international negotiation. López Portillo, in the quotation cited, talked of linking trade and immigration, whereas the United States generally seeks its quid pro quo for a trade concession in the trade field. From the viewpoint of U.S. policy makers, the successful post–World War II international organizations have been the functional ones like the General Agreement on Tariffs and Trade, the International Monetary Fund, and the World Bank, for they deal concretely in a single field. The least useful for actual decision making as viewed by the United States are such general-purpose organizations as the U.N. Conference on Trade and Development or the U.N. General Assembly itself, precisely because "everything is part of everything else." López Portillo may be logically correct, but the U.S. policy maker prefers to ask the more pragmatic question: How does one negotiate anything if everything is on the table?

There has been a certain persistence in Mexican efforts to do just the reverse, to put everything on the table at once by integrating issues for international negotiation. López Portillo's predecessor, Luis Echeverría, proposed and pushed to conclusion the U.N. Charter on Economic Rights and Duties of States, which in its way is the integrative approach to international negotiation carried to its ultimate conclusion. The charter was (and is) of no interest to U.S. policy makers except in the negative sense of getting through the process without damaging other activities in the economic field.

These differences in negotiating techniques resemble a play in which one group of actors is performing on the right side of the stage and another on the left side, both playing to parts of the audience, but the two sides and the two audiences never quite come together. The comprehensive demands of one side are met by point-by-point denials of the other.

The issues are complicated by what is now well understood in economic policy—that what is involved is a mixture of domestic and foreign affairs.[4] Trade liberalization is negotiated not solely in the ideal world of macroeconomics but also in the interplay of competing domestic interests plus the conflict between some of these interests and foreign aspirations. Decisions on trade liberalization (for example, whether to lower the level of U.S. protection on tomatoes from Mexico) are both international and domestic. The issue of illegal immigration illustrates this domestic-foreign interplay even more vividly because the stakes are higher than for a single agricultural commodity. There are significant interests in the United States that wish the flow of Mexican immigrants to continue because these workers provide labor at a price not otherwise available in the United States. The Mexican government argues that labor demand and supply in the United States are equilibrated in optimum fashion by this worker flow. The other side of the domestic pressure is from organized U.S. labor, which argues that this equilibrium is achieved at the expense of domestic workers.

One other attribute of the U.S. policy-making process worth making explicit is the effort to resolve issues at the lowest possible governmental or technical level. Issues thus tend to be debated on narrow grounds without bringing into play broader interests, of either national or foreign policy. The advantage to this procedure is that it permits examination of discrete issues based on their particular merits and defects. The main disadvantage is that it stifles conceptual breakthroughs. When each issue is a decision unto itself, and especially if it involves giving a concession to a foreign country, those seeking to block change tend to be more powerful than those trying to force change. This is one basis for the perennial complaint against the State Department, that it speaks for foreigners. The bureaucracy is intended not to be a device for originality but mostly to carry out what exists.

There have been exceptions to this generalized structure of U.S. decision making. Innovations do take place, such as the Alliance for Progress, to cite one that dealt with Latin America, but these tend to be imposed by senior political level officials able to deal comprehensively. The recent practice of economic summit meetings of the leaders of the key industrial countries is, similarly, an effort to break through the confines of narrow particularism. The summits sometimes have some value (they probably have blunted the trade protectionist drive), and they sometimes do not work (it has not been possible to coordinate macroeconomic policy at the summit, and this really is the main objective of these meetings).

Trade-offs have been attempted involving a quid in one field for a quo in another, but this is a complex process. The U.S. congressional effort to link increased emigration from the U.S.S.R. with most-favored-nation trade treatment aroused deep resentment in the Soviet Union because the two elements were incommensurate. An explicit trade-off of lower U.S. trade restrictions on a variety of Mexican exports in return for some Mexican action on illegal emigration, which is what is implied in the Mexican argument that it wishes to send goods and not people, is similarly incommensurate because different interests are involved. In addition, the time frames differ; Mexico really wishes to send goods *and* people now on the assumption that this may permit sending fewer people later. What is the present discounted price of a vague Mexican aspiration that sometime in the future fewer immigrants will come to the United States? These disparate trade-offs also entail sacrificing one group's interests for another's benefits. Such intergroup interest trade-offs are common—every import tariff or restriction does just that, but usually when the payers are not precisely identified. The trade-offs are deliberately kept implicit.

The competing styles of the two countries can be summarized as follows: What Mexico would like is for the United States to set a higher priority on relations with Mexico and then negotiate on particular issues at a high level, presidential or close to it, where the overall policy importance of Mexico can be brought to bear. Everything would not necessarily be negotiated at once, but the important trade-offs cutting across different areas would be inherent in the negotiating process. What the United States in fact does is to deal with issues mostly in isolation, generally at the technical level, and rarely to permit disparate trade-offs to influence final outcomes. Different issues may be linked intellectually but rarely in a specific negotiation.

Efforts at Integrated Negotiating Mechanisms

From time to time, efforts have been made to overcome the inertial consequences of the piecemeal approach to U.S.–Mexican relations. They have not succeeded.

The most recent such effort was the consultative mechanism brought into being in May 1977 following discussions between Presidents Carter and López Portillo during the latter's visit to Washington in February 1977. The mechanism has three main working groups, political, social, and economic, and subgroups on energy, minerals, industry, and investment; trade; finance; tourism; drug abuse; and border issues. As one reads through the public releases, the discussions under this mechanism, though substantive, add little to what can be accomplished through normal diplomatic intercourse. The discussions have dealt with complaints about one another's trading practices, Mexican requests for improved tariff preferences, civil aviation, tourism promotion, U.S. concerns about the Mexican decree on the development of its automobile industry, Mexican access to U.S. capital market, and how better cooperation can be achieved at the border region.[5] Rather than integrate negotiation simultaneously around several problem areas, the subgroups have separated issues; and this has tended to reinforce the U.S. as opposed to the Mexican negotiating mode. The consultative mechanism was reinforced, after President Carter's visit to Mexico in February 1979, but no fundamental change was made in its operating mode.

In addition to the consultative mechanism, there are other, more narrowly defined U.S.–Mexican commissions that meet regularly or as needed, such as the Cultural Commission, Joint Commission on Science and Technology, Joint Commission on Fish and Wildlife, the Border Health Commission, a Working Group on Environmental Cooperation, a bilateral Fisheries Consultative Group, a pending Working Group on Urban Affairs and Human Settlements, a bilateral Defense Commission, and the International Boundary and Water Commission (established pursuant to a treaty).

Two competing conclusions emerge from these efforts at integrated negotiation: (1) that there must be some perceived need, else the two countries would not keep trying; and (2) because each try fails, the idea itself is flawed. Why do the two countries keep trying?

The most important reason is that issues are in fact related even if negotiation is disjointed. Mexico's most severe problem is the inability to provide full-time employment for more than 40 percent of its current labor force or even to create annually more than half the number of jobs needed for the roughly 700,000 persons who seek to enter the job market each year. This set of facts, coupled with some 3,200 kilometers of contiguity with the United States, makes this a problem for the United States as hundreds of thousands or even millions of Mexicans cross the border each year, with or without papers, to find jobs. Adequate job creation in Mexico must inevitably entail intensified industrialization and the ability to export manufactured goods to the United States and elsewhere in ever-increasing amounts. Job creation, industrialization, and emigration are inextricably linked both within Mexico and in Mexico's interaction with the United States. The Mexican objection to the proposed U.S. legislation on illegal immigration is based precisely on the ground that the United States failed to take into account the impact of this restrictive policy in Mexico.

In addition, though crude trade-offs in different fields may not be practicable (such as Mexican willingness to produce and sell more oil if the United States accepts more migrant Mexican workers, or an easing of U.S. trade restrictions if in return Mexico cooperates in keeping Mexicans without documentation from entering the United States), linkages are made in the total negotiating context between nations. Can there be any doubt that the United States would not have agreed to sell sophisticated aircraft to Saudi Arabia if the United States did not need Saudi oil production? One was not traded for the other, but one would not have been traded except for the other.

Finally, if the respective representatives are senior enough and are able to negotiate simultaneously or seriatim across a range of issues, the hope is that this can blunt the force of particular pressures for maintaining the status quo. Individual interest groups would still be heard, but the context for interaction would be broader. This type of negotiating context is what Mexican leaders seem to want. Mexico's power structure involves fewer people and issues come more quickly to the top, but there is no central location in the U.S. government, short of the president, that is a counterpart to this. A common Mexican complaint is that they do not know where to go in the U.S. government, above the technical level, for resolving substantive issues; and when they do raise an issue at the technical level, it is dealt with technically and in isolation.

Would an organizational restructuring by the U.S. government make much difference? Possibly yes, but probably not. The current consultative mechanism was established precisely to overcome the lack of central location for interaction and to avoid issue atomization by making each issue part of a larger structure. The two foreign secretaries were placed at the apex of the mechanism. Still, as already noted, it has not worked. It may be that the decentralized U.S. negotiating style is inevitable, given the variety of interests that must be heard on each issue. A czar in charge of Mexican affairs might be a powerless figurehead. It may also be harder for the United States to negotiate with Mexico than with most countries because the domestic part of each negotiation is apt to be extremely important. This is what makes the illegal immigration issue so intractable.

Despite the uncertainty of the outcome of a reorganization, the current unsatisfactory state of Mexican–U.S. relations makes it desirable to look to structure as this may be impeding effective dealing with substance.

69

Alternative Structures for Interaction

The perceived shortcomings of the current U.S. structure can be summarized as follows:

1. Issues tend to be dealt with in isolation without regard for the total relationship.

2. This, coupled with the domestic ramifications of almost any negotiation with Mexico, stacks the odds in favor of inertia—or, when there is action, as in the cases of immigration legislation or buying natural gas from Mexico, more weight is given to domestic considerations than to relations with Mexico.[6]

3. Finally, except for the few issues that can be raised directly with the president, the Mexicans find themselves negotiating with the U.S. Department of Agriculture, or Labor, or Commerce, or Treasury, or Energy, and occasionally even with the State Department, but rarely with the U.S. government all at once.

It is worth repeating that these perceived shortcomings are the result primarily of substantive differences rather than organizational deficiencies. The limits placed on nonreciprocal trade concessions to Mexico do not stem from organizational shortcomings. The insistence that Mexico restrict its textile and apparel exports results from a generalized U.S. problem relating to many developing countries. Certainly some problems would have been handled differently if it were clear that the president of the United States placed great importance on good relations with Mexico and that important statements about and negotiations with Mexico were to be coordinated with a central person who enjoyed the confidence of the president. The gas price negotiations might have turned out exactly as they did (or they might not have), but the rhetoric from the United States would have been more sensitive to Mexican history.[7] Some organizational device might be considered to try to overcome these shortcomings.

The most straightforward technique would be for the president to appoint a distinguished person, familiar with Mexico, as his coordinator (or ambassador at large) for Mexican affairs. The position would not have to be permanent. It could be, but an alternative is to make it clear at the outset that the coordinator would devote, say, the next two years to across-the-board discussion and negotiation with a Mexican counterpart on the crucial issues concerning the two countries. This would differ from the existing consultative mechanism in that the person in charge would devote full time to Mexican affairs. The coordinator could report either to the secretary of state or, conceivably, to the president or to both simultaneously.

This structure, of a "secretary of state for Mexico," would certainly highlight symbolically that the United States considered its relations with Mexico to have higher priority than relations with most other countries. A coordinator for Mexico at this senior level would be unique in the U.S. structure. Even for interaction with China or the U.S.S.R., the most senior full-time officials are at lower bureaucratic levels. The most direct comparisons are the structures established to negotiate the Panama Canal treaties or disarmament agreements or the law of the sea—that is, for functional negotiations of great importance. The reason for the suggestion that this position be temporary is that sustained high-level negotiations would lose their vigor after a few years. An organizational decision of this type should not be taken unless the president really felt that U.S.–Mexican relations were so important as to merit extraordinary attention.

The clear advantage of this organizational structure is that it would focus attention on Mexico and force substantive examination of bilateral issues. The coordinator would be able to integrate issues in a way that is not now possible. The major potential disadvantage is that it might not work. The underlying substance would not alter just because there is a coordinator, and the outcomes might not change either. Is it better to have tried and failed than not to have tried at all?[8]

Other devices short of designating a senior coordinator for Mexico can be conceived. One of these is to raise the level of the officer in charge of Mexican affairs in the State Department; this person is now an office director and could be made a deputy assistant secretary. This would give the person more authority, but he/she would still be quite junior in the Washington hierarchy. This is not really comparable to the coordinator idea.

Another way to stress the importance the United States attaches to its relations with Mexico would be for the president to appoint a special commission, with a short deadline of about six months, to report back to him on substantive and organizational arrangements regarding Mexico. The disadvantage of this suggestion is the same as that for most commissions; it might be seen as a way of deferring rather than promoting action.

Another approach might not be organizational at all; this would be for the president to give the agencies some sense of the great importance that he attaches to U.S. interaction with Mexico and to state his expectation that this will be reflected in important agency actions. Conceivably this could make a difference, but its effective life is apt to be very short. An organizational change probably would be needed to reinforce the sincerity of a presidential pronouncement. The ultimate reinforcement would be some changes of substance and style in U.S. actions toward Mexico.

It might be useful to conclude with a few words on the mixture of style and substance. There are, of course, objective differences in power between the two countries that must affect the content of negotiations. About 60 percent of Mexico's exports come to the United States, whereas less than 5 percent of U.S. exports generally go to Mexico. The migrants come to the United States to find jobs and not the reverse. The per capita income in the United States in 1976 was close to $8,000, almost eight times that of Mexico. Asymmetry in relations is inevitable.

It need not be blatant, however. The organizational suggestions contained in this paper are intended to deal primarily with substance, but they could have the added benefit of improving the style of U.S. interaction with Mexico. The asymmetry that now exists in U.S.–Mexican relations is less than it used to be, and it certainly will be less still in the future. Mexican oil and gas discoveries will change the bilateral negotiating relationship. So will further Mexican development of more sophisticated industries. Future trade competition is likely to be in machinery, basic petrochemicals, steel, probably automobiles, and not just in textiles, clothing, tomatoes, and shoes. The very size of Mexico (about 125 million people by the year 2000) will add to its importance to the United States.

It is inevitable, therefore, that the Mexican connection in U.S. foreign relations will grow in importance. This is the basis for the organizational suggestions made in this paper—to recognize this importance and to give it prominence.

Notes

At the time this essay was written, the author was a senior fellow at the Brookings Institution. The views expressed in this article are his own.

[1] This paper was prepared before the position of coordinator for Mexican affairs was created and former Congressman Robert Krueger of Texas was named for the job. It cannot be said that the position has had any significant effect on U.S.-Mexican relations. It may be that the idea is flawed. The idea espoused in this article, however, has not really been given a fair test. What Sidney Weintraub has in mind is not a highly visible ambassador with political ambitions but an internal coordinator, someone to force the U.S. government to take positions on issues of U.S.-Mexican relations that are not mutually inconsistent. The kind of person contemplated is a skilled government operator with a passion for anonymity. The executive branch has not yet abandoned the position of assistant to the president for national security affairs, where the same conflict between anonymous coordination and flamboyant, public position taking exists, and probably should not abandon the idea of a coordinator for Mexican affairs until it has been tested under the right circumstances and with the right kind of person.

[2] In a press interview in Mexico City on May 4, 1978, former U.S. Secretary of State Cyrus Vance said it would not be appropriate to discuss this issue with others outside the United States until gas prices in the United States are decided. U.S., Department of State, *Bulletin* 78, no. 2015 (June 1978): 57. The Mexican price was rejected on the additional ground that it was higher than the price for natural gas from Canada.

[3] Quotation taken from David F. Ronfeldt and Caesar D. Sereseres, "Treating the Alien (ation) in U.S.–Mexico Relations," Rand Paper Series, August 1978, p. 22. Their source was an interview reported in the *Christian Science Monitor,* September 14, 1977.

[4] An excellent discussion of this theme is contained in Bayless Manning, "The Congress, the Executive, and Intermestic Affairs: Three Proposals," *Foreign Affairs* 55, no. 2 (January 1977): 306–24.

[5] "Joint Report on Status of the U.S.–Mexico Consultative Mechanism," approved by U.S. Secretary of State Cyrus Vance and Mexican Secretary of Foreign Relations Santiago Roel García, Mexico, May 4, 1978.

[6] A good illustration of this is contained in Secretary Vance's press conference of May 4, 1978, in Mexico City, cited above. Vance was asked if there were any serious discussions going on in Washington on renewing the bracero program. From time to time, Mexican leaders have raised this possibility; President Echeverría did. Vance responded: "The answer . . . is a very simple one: no."

[7] The Immigration and Naturalization Service might not have considered putting up a particularly difficult fence at El Paso to force illegal migrants to detour to other routes, an action later reconsidered, if some central coordination had taken place first.

[8] The appointment of a coordinator is my preferred organizational solution. This suggestion originally was made before President Carter's visit to Mexico, and it may be a reality by the time this appears in print.

Problems and Cooperation between U.S. and Mexican Border Cities

Frank J. Call

Problems

In order to place the following remarks in some perspective, it is necessary to sketch briefly the major problems confronting U.S. border cities. Many of these problems will be recognized as problems for Mexican border cities as well. These problems are the basis for cooperation between U.S. and Mexican border cities.

Economic. Economics is the basis for almost all of the problems in the border area. Border communities on both sides can be characterized as having soft economies, consisting of very large service sectors, based on tourism, trade, and governmental expenditures. Illegal trade, unknown in volume, involves contraband, stolen merchandise (from transistor radios to automobiles), and drugs. There is little activity, much of it declining, in agriculture, mining, forestry, fisheries, and so forth. Shrimp production in Brownsville, Texas, has dropped consistently since 1970, and the regulations imposed on the tuna fishing fleet based in San Diego have caused the catch to drop substantially. Border city economies have little economic base diversification, generally with a small manufacturing sector and a huge governmental sector. Absentee ownership is common both in the United States and in Mexico. These economies are weakened by large capital leakages.

The economies are largely underdeveloped, with a low-skilled labor pool constantly being replenished at the bottom. Although it has been said that there is no direct displacement in the labor market area by the legal and illegal immigrants, there may be indirect or delayed displacement.

The border economies have limited energy availability. Geothermal energy resources have been developed in Baja Norte, and Sonora and Chihuahua have some potential for further development. The completion of distribution pipelines will make energy more readily available on the Mexican side. The limited natural resources in the border area have a history of poor development and management, partly because of the inadequate federal and state policy on both sides.

The economies are undeveloped partly because they are isolated from the markets of both countries, though San Diego can of course, service the markets of the huge Los Angeles area and areas farther north. Perhaps a more important factor is that the population is growing faster than the economies.

There is a huge economic disparity between the United States and Mexico. The counties on the U.S. side are the poorest in the nation, but they are still richer than the border counties in Mexico, which are some of the richest in that nation. Although the states of Texas and California are quite rich, their border areas are very depressed economically.

Housing. In excess of 150,000 houses on the U.S. side of the border are substandard, even by local housing standards, which are lower than those in many other communities in the United States. There is no way of estimating overcrowding. Housing on the Mexican side ranges from poor to terrible.

Many U.S. border communities are old cities, with extremely old downtown core sections; yet these cities do not qualify for many federal programs because most of the housing was built after 1940. Only recently has there been a significant expansion in housing in border communities.

With housing standards on the Mexican frontier considerably lower than on the U.S. side, there is a constant migration to the United States. There are few demands on landlords to improve rental property or to make repairs necessary to upgrade housing, but there is an insatiable demand for housing on the border. In McAllen, Texas, when a substandard housing unit became vacant, it was condemned and bulldozed before anybody could occupy it. Unfortunately, this led to the development of *colonias* outside the city limits that did not meet plumbing or street development standards or electrical codes. After the city of McAllen was forced to annex these *colonias,* it found that it was expensive to upgrade them to meet minimum standards. In El Paso, during El Chamizal resettlement, hundreds of portable trailer-type housing units had to be brought in to accommodate the displacement.

Although many residents in substandard housing cannot afford new housing, the demand for new housing runs high and at exorbitant rates. The poor have no alternative to public housing, which often destroys residential property values and removes taxable property from the tax roles. Public housing is growing at an alarming rate in the border area.

Health. Components of the health problem include vector control, environmental health, communicable diseases, and health-care costs. In regard to vector control, mosquitoes, fruit flies, fire ants, rabies, and many other problems are no respecters of international boundaries, especially when there is a free flow across the boundaries. In the case of rabies, vectors include bats, dogs, and skunks. The border patrol does not attempt to halt their flow across the border, though these are serious problems. If one side of the border is sprayed for mosquitoes and the other side is not sprayed, a serious outbreak of disease may occur.

Air, water, and solid waste pose serious environmental health problems along the border. Recent proposals to bury nuclear waste in the Carlsbad, New Mexico, area evoked great concern from the citizens from Ciudad Juárez, Mexico, who were concerned that the depositories could be damaged by earthquakes. Some proposed disposal sites lie near fault areas in which there is groundwater transference, and some fault areas extend from the Carlsbad area into Mexico. The border area may have a continuous problem with nuclear waste, due to the large areas of low population. The border area also contains several fast-growing urban centers that may eventually be threatened by such waste disposal.

The problem of sewage treatment continues to develop at an alarming rate. The U.S. side of the border extensively treats sewage, often making it cleaner than the water the communities are taking from the river. Communities on the other side do not attempt to treat the sewage because they cannot begin to meet the demands of population growth.

Air pollution poses even more serious problems. Air quality has deteriorated beyond the ability of many border communities to restore. In the El Paso–Ciudad Juárez area, for example, natural conditions— the yoke of the mountain—prevent dispersion of many of the pollutants generated by industrial activities and by motor vehicles. The Environmental Protection Agency has restrained El Paso from developing further industry that will affect air quality. Unfortunately, there are no similar restraints in Mexico. Although the Mexicans are very concerned about the quality of the environment, jobs must come first.

There is great potential for outbreaks of communicable disease on the border, where population outstrips municipal services such as water treatment, sewers, and even solid waste disposal. Water standards are a problem not only on the Mexican side of the border but also on the U.S. side. The entire border is arid: 83 percent of all cases of amebiasis in the United States in the last five years were reported in the lower Rio Grande valley along the Texas side of the border, chiefly because of the lack of adequately treated water. Since people are obtaining water from contaminated sources, an epidemic borne by water carriers could quickly spread. Health authorities have no idea why this has not already happened.

Another element of the health problem is that residents on both sides of the border are increasingly unable to pay even necessary health-care costs. Local government will probably assume some health-care costs for their impoverished residents, but they are unlikely to continue to supply health care to nonresidents without being reimbursed. McAllen, for example, which operates its own municipal hospital, estimates that the drain on municipal funds for nonelective care of aliens is in excess of $800,000 per year. Nonelective care includes injuries, accidents, sudden sickness, and childbirth. In Southern California, hospitals have been forced to close because they have been unable to meet these expenses. Clearly, there is a need to develop a mechanism that will reimburse these public hospitals.

Drug abuse is a growing problem on both sides of the border. Its rate of growth has many professionals concerned that there may never be adequate resources for either prevention or treatment programs. The huge transient population makes it difficult to keep track of known abusers. The border offers an ideal hiding place for them.

Education. On the U.S. side of the border, educated young people are migrating away from border areas in search of employment and opportunities that do not exist there. Probably the reverse is true on the northern frontier of Mexico, where Mexicans come in search of opportunity. Such migration tends to breed underemployment, which can be a problem as devastating as unemployment.

Part of the education problem is the massive overcrowding of schools, which exists on both sides of the border. The school districts on the U.S. side are unable to cope with this growth through current taxation. Some school districts cannot finance quality public education. There are constitutional limits to bonding for new school construction. The situation is generally the same in Mexican border communities. Some communities have split schedules, with morning and afternoon sessions. Overcrowding is far more serious in Mexican border communities that have experienced rapid population growth, especially among the younger people. U.S. courts are in disagreement over how to pay for the education of aliens. The Organization of U.S. Border Cities, under contract to the Southwest Border Regional Commission, is currently trying to determine the impact of resident alien and migrant school children on border school districts. It is hoped that this study will lead to an allocation formula that would allow up to $30 million worth of new school construction in the border region on the U.S. side, but that would not solve the problem on the Mexican side.

Criminal Justice. Border communities are noted for a high rate of petty crime, such as purse snatching, and shoplifting but there are also more serious crimes. In San Diego serious assaults on Mexicans, both legal and illegal, are increasing rapidly. Most assaults occur while people are crossing the San Diego–Baja Norte portion of the border. Police departments of the border believe that stolen merchandise goes both ways: they say that merchandise fenced on the U.S. side is often stolen in Mexico; merchandise, autos, and construction equipment fenced on the Mexican side of the border are stolen in the United States.

The problems of drug abuse, discussed under health problems, have criminal implications. Many drug abusers resort to crime to support their addictions. More burglaries are committed in the border area than in any comparable population area in the United States. Most of this burglary finances drug abuse. A further consequence of drug abuse, the smuggling of firearms into Mexico in exchange for drugs, could have longer-term significance if these arms are used for ideological purposes.

Compounding Factors

Perhaps the most important factor compounding the problems we have briefly reviewed is the lack of continuous policy input at the national level. The Organization of U.S. Border Cities was established to act in a united fashion in support of greater attention to the needs of the border area.

The inability to initiate more communications between the sister cities of the border on a one-to-one basis also compounds the problems of the border. This problem is partly due to differences in the structure of government, but mainly to the current interpretation of international law—that the nation-states can make only formal communications. Many needed communications are so minor that they hardly warrant diplomatic transmission.

Sister cities are not allowed to make binding agreements at the local level. It has been said that the differences between the English common law system used in the United States and the Roman law tradition used in Mexico prevent or at least hinder the making of legal agreements, but empirical observation shows these differences to be small. Worldwide, there continue to be many interactions between the English common law tradition and the Roman law tradition.

Border problems are further compounded by the inability of the local governments on the U.S. side to finance the foreign policies of the United States and the Republic of Mexico. Costs of policing the border and of providing education and health care under our federal system should be borne by income taxes, customs duties, and the like. Border residents, however, unfairly carry much of the financial burden of U.S. foreign policy vis-à-vis Mexico. If these local expenditures were offset by some other financial advantages, then these communities would not be among the poorest in the United States. Because most federal block grants are allocated on the basis of either population or unemployment, perhaps assistance to border communities should not be calculated on the basis of the figures for only one side of the border. Most observers believe the border communities have interdependent economies. Brownsville, Texas, for example, is eligible to receive block grants relative to its population of 80,000, but that population is supplemented daily by nearly 60,000 Mexicans who come there to work, shop, or spend leisure time. The difference between 80,000 and 140,000 in terms of federal block granting is significant. San Diego may show official unemployment rates between 8 and 10 percent, while Tijuana, Mexico, which has a population nearly the size of San Diego, has an unemployment rate in excess of 30 percent. These are interdependent cities to some degree; they should be assisted with that fact in mind.

The problems of the border are unique and dynamic, totally unlike those of the longer-established inland communities with stable populations. Unfortunately, little federal attention is paid to these problems, and most federal grants and programs do not work well in the border area, mainly because of a lack of united political strength.

Examples of Cooperation

There are some positive examples of cooperation along the border. The prisoner exchange treaty (which was negotiated at the highest diplomatic level between the two countries) was an example of a successful approach to a problem that seemed unresolvable. Another example is the International Boundary and Water Commission (IBWC), established by conventions between the two countries. This commission, which has authority solely with regard to water and boundaries, has clearly been a success—without the problems normally associated with negotiations in these areas. Many border residents feel that the powers of this commission should be broadened to include groundwater withdrawal. Water shortage is one of the most serious problems facing the border right now. The lower Rio Grande valley is 400,000 acre-feet short of surface water every year. The Mexicans are damming the Rio Conchos, which supplies nearly 100 percent of the flow from Big Bend on the Rio Grande down to Amistad Reservoir. Some medium will be necessary to deal with groundwater resources. The U.S. and Mexican sections of the IBWC are exchanging data on groundwater withdrawal for parts of the border and could expand this activity.

Another formal organization is the Pan American Health Organization (PAHO), sponsor of the U.S.–Mexico Border Health Association. Most border residents feel this organization has been successful. It has provided for accurate health record keeping, and it has developed a public forum for the two countries to discuss health issues. PAHO, which is supported financially by both countries, has some capability to work out formal agreements.

Another example of cooperation on the border is tourism development resulting from the consultative mechanism. Clearly there have been some successes even though no local people are part of the consultative mechanism. Perhaps the advisory groups or the subgroups of the consultative mechanism can be enlarged to include participation by people along the border.

Another example of cooperation is the Customs Brokers Association, which works in an informal way. It has been very successful in working with the federal agencies to speed the handling of trade between the two countries.

There is also some optimism about the Southwest Border Regional Commission and its Mexican counterpart. These two entities are expected to do some planning together, but they offer no panacea. The solution to the problems in the border region is partly political, partly social, and partly economic, but the charge of regional commissions in the United States is strictly economic.

Other examples of cooperation on an informal level include the tourism associations that promote the border as a final destination for travel. Regular Chamber of Commerce programs between sister communities have strengthened ties between the commercial sectors and have led to a better understanding of changes in policies between the two countries. The Maquila Association has worked diligently to remove obstacles to the development of this program in both Mexico and the United States.

On a more formal level, an Environmental Protection Agency study of air quality is now being conducted between San Diego and Tijuana. There has been talk of a similar study for the El Paso/Ciudad Juárez area.

Many residents of the border are encouraged that the border resource centers are begining to develop. The San Diego center, directed by Dr. Norris Clement, is especially encouraging because it is concerned with the border problems on a binational basis, and not just on the U.S. side. One of the projects of Dr. Clement's border resource center is an input/output model—an econometric, mathematical tool to judge the effects of changes on the economies of both Tijuana and San Diego. The Border State University Consortium for Latin America (BSUCLA) is a consortium of universities dedicated to providing information about border problems. Universities on the Mexican side may be able to participate in such an endeavor. An example of cooperation between the universities was seen in Ciudad Juárez, Mexico. A group of twenty-six students in the University of Juárez's planning program (master of arts program), were required to take a seminar in urban planning, but the university lacked the necessary teachers and resources. The university joined with the University of Texas at El Paso, New Mexico State University, and local citizens on both sides of the border to provide professional assistance. The seminar became fully accredited and the students did not have to go to Mexico City for this final semester.

Another example of academic cooperation is the Association of Borderland Scholars (ABS). The ABS is similar to the regional associations of university professors. The scholars of the borderlands have firsthand knowledge of their communities, but they have been largely neglected by federal agencies dealing with border problems.

Examples of binational planning include the Railroad Relocation Project in Brownsville, Texas. It involves an effort to relocate U.S. and Mexican railroads out of Brownsville and Matamoros, to less-developed outlying districts, where they will not pose problems of congestion and public safety. This project has involved planning between local officials, state officials from Texas and from Tamaulipas State, and planners from Washington and Mexico City. The U.S. appropriations act of $24 million for this railroad relocation specifically allows the money to be used in assisting the Mexican government in relocating its facilities.

A railroad relocation project takes from nine to twelve years from initiation to implementation. It requires a massive planning effort involving thousands of variables, including the handling of toxic chemicals and explosives, speed, right of way, environmental protection, population growth, and the like. This railroad relocation project was an outgrowth of "Intercambio," an informal effort between residents of the lower Rio Grande valley of Texas and their Mexican counterparts to plan together for future development. This was a successful program that fell into disuse when the principal people involved left public office. It could be revived.

The city of El Paso, realizing that mosquitoes do not respect international boundaries and that the city of Ciudad Juárez lacked the equipment and personnel needed to spray, offered its trucks, personnel, and spraying equipment. There was concern that when the trucks and the personnel went across the border they would have no legal standing. If the workers were injured or the trucks or equipment damaged, there might be no legal way to collect insurance. An informal agreement between the two communities resolved the problem: the spraying is now called a training session. This solution allows El Paso to retain its insurance coverage. Other examples of cooperation include rabies eradication programs. In the border region, dogs, cats, and other pets pose a far less serious rabies problem than do skunks, bats, and coyotes. PAHO has taken over the rabies eradication program.

The Texas legislature has enabled fire engines or any vehicles of public safety to pass across the border and still be protected by insurance. There is some question whether this measure is legal, but it does help local U.S. public officials in deciding whether to send equipment and personnel when there is a fire or a natural disaster in a counterpart community across the border.

There are other significant examples of informal cooperation. The Inter-American Council, which serves McAllen, Texas, Hidalgo, Texas, and Reynosa, Mexico, is composed of businessmen and civic leaders who attempt to resolve problems between local units of government and the citizens. In Brownsville-Matamoros a similar group is called the International Council; in El Paso-Ciudad Juárez this council is called the Intercity Group. One outstanding example of cooperation of two communities can be seen annually in Laredo–Nuevo Laredo on Washington's birthday. There are huge celebrations between the two communities, and people pass freely across the border to participate in them. On the Mexican Independence Day there was a *grito* in El Paso as well as in Cuidad Juárez. One could continue to describe such examples almost indefinitely.

The Fronteras Program has been successful in promoting understanding between Southern California and Baja Norte. This program, a bicentennial project, is now being funded by the city of San Diego. Another successful regional program, the Commission of the Californias, was established in 1964 to improve relations between Southern California and Baja Norte. It has been taken over by the lieutenant governor of California, who has given it even more emphasis. As a result, the De la Madrid government in Baja California Norte has also given it more emphasis. The New Mexico Border Commission is similar to that of the Commission of the Californias except that there is more emphasis on tourism development and port development. It has also facilitated cattle exports from Mexico and the processing of food exports from Mexico. The Good Neighbor Commission in Texas has as one of its main objectives the improvement of relations between Texas and its neighboring states in Mexico.

There are a number of private foundations and religious groups that help people on both sides of the border with informal programs. These programs, which help those who are unable to help themselves, are far too numerous to mention. There are also binational conferences, an example of which is the Substance Abuse Conference held in 1978 at Piedras Negras. Health professionals on drug abuse from both the United States and Mexico participated in this conference.

With the exception of arrangements such as the International Boundary and Water Commission and the Pan American Health Organization, there are few formal relations between Mexico and the United States. Most relations between the two countries or between two communities at the border are informal and have no binding force.

When both El Paso and Ciudad Juárez elected new mayors, the Organization of U.S. Border Cities brought them together as early as possible to discuss common problems. Joint luncheon meetings were set up, and six hours of discussions were filmed for television, in Spanish and English, and shown both in the United States and in Mexico. These documentaries, which covered problems of economic development, transportation, health, immigration, and criminal justice, proved useful in explaining the situation on both sides of the border.

Mexican cities may need an organization like the Organization of U.S. Border Cities and Counties, which cannot, of course, try to organize these Mexican cities. Mexican *municipios*, however, lack the autonomy of U.S. cities and are therefore more difficult to organize.

To sum up, there is no power to negotiate in the local public interest, that is, in terms of protection of equipment and personnel. There is no local ability to protect property and lives that go across the border. Contradictions between the Roman law tradition and the English common law tradition seem to be of minor consequence. Executives on the two sides of the border differ in their power to translate wishes into programs. U.S. mayors, with approval of their city councils, can implement programs, raise money, and spend it. The *presidente* of a municipio in Mexico, which receives most of its funds from the federal government, has little direct power to translate wishes into programs. Binational planning at present is limited to a few examples at the local level. At the federal government level, most binational planning centers on general strategies or changes in direction of government, rather than planning for implementation. Communication at the local level is usually informal. Local governments have limited access to federal decision making, and border residents sense a reluctance to work on basic problems at the national levels. Programs are largely ceremonial, promising great results but producing little. In the case of water, for example, some combined resource development strategy is needed to work on basic problems, but the Department of State and others making federal policy show little sensitivity to these problems. A common concern for the environment, however, offers some hope.

Crime and Violence in the Border Area

Many border residents are becoming aware of reasons for concern that overshadow other problems. On the border in Mexico, one sees the landless poor, the squatters in colonias and the dwellers in cardboard villages, without water, without jobs. One sees the guns-for-drugs trade continuing, as well as constant drug-related homicides. There have been shoot-outs with the 23rd of September League and other terrorist groups and a factory manager in Ciudad Juárez was shot to death by terrorists. There have been assaults on tourists. The high crime rates offer a potential for organized crime.

Border residents remember the infamous jeep-pulling contest in El Paso. A jeep stalled in the middle of the river with 500 pounds of marijuana in it. The Mexican Customs agents on the Mexican side hooked on to it, and so did Customs Service on the U.S. side, and each tried to pull the jeep to its side of the river. The national media reported the humorous circumstances, but there was a large amount of firepower on both sides, and a helicopter circled overhead. Children were among the large number of spectators on both sides of the river. If a shot had been fired or if someone had thought a shot had been fired, there could have been a very serious incident.

Violence is especially high between San Diego and Tijuana, with killings, rapes, and assaults on aliens. According to the Mexican press, automatic weapons were found during a recent incident in Matamoros. Arson and homicide are widespread, and the Ku Klux Klan has threatened to deal with the aliens. One hears regularly about the Mexican police crossing to the U.S. side in hot pursuit with guns blazing. Countless Mexican aliens have died crossing the border in one way or another.

Other problems pale beside the potential of a border erupting in violence. The factor that might unite all elements is U.S. immigration policy, which forces the return of many Mexican citizens to border communities that cannot absorb them. If alien legislation were more lenient, however, it could result in harassment of the new resident aliens by Mexican Americans. A newspaper in San Diego reported that many assaults on illegal immigrants there were by U.S. citizens of Mexican-American descent.

The border seems to be a powder keg that could explode at any time. The challenge is to develop greater cooperation, understanding, and a sense of partnership. Border residents must begin to work together.

Observations and Recommendations

The federal government should encourage more participation at the local level in border policy development. Local residents want to see more intensive analysis of the impact of policy initiatives. An advisory group on policy development and policy formation should be established.

All future policy initiatives with Mexico should stress an equal partnership approach to dealing with problems. Limited treaty-making or, at least, agreement-making power should be delegated to the local level in the interest of public safety. Such power should not abridge the power of the U.S. government in its dealings with Mexico. These will be strictly local agreements, for either the short term or the long term, depending on the local needs. Because there is some protocol involved in this process, such limited treaty-making or agreement-making powers should be negotiated at the highest levels.

The federal government should encourage greater cooperation and communication among individuals and governments of the two countries. The federal government should encourage binational planning. This step may require incentives and negotiations at the State Department level.

The needs and wishes of the border area should be considered when new policy is being developed or existing policy is being changed. Great emphasis should be placed on minimizing the negative impact of policy implementation between the two governments.

Part
Two

Problems and Issues: The Content

U.S.–Mexican Border Public Health: A Policy Analysis

Reuel A. Stallones and Lorann Stallones

In discussing contemporary (1945–1970) problems in relations between Mexico and the United States, Karl Schmitt divided the field into peripheral and central issues.[1] Matters related to health and disease were relegated to the peripheral class, and the few diseases that Schmitt mentioned (Venezuelan equine encephalitis, screwworm infestations, and hoof-and-mouth disease) are of economic significance but rarely affect human health. Concern for human health is not readily transmuted into transcendent policy; the hazards are often occult, and the problems are so diverse that they do not lend themselves to generalized solutions. Thus policy is likely to represent the summation of specific program activities, the result of actions rather than their determinant.

The border between Mexico and the United States is permeable to people, animals other than man that may be vectors or reservoirs of disease, inanimate substances carried by air or water or transported in commerce, and ideas, knowledge, and attitudes. Although the contrasts in occurrence of disease between the two countries are striking (see table 1), they are much less marked along the border, and, in some places, little discontinuity is apparent.

Although the paired border communities have not been major industrial centers, they have grown enormously, and shared problems of pollution of air and water have been growing concerns. The provision of personal medical services raises a series of difficult policy-related issues. Our medical-care system does not respond well to the needs of people who are poor, nomadic, or of an ethnic minority. If all three characteristics apply to a people and they are also nationals of another country who entered the United States irregularly, they are likely to find themselves barred from access to the services they need.

Problems related to health and disease affecting relations between Mexico and the United States are overwhelmingly concerned with the importation of infectious diseases from one country to another. The risk of transferring a disease is a joint function of the volume of traffic across the border and the relative frequency of the disease in the two countries. Fortunately, tourists, immigrants, and transient workers are all, by dint

TABLE 1

AGE-ADJUSTED DEATH RATES PER 100,000 POPULATION FOR
SELECTED CAUSES FOR MEXICO AND THE UNITED STATES, 1974

Cause of Death	Mexico	United States
All causes combined	718.3	454.0
Typhoid fever	3.5	0.0
Diarrhea	72.2	1.1
Tuberculosis	16.3	0.8
Malignant neoplasms	40.4	77.8
Diabetes mellitus	16.4	7.3
Nutritional deficiency	9.1	0.5
Ischemic heart disease	21.5	120.2
Stroke	25.5	35.8
Pneumonia	75.9	12.4
Cirrhosis	22.7	1.6
Ill-defined condition	84.1	11.6
Motor vehicle accidents	16.2	19.8
All other accidents	35.1	21.3
Suicide	2.3	9.1
Homicide	24.3	9.1

SOURCE: Pan American Health Organization, *Health Conditions in the Americas,
1973–1976,* Scientific Publication no. 364 (Washington, D.C., 1978).

of circumstance, relatively healthy; but nevertheless they may easily
carry infections that are latent, chronic, or incubating. The number of
border crossings is enormous, nearly 300 million in 1971.[2] The interchange between the paired cities along the border from
Brownsville–Matamoros to San Diego–Tijuana is so great that each pair
should be considered a single community for epidemiological purposes.

Communicable disease reports from the border are sprinkled with
anecdotal accounts of exchanges of disease between the two countries.[3]
In July 1976 three cases of typhoid fever occurred in residents of Phoenix
shortly after they had returned from attending the funeral of a relative
in Hermosillo. Major epidemics of typhoid fever occurred in Mexico in
1972 and 1974, mostly in Hidalgo and the Federal District; and in 1972,
of forty-nine cases that occurred in the United States, 90 percent were
traceable to Mexico. During the period 1967–1972, thirty-nine cases of
brucellosis were reported among U.S. residents in the counties along
the border; twenty-nine of these were linked to sources in Mexico,
sixteen had eaten unripened goat cheese, seven had used other dairy
products from Mexico, and six had traveled in Mexico but did not

provide a clear history of eating suspect food. In recent years, vector-borne diseases of humans have been more a potential than a real hazard. In 1972 Venezuelan equine encephalitis invaded Texas from Mexico but presented mainly a threat to horses. Epidemics of dengue in the Caribbean in recent years are a continual threat to both the United States and Mexico, but should it reach either, the threat to the other is augmented; this is an especially delicate problem because although the Latin American countries have devoted great effort to controlling the vector *Aedes aegypti,* they have been exposed to the risk of having these mosquitoes imported from the United States, where control efforts have been lackadaisical at best.

Cooperation between the two countries for the control of disease transmission is complicated by the fact that program responsibility in Mexico is centralized in a federal agency, the Secretariat of Health and Welfare, and in the United States it is distributed, sometimes capriciously, between the federal Department of Health, Education, and Welfare and the health departments of the states. In 1902 a multilateral treaty organization was established, known since 1958 as the Pan American Health Organization (PAHO), to promote public health in the Americas. This organization opened a field office in 1942 in El Paso, Texas, which was especially concerned with health and disease along the border. Under the general auspices of PAHO, and with the blessing of officials of both countries, a voluntary organization of public health workers, the U.S.–Mexico Border Public Health Association, was formed in 1943. Through annual meetings and special study groups, the association has played an active role in the exchange of information and the promotion of collaborative programs. The interaction of these various agencies is well illustrated by some specific examples.

Case Study: Rabies

Rabies is a viral disease that survives in wild-animal reservoirs, mainly bats, skunks, and foxes, from which it is introduced into urban dog populations at irregular intervals. Although sporadic cases occur in people through contact with wild animals, the outbreaks in dogs constitute a far more serious threat and stimulate control activities. The urban dog populations consist of feral animals and owned dogs attached to a defined residence, but the distinction between the two groups is strongly influenced by human culture. If owned animals are registered and immunized, they serve as a buffer between people and the feral dog population. Control of wild-animal populations is extremely difficult, and therefore rabies control programs emphasize immunization of house dogs and capture and destruction of strays.

Because wild animals move freely across the border between Mexico and the United States, and stray dogs may easily cross from city to city, rabies provides an example of a problem that calls for a high degree of collaboration between the health authorities of the two countries. Intensive control efforts are moderately expensive and, except during significant outbreaks, have not commanded a high priority in the allocation of the limited resources available in Mexico. Recurrent explosive outbreaks of dog rabies occurred along the border in the 1950s and 1960s; and in 1966 a specific program was initiated to attack the problem. PAHO was selected to serve as the intermediary between Mexico and the United States, and both governments signed letters of agreement with PAHO to implement the project. Through the Center for Disease Control (CDC), the United States provided funds to PAHO, and these were transferred to Mexico for the support of rabies control activities in the border cities. The Secretariat of Health of Mexico was the recipient of the money and reported annually to PAHO. Technical assistance was provided by the staff of the PAHO field office in El Paso, Texas. During a nine-year period, from 1966 to 1974, the allocations from CDC amounted to nearly $1.5 million, and with this assistance, well-organized and aggressive control programs were maintained in all of the major Mexican cities on the border. In the United States, no mechanism exists for centralized administration of programs in the border states; immunization of dogs is performed almost exclusively by veterinarians in private practice; and control of stray dogs is usually based on nuisance abatement and may be the responsibility of police or health departments or other agencies.

Rabies virtually disappeared along the border in the late 1960s and early 1970s, but in 1973 and 1974 a major outbreak occurred in El Paso, Texas; Doña Ana County, New Mexico; and Ciudad Juárez. In evaluating these circumstances in retrospect, the resurgence of dog rabies in Ciudad Juárez in the presence of a vigorous rabies control program raised strong doubts as to the effectiveness of this approach. In 1975 a binational study group of three Mexicans and three U.S. nationals was appointed to survey the program and submit recommendations to the director of the CDC. The report of this group served as the starting point for a gradual disengagement,[4] and financial support is expected to end.

In this case, the interests of the United States were judged to be served by providing financial support to Mexico for a specific disease control activity. The availability of a multinational health organization to serve as a conduit for the funds has some obvious advantages in the administration of the program. The program should be maintained in perpetuity, however, as the probability of reintroducing the disease from an uncontrolled wildlife reservoir is undiminished; and, when recrudescence of the disease raises questions about the effectiveness of the program, its discontinuance or redirection raises additional problems. One of the important policy lessons to be drawn from this experience is the need to consider, before a program is initiated, how it might be terminated gracefully.

Case Study: Tuberculosis

The morbidity and mortality rates for tuberculosis have long been higher in Mexico than in the United States, and thus concern about the potential importation of the disease by persons crossing the border to work in the United States led to the development of an x-ray screening program. For many years, applicants for work permits were required to be examined and cleared by officials of the U.S. Quarantine Service. In 1967 the Quarantine Service was transferred to the Center for Disease Control, and this led to a thorough assessment of the tuberculosis control program.[5] A special Binational Tuberculosis Commission was established, and the commission recommended that a pilot project be established to screen applicants in the health center in Ciudad Juárez.[6] This was begun in 1970, and in 1971 the activity was extended to several other Mexican border cities. Although the pilot project was considered successful, close scrutiny of the activity led to the conclusion that no serious problem of disease transmission existed, and in May 1973 the screening requirement was dropped.

This case again illustrates the value of cooperation and joint action by the health authorities of the two countries. Given ordinary rigidity and resistance to change, neither the transfer of the responsibility for x-ray screening to Mexican clinics nor its termination could have been expected. An important consideration in the successful resolution of this issue would seem to be the careful concentration on the scientific components of the problem.

Policy

The first formal efforts to limit the spread of disease between countries began over 500 years ago. Quarantine restrictions had the advantage of seeming inherently logical; the disadvantages were that they caused personal inconvenience, economic loss, and strained relations and were rarely effective. One of the more notable lessons of infectious disease epidemiology has been the increasing appreciation that a marked decline in disease frequency is often the result of modification of the ecological circumstances that had previously fostered the transmission of that disease. Therefore, the transmission of disease across national borders should not cause undue alarm, because with a few exceptions, major epidemics are not likely to occur. Along the U.S.–Mexican border, this philosophy has prevailed, and restrictive programs have been supplanted by efforts to increase the dissemination of information and to encourage joint activities to reduce the hazards of disease in both countries.

Relations between the United States and Mexico are inevitably colored by the suspicion and mistrust generated in the past, and public health concerns cannot be dealt with in isolation from that past. Infectious diseases tend to move from places where the frequency of disease is high to places where it is lower, and, for many infections, this movement is from poor to affluent communities. Therefore, considerations of disease control may become linked with concerns such as economic exploitation. To refer discussion of these problems to binational study groups and meetings of scientific associations allows them to be addressed relatively dispassionately, with scientific objectivity. If agreement can be reached in these forums, then the more emotionally charged issues may be avoided entirely.

Summary

The major causes of death in the United States—heart disease, stroke, and cancer—do not play a major role in border relations between the United States and Mexico.

The large number of people who cross the border between the United States and Mexico serve to carry infectious diseases back and forth. Control of disease transmission through quarantine restrictions or by screening examinations of travelers is expensive, annoying, and relatively ineffective. This approach has been replaced by programs for disease prevention based on the free exchange of information and on cooperation.

The risk of infectious disease has steadily declined on both sides of the border, and in the future disease problems related to environmental pollution will command the attention of public health agencies as industry expands in the border cities. The mechanisms of collaborative study and scientific discussion that have been successful for infectious diseases are being applied to environmental problems. The economic problems related to environmental pollution tend to be focused on the loss of income to the industries involved, however, whereas economic concerns related to infectious diseases focus on man-hours lost and direct costs of treatment.

This shift in emphasis will require that the base for policy formulation be extended beyond the biomedical community.

Notes

[1] K. M. Schmitt, *Mexico and the United States, 1921–1973: Conflict and Coexistence* (New York: John Wiley, 1974).

[2] H. R. Alvarez, *Health without Boundaries* (Mexico: United States–Mexico Border Public Health Association, 1975).

[3] *Border Epidemiological Bulletin* (Field Office, U.S.–Mexico), PAHO Monthly Epidemiological Reports and Special Reports, 1973.

[4] *Binational Border Rabies Review Committee, Final Report* (Atlanta, Ga.: Center for Disease Control, 1976).

[5] Joseph Giordano, director, Quarantine Division, Center for Disease Control, Atlanta, Ga., personal communication, 1978.

[6] *Border Epidemiological Surveillance Tuberculosis Bulletin,* no. 6, April–June 1973.

Review of the Health Situation: U.S.–Mexican Border

An HEW Report
excerpted by Stanley R. Ross

The following excerpts are taken from a report described by Dr. Julius B. Richmond, assistant secretary for health in the Department of Health, Education, and Welfare and surgeon general, as "the first step in a new period of expanded mutual cooperation in health between the United States and Mexico, with the assistance of the Pan American Health Organization (PAHO)." The purpose of the report was to identify major health problems in the border area that can benefit most from bilateral cooperation and to offer recommendations for solving these problems.

• • •

In 1942, the Pan American Sanitary Bureau opened a Field Office in El Paso, Texas, to respond to the wishes of the United States and Mexico for the control of venereal diseases, tuberculosis, and other diseases in the border area. In 1943, the Pan American Sanitary Bureau organized a meeting in El Paso, Texas, and Ciudad Juárez, Chihuahua, to discuss matters related to the health problems of the border area. During this meeting it was decided that a United States–Mexico Border Health Association would be created to serve as a forum for the interchange of ideas between health professionals of both countries who had an interest in the health problems of the border area. At the same time, the Association would serve as a stimulus to create and develop local binational committees and to promote personal contacts between authorities of both countries.

Since the creation of the Association, the Field Office of the Pan American Sanitary Bureau has assumed the responsibility of Secretariat to this Association and has continued, together with the Association, to respond to needs of the region. In addition to the promotion and support it provides to the meetings of the Binational Councils, the Association holds an annual meeting in which scientific presentations are made. This meeting serves as a forum for the joint discussion of problems of common interest. At these meetings resolutions are adopted and recommendations are made which are transmitted to the authorities of both countries for their possible implementation. . . .

Because the health authorities of the United States and Mexico have become increasingly concerned about the health problems of the communities along the U.S.–Mexico Border, high priority has been given to the development of cooperative health programs which would benefit all communities of this region.

In order to foster greater cooperation in this area, the Under Secretary for Health and Welfare of Mexico, the Assistant Secretary for Health/Surgeon General of the United States, and the Director of the Pan American Health Organization participated together with a selected group of experts in a meeting that was held in Reynosa, Tamaulipas, Mexico, on April 18, 1978. That meeting was held in conjunction with the annual meeting of the Border Health Association.

The Border Health Planning Team was instructed to obtain available information in all areas related to the field of health and develop a profile of the health status in the border area. Due to the time limitation, generation of new data was not undertaken. Major contributors to this data gathering effort were the State Health Officers of both countries and other individuals and organizations in the ten U.S. and Mexican sister states. This planning effort and the resulting document are an achievement in trilateral cooperation.

. . . The first task of the Border Health Planning Team was to define the geographic boundaries of the border area. . . . For pragmatic reasons . . . only the political entities that have a common border with the neighboring country were included in the analysis.

Border Profile

A. General. More than 3,100 kilometers of border are shared by the United States and Mexico. The Border is formed by six states on the Mexican side (North Baja California, Sonora, Chihuahua, Coahuila, Nuevo León and Tamaulipas) and four on the United States side (California, Arizona, New Mexico, and Texas). Thirty-six Mexican municipalities are contiguous with 23 U.S. counties.

The border region consists of arid sandy plains. . . . The climate is generally hot and dry. . . . Average annual precipitation is less than 500 mm. In the Colorado River basin it is less than 50 mm. . . .

The vegetation of the area is varied; some regions are primarily grasslands, others are barren, still others have subtropical meadows. A common plant in the area, *Larrea tridentata,* is intimately linked with the fungus *Coccidioides immitis,* which produces the dusty fomites responsible for the transmission of coccidioidomycosis, or valley fever.

97

Wildlife consists of wild dogs, wolves, coyotes, skunks, squirrels, and some reptiles. Cattle, swine, goats, and poultry, which are raised for market, serve as reservoirs for bacteria, parasites, and other disease vectors that are implicated in the transmission of tuberculosis, brucellosis, rickettsia, and viral diseases, etc. Rodents infected with pasturella pestis have been found in New Mexico and Arizona. Although it has not been investigated, it is conceivable that they may also be found on the Mexican side of the Border.

Aedes aegypti, the vector of yellow fever and dengue is found in the northeastern zone (Coahuila, Nuevo León, Tamaulipas, and Texas). Culex, anopheles, psoraspora and the vectors of various types of encephalitis are also found along the Border.

B. *Cultural Factors.* The cultural patterns of the U.S. and Mexican border states are profoundly influenced by the social and demographic conditions which are peculiar to the area. Border stations along the U.S.–Mexican line record about 82 million crossings every year. This heavy flow of traffic includes tourists and residents of both countries who cross the Border for work, recreation or to visit family members who live on the other side. While there are many Mexican citizens who maintain a permanent residence on the United States side of the Border, there are few citizens of the U.S. who reside in this part of Mexico. There are, however, thousands of U.S. citizens who spend hours or weekends in Mexico as tourists.

One result of this constant migration between Mexico and the United States is that all of the communities along the Border show the influence of both countries and both cultures. Clothes and other consumer goods produced in the United States are popular in Mexico. The Mexican population watches U.S. television programs and listens to U.S. radio stations. Eating habits, architecture, and music on the U.S. side of the Border show the influence of Mexico. These reciprocal influences are widely recognized. Economists can demonstrate the economic interdependency of the border communities. Health planners must also recognize the importance of this intense interaction and develop health programs which promote the positive aspects of the bond between Mexico and the United States.

C. *Demographic Factors.* According to the latest available data, the population of the border area was 3.3 million on the U.S. side in 1975 and 3.2 million on the Mexican side in 1978. Population growth has been rapid on both sides of the Border. . . .

The U.S. Census Bureau's population projections for the four border states indicate continued growth through the year 2000 at rates well above the national average. Under the assumption that the 1965–75 migration trend continues, the following projections were made.

Population projections are not available for the Mexican border states; however, the population of these states can be expected to double in 20 years if their growth rates are equal to the rate of natural increase for the entire country. In fact, the border population more than doubled between 1950 and 1960, and increased by 78% between 1960 and 1970. . . . A doubling of the population in 20 years is a conservative estimate in view of the rapid growth of the past two decades.

Migration and natural increase probably contribute in equal amounts to the high growth rate of the border area. The birth rates in Mexico range from 38.1 to 49.2 for the border states. In 11 of the 23 U.S. border counties, the birth rate was over 20 and in one Texas county, it was 33.5 in 1976. (The U.S. average was 15.3 in 1977.) The higher birth rate and lower life expectancy in Mexico (65 vs. 73 years in the U.S.) suggest a slightly different age structure in Mexico which must be taken into account when planning health programs.

The majority of the population on both sides of the Border lives in urban areas. In Mexico, 94% of the border population reside in urban areas of 2,500 or more. Approximately 88.7% of the population reside in only 12 municipalities.

In rural areas, population groups are often separated by considerable distances. Many of the smaller municipalities are isolated in mountainous or desert areas. Both distance and isolation impose major barriers to the provision of health services and accessibility to them.

While the problems of accessibility and provision of services would appear to be easier to solve in urban areas, lack of transportation, limited financial resources, and social distance may make urban health services equally inaccessible to some population subgroups.

The rapid increase in the population on both sides of the Border has seriously hampered health planning efforts. Marginal settlements have mushroomed on the outskirts of Mexican border towns. These areas are often without municipal services of any kind. The lack of water and sewerage systems, refuse collection services, and basic health services poses serious problems for the community. The low income areas of border towns on the U.S. side are seriously overcrowded. Undocumented immigrants frequently find refuge in these areas. Health problems are often ignored until they become so serious that emergency treatment is required. Health statistics from both sides of the Border indicate that many people use hospital emergency health rooms for basic health services.

D. *Economic Factors.* In 1978 per capita GNP was estimated at $7,890 in the U.S. versus $1,090 in Mexico. This relative difference in wealth is less pronounced in the border area, for the U.S. border area includes some of the poorest counties in the country, while the Mexican border area is among the more prosperous regions of that country. Nevertheless, the contrast between the countries is striking, and provides sufficient incentive for thousands of Mexicans to cross the border. . . .

Income levels and educational status can often be positively correlated. The border areas of Mexico demonstrate higher levels of educational attainment than the nation as a whole while the U.S. border areas are below national averages.

A study undertaken by the New Mexico State Health Agency and the Center for Disease Control (CDC) in 1976 demonstrated the positive correlation between socioeconomic level and health. Birth rates, infant mortality rates, and the incidence of both tuberculosis and gonorrhea were inversely correlated with socioeconomic level. The morbidity and mortality patterns of other border areas also reflect this relationship.

E. *Mortality.* The collection and analysis of border area vital and health statistics are seriously hampered by the mobility of the population, the absence of uniform reporting systems among the states and on the two sides of the border, and the fragmentation of data gathering and processing efforts according to geopolitical areas.

Some information (primarily concerning communicable diseases) is exchanged by direct contact among border health personnel and through the PAHO Field Office. However, the complexity and multiplicity of health systems, particularly in the United States, the language differences, and the difficulty of comprehending the other country's data systems discourage cooperative efforts of area health officials.

Mortality rates are similar on both sides of the Border. . . . Differences in the leading causes of death probably reflect the differences in the age structure of the population as well as differences in social and economic development. The United States border counties demonstrate the same mortality profile as the country. In 1976, heart disease, cancer, cerebrovascular disease and accidents were among the leading causes of death. Influenza and pneumonia, diabetes mellitus, and in one county (Terrell Co., Texas) enteritis also appeared among the leading causes of death. In Mexico, influenza and pneumonia, cerebrovascular disease, enteritis and other diarrheas, diseases of infancy and perinatal diseases, and accidents are the most frequently reported causes of death.

. . . The causes of infant deaths in both countries included congenital anomalies, perinatal morbidity, and influenza and pneumonia. However, in Mexico, enteritis and heart disease were also reported among the leading causes of infant deaths, while in the U.S., accidents and ill-defined conditions and symptoms were frequently reported. There is some question as to the accuracy of reporting of infant mortality on both sides of the Border. . . .

F. *Morbidity.* The collection and analysis of information which would provide an accurate morbidity profile of the border area are hampered by the absence of uniform reporting procedures on both sides of the international border. Epidemiological surveillance activities are well-developed in both countries; however, the data collected by the various state agencies cannot always be disaggregated to present information specific to the border area.

Health officials in both countries agree that some of the major concerns in recent years have been venereal disease, rabies, the chronic degenerative diseases, vector-borne diseases, teenage pregnancies, accidents, alcohol and drug abuse, and environmental health problems of all kinds. Venereal diseases have been a major concern of border health authorities for many years. Animal rabies is reported more frequently in the U.S. border counties than it is in the border states. . . .

Despite the importance of the chronic degenerative diseases as leading causes of death, particularly in the United States border areas, there is little epidemiological information available concerning their prevalence. In both countries, the specialized programs and facilities for diagnosis and treatment of chronic diseases are concentrated in a few major cities and large academic institutions. Further investigation is necessary if a comprehensive border health profile is to be developed relative to these diseases.

The vector-borne diseases, such as malaria, dengue and encephalitis, present cause for concern, not because of their high prevalence, but because of the potential threat represented by the presence of the disease vectors in the border area. . . .

Teenage pregnancies appear to be increasing in the border areas. This probably reflects changing patterns of teenage sexual behavior and may indicate need for changes in the design and delivery of family planning services. . . . Access to sex education, maternal-child health, and family planning services is limited, particularly for low income women. . . .

Accidents were among the leading causes of death for all age groups in the border counties of Mexico and the United States in 1974. Traffic congestion in the border area is often aggravated by the lack of uniform road signs and ignorance of local traffic laws by visitors from the other side of the Border. Emergency services are not available in rural areas and are not accessible to all even in urban areas. Ambulance services in the U.S. are often private and very costly. In Mexico, the Red Cross provides free ambulance service. Recovery of costs incurred for emergency medical treatment of Mexicans on the U.S. side is often complicated, for there are no existing agreements concerning the reimbursement of the government or private sector health facility for treatment provided on an emergency basis.

Alcohol and drug abuse are among the major health problems of the border area. Available statistical data give only a suggestion of the extent of this problem. The use of marijuana and inhalants is common among young people in both countries. . . .

There has been substantial cooperation between Mexico and the U.S. in various attempts to control the production and movement of drugs. A binational center for the treatment of drug addicts is operating in Nogales, Arizona. There is a need for more binational efforts as well as trained personnel who can function in a bicultural, bilingual environment.

Environmental health problems in the border area range from the acute diseases caused by inadequate supplies of water to illnesses which develop after long-term exposure to atmospheric or industrial pollutants.

In the six Mexican border states, the proportion of population that does not have access to running water in the home varies from 18.5% to 34% of the population. In the four U.S. border states the majority of the population has adequate supplies of potable water. In both countries the quality of the water is monitored for chemical and bacterial content. In the rural areas of both countries, the major source of water is wells. An increasing problem in the area, however, is the contamination of the water by pesticides and other chemical substances.

The proportion of the population of the six border states whose homes are not connected to a sewage line varies from 24.9% to 46.4%. In rural areas the proportion varies from 12.3% to 28.5%. Wastewater processing systems are available in the U.S. border states and cover the needs of most of the population. Despite this, hepatitis is still a problem in some areas of the region.

There are community wastewater problems in some regions of the border, where communities discharge raw effluents directly into the rivers. These problems, which are increasing, are serious as health problems because downstream areas utilize the water for human consumption and recreation.

An agreement between the states of California and Baja California allows San Diego to treat a portion of Tijuana sewage on an emergency basis. However, because of limited capacity and the increasing load from Tijuana, a further cooperative effort in the treatment of municipal wastewaters will have to be developed.

In both countries, the disposal of solid waste is achieved by landfill, incineration or some other sanitary method. In Mexico the percent of the population which does not have access to solid waste collection systems ranges from 20.9% to 49.8% among the urban border populations. There are some air pollution problems associated with improper operation of dumps along the border which have to be addressed.

With regard to atmospheric pollution there are both stationary and mobile sources of pollution that create health problems on both sides of the border. The State of California has very strict standards for the emission of vehicular gases. The other three states of the border also have standards for vehicle emissions, but their regulations are less strict.

The U.S. has adequate federal legislation to maintain good environmental health standards. However, because insufficient resources are devoted to inspection and enforcement, violations of standards occur.

State	1975 Pop. (mil)	2000 Pop. (mil)	25-Yr. Change
Arizona	2.2	3.45	+56%
California	21.2	28.1	32
New Mexico	1.1	1.4	23
Texas	12.2	16.65	36

There is a signed agreement between the United States and Mexico which gives the responsibility for border water problems to the International Boundary and Water Commission, which has been operating for many years in El Paso, Texas. Both governments have recently signed an agreement between the Sub-Secretaría del Mejoramiento del Ambiente of Mexico and the Environmental Protection Agency of the United States for border area cooperation in environmental programs. As part of this agreement, an inventory of environmental problem areas will be made.

Programmatic Recommendations

A. *Introduction.* The programmatic recommendations . . . are oriented toward specific problem areas that are thought to call for priority attention.

1. Urban focus for collaborative programs. Given the heavy concentration of populations in urban areas, programs directed to those areas could reach large numbers of people at relatively low per capita costs. In addition, some of the problems of greatest concern to the two countries are localized in urban settings around major border crossings.

103

In order to focus initiatives more strongly, therefore, consideration should be given to concentrating attention on three or four pairs of sister cities along the Border. Such focusing could simplify planning and coordination. Effective programs could subsequently be extended to other areas.

While this urban-oriented strategy would serve a binational collaborative effort, the rural population would benefit minimally from it, and equity in the distribution of services should be seen as important along with efficiency. Careful consideration should also be given, therefore, to selected programs that would reach into the rural area.

2. Primary health care for underserved populations. Both the United States and Mexico have endorsed the [World Health Organization] WHO-sponsored statements on primary health care. Both countries are committed to the extension of primary care to under- and unserved populations and both have active programs under way. The program directions proposed for the border area should contribute to the achievement of this objective. While the provision of primary health care can be considered a priority on both sides of the border, to what extent can it serve as a unifying strategy?

3. Coordination within and between health systems. The health system problems identified in this report demonstrate the need for multi-organizational participation in the improvement of health along the Border. The systems of both countries involve multiple levels of government in program planning, financing, and execution. This is especially the case in the United States, where responsibilities for health are spread among municipal, county, state, and federal governments. Careful attention must be given to coordination, both within the United States and between the United States and Mexico.

B. *Recommendations.* In this study a number of specific categorical problems have been singled out as needing special attention. To facilitate programmatic approaches, the categorical recommendations have been grouped into four clusters:

Communicable Disease Control
Health Services Delivery
Environmental Sanitation
Systems Development, Planning and Evaluation . . .

The recommended activities call for a variety of forms of cooperation between the United States and Mexico. In some cases unilateral activity is required, which should be complementary to the other side—such as development of facilities and manpower resources. Others call for joint collaboration and sharing. . . . The clear need is for forms of cooperation, practically adapted to existing structures, that will be effective in addressing the problems of concern to the two countries.

• • •

In his letter of transmittal for this report, Dr. Richmond remarked that "because of the international nature of the health problems in Border cities, cooperative efforts in both planning and development of health programs can provide great benefits to both countries. The success of such efforts requires the active support and participation of segments of the health sector working along the Border. We believe that there are many programs ongoing or in the planning process on the State and local level which, in their present form, with modification or new emphasis, could be part of the programming with our Mexican colleagues. Due to the importance of conditions along the Border and our relationships with Mexico generally, the possibilities of Federal funds for new programs, although not currently available, should not be precluded for the future."

Law Enforcement and the Border

Joseph Staley

Mexico and the United States are confronted by some major problems in the area of law enforcement. The following discussion examines possible solutions to these problems and presents various policy options and alternatives. Although the major emphasis is on problems arising out of the movement of people and the enforcement of immigration laws, some attention is also given to general crimes, the drug traffic, arms smuggling, auto theft, and juvenile delinquency.

Migration

General Problems of Enforcement of Immigration Laws. The power to control immigration is unquestionably a sovereign power and exclusively a federal power in the United States. Immigration laws in the United States are difficult to administer and enforce, in part because of the constitutional and inherent rights enjoyed equally by citizens and non-citizens. Examples of those rights are freedom from unreasonable search and seizure, freedom of movement, freedom of privacy, and freedom of travel. Such rights must be maintained and should not be modified or changed.

The removal or deportation of aliens under U.S. law is civil action; thus questioning, rules of evidence, representation, hearings, etc., follow the rules of civil procedures. Court decisions have imposed more restrictive guidelines in these matters: for example, the government must show that a person is an alien and subject to deportation by "clear, unequivocal, and convincing evidence." Thus the requirement is closer to the "beyond a reasonable doubt" rule of criminal law than to the requirement for a "preponderance of evidence" in civil law. Immigration law states that "a person may be represented by counsel of his choice and expense." This is often interpreted, however, as denying equal protection under the law. Furthermore, there is disagreement as to whether counsel should be furnished by the government for those who cannot afford to pay for it.

Illegal entry, false claim to U.S. citizenship, knowingly harboring and concealing an alien illegally in the United States, and transporting an alien known to be illegally in the United States—these are all considered criminal violations. Thus the deportation process is often inter-mingled with possible criminal prosecution. This makes it very difficult to decide whether a case should be handled as a deportation proceeding or presented to the respective U.S. attorney for possible criminal pros-ecution. For these reasons court decisions in recent years generally hold that criminal case procedures such as reading a person the *Miranda* statement, having reasonable cause for questioning, etc., must be used at immigration stops and during questioning. A strong minority opinion in the case of *Almeida-Sánchez* v. *United States* held that the Immigration and Naturalization Service (INS) could obtain criminal search warrants from a U.S. magistrate or judge for places of employment or residence if there was probable cause to suspect the presence of illegal aliens. Another complication is the fact that in cases of smuggling, harboring, or concealing aliens, the aliens are considered "the evidence or fruits of the crime," but there are on record strong opinions in several cases stating that persons cannot be considered so under constitutional law.

The Immigration and Naturalization Service can issue administra-tive warrants to locate undocumented aliens. The right to enter private buildings, residences, etc., could easily be denied, however, and then the only recourse would be an attempt to obtain an order from a federal court. Once such an order has been obtained, further denial of per-mission to search the premises could be held as "contempt of the court."

Under immigration laws only an immigration officer has the au-thority to enforce the administrative (civil) deportation action (8 USC 1357). Other federal, state, and local officers usually notify the local INS office when an alien, particularly a nonresident alien, is being held for other than immigration law violations. If he has been interviewed and documented to be unlawfully in the United States, an order will be issued by the INS to show cause why the alien should not be deported, a warrant of arrest will be issued, and a hold will be placed for the INS when the other charge has been disposed of by conviction or release so that deportation proceedings before an immigration judge can be held.

If the Congress and the administration really desire to enforce immigration laws, consideration should be given to amending the law to authorize federal, state, and local enforcement officials other than immigration officers to hold a suspected undocumented alien for a short period for a determination of the individual's immigration status. This proposal would be highly controversial, with ethnic groups and strong civil rights advocates likely to consider it as being potentially discrimi-natory.

False Documents. Falsification of birth records, counterfeiting of various immigration documents, assuming the identity of a person born in the

United States, and oral false claims to U.S. citizenship are the most troublesome areas for immigration law enforcement. The INS, aware of this problem, is now in the process of converting certain documents to a more secure system under the "ADIT" program. The resulting identification document for permanent resident aliens and for holders of nonresident alien border crossing cards will greatly benefit speedy and proper identification. The system will be based on the most modern computer and coding technology available.

Records of births, marriages, and deaths are maintained by state and local agencies. The record systems in the various states vary widely in effectiveness, although uniform birth and death registration statutes have been recommended for years. There are few, if any, jurisdictions that even match birth and death records. This leaves the door open for obtaining the birth record of an individual born in the United States and assuming that person's identity as a U.S. citizen. Until a recent amendment to the social security laws, no proof of U.S. citizenship or identity was required to obtain a social security account number. No questions were asked, and assumed names and identities were not discouraged. As a result of recent changes in the social security law, some proof of U.S. citizenship or of the right to accept employment, if an alien, is required before an account number will be assigned. This is clearly an improvement.

A committee within the Department of Justice conducted an extensive survey and issued a report in November 1976 entitled "The Criminal Use of False Identification." This report suggested the extent of criminal activities in the use of false identification, not only for immigration but for other purposes as well. Under federal law it is a felony to claim falsely to be a U.S. citizen for illegal purposes (8 USC 911).

Notwithstanding the evidence presented by this study, it was concluded by its authors that a federal law requiring a national identification document should not be enacted. It was felt that such a requirement might constitute an invasion of the constitutional rights of freedom of privacy. The study suggested, however, that this approach might require further study in the years ahead. The report also recommended that the states should move in the direction of an improved and more uniform system of maintaining vital statistics.

Thousands of oral or documented false claims to U.S. citizenship are discovered annually by INS officers, and the number is growing. As undocumented aliens remain in the United States for longer periods and learn the language, customs, and how the local system functions, false claims to U.S. citizenship become much more likely.

Obviously this is an important area for policy change based on a prior comprehensive study of the problem. Most European countries now require national identity documents. Such documentation could protect the law-abiding citizen without forfeit of individual freedom. At present the social security card is the closest thing to a national identity document that the United States has, and it is widely used for a variety of identification purposes. If proper and trustworthy evidence were required before issuance of a tamper-proof, secure card, the social security card could greatly alleviate the problem.

This proposal has met some objections, however. To replace millions of outstanding cards would represent a major undertaking and cause considerable expense. Most racial groups have no objections to identification documents if required of all persons but rightfully have strong objections to requiring identification of a segment of the population because of racial characteristics, manner of speech, etc.

Smuggling of Aliens. The smuggling and the transporting of illegal aliens on the southern border have increased dramatically over the past decade. In 1970 8.4 percent of the 218,000 illegal aliens found in the United States had been smuggled. In 1978 over 130,000 of the aliens detained were found to have been smuggled. Smuggling is a lucrative endeavor that is carried on by friends, amateurs, and highly professional organizations. The cost for being transported into the United States illegally varies from a few dollars to $1,000 or more for each person smuggled.

The average potential illegal entrant, with limited education and unfamiliar with the border areas and law enforcement, seeks information to effect successful legal entry and, thus, is easy prey for the smuggling rackets. The smuggling operation encourages reentry by apprehended smuggled aliens who are desperate on being returned to Mexico without earnings from the United States and who face the impossibility of repaying the creditor who originally lent them the money to enter the United States.

Despite the use of more sophisticated detection and aerial observation equipment to locate illegal entrants, smugglers take advantage of restrictions imposed by the courts regarding checkpoints. Confident in their knowledge of the enforcement limitation, smugglers have succeeded in virtually eliminating any element of surprise.

Illegal aliens now tend to seek large-city employment opportunities and assimilation in the big city. To reach that destination rapidly requires arrival at major transportation terminals within hours after illegal entry. Understaffed antismuggling personnel cannot cover transportation routes in a manner that would discourage the large-scale illegal operations.

Smuggling is carried out often under the most inhuman conditions. Not infrequently the smuggled alien loses his life at the hands of the smuggler. A few years ago an abandoned U-Haul truck was found in San Antonio. When opened, it was found to contain forty-three Mexican nationals jammed against the locked back of the truck. Three died from the experience, and twenty-six were seriously ill. Another instance of such treatment occurred when twenty-two aliens were found near Rio Grande City standing in several inches of oil in an 8-foot by 6-foot compartment of an oil transportation truck. At Laredo, 124 aliens were found in two mobile homes being smuggled to Houston.

Smuggling and transporting are lucrative activities. Various schemes are used in the collection of exorbitant fees. One such arrangement is "go now, pay later." After a small down payment is made, the smuggler or his representative continues to collect as long as the alien is illegally in the United States. The alien pays dearly, always under the threat of being reported to the immigration authorities.

Another scheme is a "package deal." The smuggler not only smuggles the alien across the border and transports him to prearranged employment in the United States but also furnishes counterfeit or altered documents—social security card, driver's license, and a birth or baptismal certificate showing U.S. citizenship.

Getting at the principals involved presents a very serious enforcement problem. Often a low-priced automobile is made available for a group, and one of the group drives. In other instances, illegal alien teenagers younger than seventeen years old drive the transporting vehicle because they are practically immune from prosecution. Similarly, female transporters, often with small children, are used to avoid prosecution. Those responsible for the operation often remain abroad and thus cannot be arrested and prosecuted in the United States. Over 50 percent of the smuggling activity takes place within 50 miles of the Pacific Ocean with organized rings operating in this area.

The requirement of holding all smuggled aliens as witnesses in a smuggling prosecution case, as required by court decisions, causes a serious problem of detention. The material witnesses must be held in jails (often in very crowded conditions), sometimes for several weeks while awaiting the trial of the smuggler. By statute these witnesses can be paid only one dollar a day. This practice has been criticized by Mexican officials. Usually the smuggler is free on bond, though occasionally he is housed with the potential witnesses.

This matter needs improvement: realistic witness fees should be authorized, special housing facilities provided, and smugglers brought to trial speedily. Defenders of smugglers should be required to limit the number of witnesses to be held by requiring prompt interviews to locate vital witnesses. To return the witnesses to Mexico or to release them pending trial are two alternatives that have not proved feasible. In the former instance it is found that witnesses tend not to return at trial time. In the latter, there is a tendency for them to disappear or to take a job, and this provokes criticism.

Mexico has been very cooperative in the effort to prosecute alien smugglers. A recently amended Mexican law authorizes the prosecution of smugglers. This foundation for cooperation should be developed further, a goal that can be accomplished only through cooperation between federal prosecutors in Mexico and U.S. immigration officers. There have been other encouraging developments: in 1978 INS established a National Anti-Smuggling Division in the service and assigned additional personnel to this effort; Congress has authorized additional federal judges and prosecutors; and of great importance is the passage of a law authorizing the seizure of aircraft, boats, and vehicles used in smuggling aliens. It has been found that vehicles with specially built compartments are used over and over again after being identified in smuggling operations.

It is this writer's view that the complacent attitude of immigration law enforcement should be replaced by a legal, controlled temporary workers program, if such workers are needed. In our society and form of government, laws should be enforced or changed. Prosecution of undocumented workers is at best a dubious deterrent to illegal entry. Less than 5 percent of the undocumented aliens subject to prosecution are prosecuted. Even this number puts a severe strain on local jail facilities and is very costly to the government ($7 to $50 or more per day). Often it is the families who suffer most when the breadwinner is incarcerated. Usually an undocumented worker must be a chronic repeater, make a false claim to U.S. citizenship, resist arrest, engage in smuggling, etc., before prosecution is instituted.

If an alien has been in the United States since 1948 and is of good moral character, permanent residence can be granted (Registry Proceedings). Suspension of deportation can be granted if *extreme* hardship can be proved and if the alien has been in the United States for seven to ten years (8 USC 1254). Economic hardship alone is not sufficient. Although it seems to benefit those who are not caught, no doubt this 1948 date for registry should be advanced to a more realistic date. If an undocumented alien has remained in the United States for a number of years, argument can be made that as equities are established in the United States removal would constitute a severe hardship.

Certain discretionary relief from deportation is possible, but to adjudicate such applications is time consuming and expensive, not only to the alien but to the government. Discretionary authority rests with the district director, who can institute deportation proceedings in many cases. This discretionary authority should be limited by providing clear statutory mandates. Otherwise it is impossible to have uniform decisions throughout the United States. Immigration laws must be enforced in the most humanitarian manner. Too much discretionary authority in regard to the enforcement of laws creates an intolerable situation, however.

The replacement of fencing in the El Paso and San Ysidro areas has received considerable comment in the past year. Fencing has existed in both the Mexican and the Canadian border areas for many years. Such barriers exist worldwide between countries that share the same land borders. It is the only practical way to prevent entries at other than ports of entry on land borders.

Without a completely open border, there must be border demarcations. It is impossible to staff such areas adequately with personnel to ensure entry at designated points. Such barriers are equally important to both nations. Smuggling of merchandise and illegal entries go in both directions. Improved fencing will not solve the illegal entry problem, but it will deter nuisance crossings by juvenile delinquents, criminals, etc., by denying ready access and easy escape for thieves, burglars, and smugglers. It also hinders the carrying out of demonstrations.

Maintenance is needed to make fences more effective barriers. Many times they are cut, dug under, or easily climbed. But at the same time these barriers should be constructed so as not to injure those who attempt to climb over. Many fewer nuisance crossings occur in Texas along the Rio Grande—even though it is shallow or practically dry at times—than along the land border to the west. Such barriers should be constructed with the acceptance and approval of both nations and should create as few international complications as possible. By midsummer of 1979, after the controversy over the matter had subsided somewhat, construction began on the replacement of the dilapidated barrier separating El Paso from Ciudad Juárez. In addition to the two and a half miles of chain-link fence being installed in the El Paso area, an additional five and a half miles of fencing are to be erected between San Ysidro, California, and Tijuana, Mexico. Immigration authorities assured the public that the design of the fences had been changed to eliminate potentially dangerous features.

Two final questions related to immigration law enforcement merit mention. First, there should be federal legislation requiring a person to identify himself to federal officers without probable cause or reasonable suspicion of a criminal or civil law violation. This procedure is the law in some states (California, for example) under police power. It would seem not to violate any constitutional right and would be of invaluable assistance in immigration matters. The strongest opposition to this proposed legislation comes from employers of illegal aliens and from ethnic groups, who base their objections on possible discrimination. Ironically, the latter are those most subject to harm by substandard wages and working conditions. Second, a provision should be made to impose a penalty—either criminal or civil (sanctions)—on employers who knowingly hire undocumented aliens. Without such legislation, it will continue to be impossible to enforce the immigration laws of the United States. This writer believes that such a law could be administered without any discriminatory complications.

Crime and the Border

Any international border creates conditions that are conducive to all kinds of crimes (theft, robbery, assault, murder, rape, prostitution, etc.) as the perpetrators of crimes escape detection or prosecution by going from one country to another, thus avoiding the jurisdiction of police authorities. With the vast increase in population and development along the Mexican–U.S. border in the past thirty years, it is inevitable that criminal activities would increase. The differences between Mexico and the United States in standards of living, pay scales, language, customs, judicial systems, and other factors compound the problem. In Mexico, as in the United States, local, state, and federal agencies are involved in law enforcement activities. This results in some duplication of effort and often in inadequate funding and training.

The tremendous movement of Mexican nationals to border cities in search of employment and possible illegal entry into the United States is also a contributing factor to crime. Undocumented workers seeking employment are more often the victims of crime than its perpetrators. Border areas of concentrated illegal entries, such as the 40-some miles of border south of San Diego, where over 50 percent of all illegal entries occur, the El Paso–Ciudad Juárez area, and to a lesser extent other sister-city areas on the border, often become almost a no-man's-land after dark. Local police along with federal border patrol officers must have task forces on duty to protect the illegal entrants from being victimized by criminals from both Mexico and the United States.

The attorneys general from the four border states (California, Arizona, New Mexico, and Texas) have sponsored conferences on crime and the border at San Diego, El Paso, Albuquerque, and Phoenix, in April 1977, October 1977, April 1978, and June 1980 respectively. Discussions and workshops in many facets of binational law enforcement were held, and the reports of these meetings are available.

Local, state, and federal agencies from both countries emphasized the absolutely essential close cooperation and liaison between agencies at all levels of government. This must be a continuing process, as many of the officials are periodically changed through the political processes as well as through transfers of civil service personnel in both countries. Communication and the exchange of information are also essential. Fingerprint information from the Federal Bureau of Investigation, data from the National Criminal Information Center, and state police information identifying criminals must be exchanged. The establishment of an intelligence center at El Paso (EPIC) primarily for combating drug traffic but also for coping with false documents, smuggling, etc., is a step in the right direction and should be expanded.

There is no general extradition treaty between the United States and Mexico. It is usually not difficult, however, to return a national wanted on criminal charges by either country to the other country. Those suspected of immigration law violations are delivered to appropriate authorities when deported. If the suspect has dual nationality or legal residence, it is often impossible to extradite him.

Claims for asylum in the United States for political reasons are being made as radical groups including Communist or Communist-oriented organizations begin appearing in Mexico. The validity of such claims between friendly democratic governments and whether the asylum is based on escape from criminal prosecution rather than on political persecution may become an extremely critical issue in future years.

Drug Traffic. Not all law enforcement problems in the border area are related to the movement of undocumented workers. The production of and the trafficking in drugs in Mexico for shipment to the United States have been and continue to be a substantial problem. It was the extensive use of drugs in the 1960s that brought a revitalization of the drug business, but it was the 1972 severance of the "French connection" that brought the "Mexican connection" to full flower. Amphetamines, marijuana, and Mexican "brown" heroin flowed across the border in response to the large and highly profitable market there. Finally, in response to inordinate pressure applied by the United States and recognition that Mexico too was experiencing a growing drug problem and that there was a link between some of the drug traffic and arms for rebel groups, the Mexican government energetically responded with a campaign both to destroy the drug-producing plants in the fields and to interrupt the movement of the drugs themselves. The campaign, begun in 1976 and known as Operation Condor, involved locating and spraying marijuana pastures and opium fields and seizing drugs in transit. The success of these efforts, combined with a preference for Colombian "gold," led to the South American nations' supplanting Mexico as the major supplier of the American drug market. Drug smuggling from Mexico remains a problem of important dimensions, and even some of the Colombian production finds its way through Mexico en route to illegal entry into the United States.

The eradication of drug-producing crops and the combating of the drug traffic in Mexico are examples of what can be done through mutual cooperation. Beyond that, law enforcement authorities emphasize the need for authority to confiscate vehicles—cars, trucks, and planes—when they are involved in illegal operations rather than to release them for reuse in subsequent smuggling efforts. It is argued that this would be a crippling blow to smugglers of aliens as well as of drugs. Others cry out against protection for the drug traffickers in high places in state and local governments in the United States. They point to the lack of equipment and personnel to cope with the problem and stress the urgent need for cooperation and coordination among the agencies that have responsibility for the execution of the law. The United States must continue to cooperate with Mexico, which has quite correctly described its effort as the "Permanent Mexican Campaign against Narcotics."

Arms Smuggling. Not unrelated to the drug issue is the matter of arms smuggling. Measures were taken by Mexico in 1971 restricting the sales of guns and requiring their registration in an effort to "depistolize" the country. The new regulations helped to augment the black market in guns. The customers include government departments seeking to avoid red tape, Mexican businessmen providing for their own and their families' protection, urban guerrillas, and narcotics traffickers. The smuggling of arms is lucrative and the return fairly high for the risk involved.

The United States clearly is the source of many of these weapons, although some weapons from the Communist world also have been seized. Many of the weapons are stolen from U.S. arsenals. And there seems no reason to doubt that much of the Mexican gun trade involves the trading of guns for drugs. Here again there is need for cooperative effort by both nations in their own respective interests. The Mexicans would like to see stricter control on the sales of arms in the United States and more effective communication between those U.S. authorities responsible for the control of shipments of arms, ammunition, and munitions, and Mexican authorities.

Stolen Vehicles. The theft of automobiles and other vehicles is probably the next most serious problem facing criminal law enforcement officials in both nations. The problem is as old as the mass-produced automobile. In fact, the movement of stolen U.S. vehicles to Mexico had become an acute problem by the time the two nations signed Convention No. 914 in 1937. Border cities have a below-average recovery rate of stolen vehicles, and estimates of the number of stolen vehicles likely to go to Mexico each year range from 5,000 to 10,000. Illegal importation of stolen vehicles robs the Mexican government of legal duties and is in direct competition with the expanding Mexican automobile industry. The traffic in stolen vehicles is very closely interrelated with many other crimes. Several stolen-vehicle rings have been reported operating in the Tijuana–San Diego area. Such vehicles also often carry other stolen or contraband items being illegally introduced into Mexico.

Stolen vehicles include automobiles, vans, light trucks, tractor-trailers, excavating machines, and airplanes. The magnitude of the problem can be read in the claims statistics of insurance companies. Obviously here is another area requiring international cooperation. In the past this has been most effective in the immediate border area, whereas recoveries in the interior of the country, which comes under Treaty process, have been notoriously less frequent. Obviously cooperation is in Mexico's own interest, and the past few years have been marked by a significant increase in the number of vehicles returned. C. C. Benson, manager of the National Automobile Theft Bureau in Dallas, Texas, informed the Second Conference on Crime and the Border that 1977 had been the best year in this regard in his thirty years of experience with the problem. Other sources also underscore the cooperation of the López Portillo administration. During March–April 1977, for example, forty-two stolen aircraft were returned, compared with a total of sixteen during the preceding three years. Obviously, better communication for both the exchange of information and consultation would help. Recent reports on the numbers of stolen vehicles returned are encouraging.

Juvenile Delinquency. Problems stemming from juvenile delinquency are frequent on both sides of the U.S.–Mexican border. Having access to an international boundary facilitates the escape of those fleeing prosecution. There are increasing reports—and evidence to support such reports—that Mexican children are crossing the border to engage in crimes of a felonious nature, mostly burglary. The offenses also include shoplifting, mugging, car theft, and prostitution. Juvenile gangs from both sides of the border have engaged in "raids," after which they retreat to the "sanctuary" of their own border. There is also good reason to believe that some of this delinquent behavior is organized by criminal groups. The problem is proving increasingly costly and very difficult to deal with.

The prosecution of border criminals in general poses some special difficulties. When the victims of crime are aliens in the United States, they are often fearful of the consequences of reporting crime, even serious crime. They fear that contact with American judicial authorities

116

will result in their deportation. Alien witnesses similarly are reluctant to give testimony. Because there are no funds to house alien victims or witnesses, both frequently have vanished by the time the case—delayed by crowded calendars or by the defense's tactics—comes to trial. Similarly, alien defendants disappear when released to await trial, often without even having been so identified.

The problem with juvenile delinquents from Mexico is even more complicated. Under the American judicial system, juveniles often are handled separately from adults and generally are accorded lesser punishment than adults who commit similar offenses. Treating foreign juvenile offenders more severely than nationals would be undesirable. Public relations and cost considerations often encourage prosecutors to defer prosecution and to turn the youngster over to the border patrol for deportation. This is an important issue, requiring study and continuing and strong cooperation with Mexican authorities.

Enforcement of Import Duties and Restrictions

The Bureau of Customs of the Treasury Department was one of the first federal agencies established in the United States, and for many years import duties were the principal source of revenue for the federal government. Today, such duties are still a source of revenue, $6 billion last year, but this sum represents a small part of the federal budget. Tariffs still play a vital role in protecting American industry from unfair competition from abroad, however.

The Bureau of Customs cooperates with and assists numerous government agencies in administering and enforcing over 400 statutory or regulatory requirements relating to international trade. These include provisions of the Anti-Dumping Act; countervailing duty, copyright; patent and trademark provisions quotas; marking requirements for imported merchandise; interdiction and seizing of contraband, including narcotics and dangerous drugs; processing of persons, carriers, cargo, and mail into and out of the United States. There is no export tax, and there are few regulations on exports. Even inspection of departures from the United States is practically nonexistent except in war or time of national emergency.

Customs and immigration officers working jointly are important elements in international relations. Often they are the only federal officials that persons entering the United States ever contact. Their complex duties must be carried out courteously, quickly, and efficiently. Though the latter are principally concerned with the illegal human entrant, the former must be concerned with a wide range of goods entering the country both legally and illegally. It is the customs officer who must

117

see that appropriate duties are imposed when the traveler exceeds his duty-free allowance, when a businessman imports items from abroad, or when a nation exceeds the quota imposed on particular items to protect domestic producers.

The customs officer also is concerned with the importation of drugs and other restricted substances; and he must be concerned with the illegal entry of historical materials—for example, pre-Colombian artifacts—which properly belong to the neighboring country's patrimony. Though Mexico has laws restricting the removal of such items from the country, a recent treaty makes it incumbent upon U.S. officials to seize such items when possible. This has occurred in the case of some very large items, but the illicit traffic continues because the trade is very lucrative. Mexico has appreciated U.S. efforts in this area. Another lucrative business is the traffic in parrots and other tropical birds. Smuggled parrots come across, often quieted by tequila or a mixture of tequila and corn mash. For the parrot smuggler the profits are high and the risks low. Pound for pound the bird is worth more than marijuana, and the record suggests that it is five times as hard to get a conviction on smuggled birds. Two recent outbreaks of Newcastle disease affecting chickens in Southern California put the matter in a different light. Millions of chickens had to be killed in order to bring the epidemic under control. This trade poses difficulty because it is not against Mexican law to export the birds.

This problem also cuts the other way. Mexico has a similar set of customs laws. The long, relatively open border is difficult to control, and low-paid *aduana* agents are susceptible to the *mordida,* or bribe. There is no doubt that contraband trade undercuts the protectionist tariffs intended to encourage import substitution production by raising prices significantly on imported items and protecting and promoting the competing Mexican producers. Furthermore, such illegal imports undermine Mexico's international balance of payments and are a matter of considerable concern to Mexico's leaders. Included are automobiles—many of them stolen—television sets, other electronic items, jewelry, liquor, etc. Because the exportation of such items from the United States is lawful, it is difficult for U.S. officials to be responsive to this concern of Mexican officials. The picture is further complicated by the existence of duty-free shops in the border region and by Mexican concessions to the border region of their country to import certain items—normally purchased abroad—duty free to entice the consumer to buy what he needs on the Mexican side of the border.

Beyond law enforcement is the whole question of access to the U.S. market. Mexico, which buys two-thirds of its imports from the United States, has a very real need to increase its exports to that country. When

American labor protests, however, that the assembly plants of border industry mean exporting jobs to take advantage of cheap labor, when reduced quotas are imposed on importations to assist a domestic industry, and when farmers protest the importation of Mexican fruits and vegetables and attempt to block the movement of such produce at the international bridges, then trade relations become a part of law enforcement and have significant impact on the relations between the two nations.

Conclusion

Obviously the solution or amelioration of most of the law enforcement problems touched upon in this paper will depend to a very large degree on the improvement of conditions on both sides of the border and most particularly in Mexico. Beyond that, the improvement of all phases of law enforcement must be on an equal-partner basis. Problems must be dealt with—and issues must be resolved—through mutual efforts without infringement on Mexican sovereignty. There must be continuing and improved liaison at all levels of government as well as the establishment of personal relationships between law enforcement officers in one country and their counterparts in the other so that the laws of each country may be properly enforced in an atmosphere of international friendship and understanding.

This writer firmly believes that the continuance of a strong, democratic, and stable government in Mexico is in the national interest of the United States. Furthermore, I am convinced that the betterment of the Mexican people as a whole is an essential ingredient for such continuance. Accordingly, it is in the interest of the United States to adopt a "special relationship" with Mexico that would include favorable immigration laws, easier access to the U.S. market through lowered import duties and reduced trade restrictions, and such other economic and technological assistance as may be needed by Mexico in a form acceptable to the Mexicans.

References

Avante Systems, Inc., and Cultural Research Associates. *A Survey of the Undocumented Population in Two Texas Border Areas.* San Antonio, 1978. Report submitted to the Southwestern Regional Office of the U.S. Commission on Civil Rights.

Benson, C. C. "Stolen U.S. Vehicles and Mexico." Paper prepared for the Southwestern States Conference on Crime and the Border, San Diego, April 21–23, 1977.

Chapman, Leonard F., Jr., and Leonel J. Castillo. "Selected Speeches by the Commissioners of Immigration." Collection of processed papers from the file of the district director of the Immigration and Naturalization Service, San Antonio.

Flores, Roy, and Gilbert Cárdenas. *A Study of the Demographic and Employment Characteristics of Undocumented Aliens in San Antonio, El Paso, and McAllen.* August 23, 1978. Report submitted to the Southwestern Regional Office of the U.S. Commission of Civil Rights.

Schons, Gary, and Stephen W. McGee, comps. "Mexico: Administration of Law Enforcement." San Diego, 1977.

Southwestern States Conferences on Crime and the Border. "Full Text of Resolution: First and Second Conferences Held in California and Texas." Austin, Texas, 1978.

State of California, Office of the Attorney General. "Manual for the Southwestern States Conference on Crime and the Border, San Diego, California, April 21–23, 1977."

State of Texas, Attorney General. "Second Conference on Crime and the Border." El Paso, October, 2–5, 1977, 1978.

"Summary of Certain Provisions of U.S. Immigration Law." From the file of the district director of the Immigration and Naturalization Service, San Antonio.

U.S. Department of Justice. *Preliminary Report: Domestic Council Committee on Illegal Aliens.* Washington, D.C., 1976.

U.S. Department of the Treasury. "U.S. Customs Service," *Department of Treasury News.* Summary of the duties of the U.S. Customs Service.

Younger, Evelle J., attorney general of California, to the president of the United States, May 20, 1977. Copy from the file of the district director of the Immigration and Naturalization Service, San Antonio.

The Migration Issue in U.S.-Mexican Relations

David S. North

One of the most complex, acrimonious, and potentially intractable aspects of relations between the United States and Mexico, two adjacent and basically friendly nations, is the question of migration. Nowhere else in the free world is there a boundary between two nations of such remarkably different levels of wealth. The combination of the differing economies, Mexico's rapid population growth, and a loosely controlled border has created a northward movement of migrants that has become a major issue between the two nations.

In this paper we will briefly examine the widely divergent definitions of this issue that prevail in the United States and in Mexico, review the current status of the phenomenon, and outline the policy options available to the two nations.

Definitions

One of the fundamental difficulties with the binational dialogue on migration is that the official definitions of the subject are quite different from each other. To some extent the views of the U.S. and Mexican governments conflict, but perhaps to an even greater extent they simply pass each other in the night. The dialogue on the U.S. side is complicated by a substantial stream of academic and Chicano arguments and definitions that are often close to those of the government of Mexico; there is no visible comparable phenomenon within Mexico.

Thus the matter of migration is an issue on which the Mexican leadership is united and the American leadership is not. It is a matter of great importance to the government in Mexico City but of lesser importance to the government in Washington. In Mexico, the matter is viewed from a historical perspective—that movements of persons across America's southern border are really movements between two areas that were, for centuries, governed by Mexico City. The official U.S. position looks at the present (and at the future) and pays little attention to the past.

The U.S. view of migration tends to be legalistic, considering all

121

persons crossing the southern border as falling into three broad classes: legal immigrants, legal nonimmigrants, and illegal or undocumented migrants. The Mexican tendency is to ignore these distinctions and to regard all migrants and would-be migrants simply as human beings.

To the U.S. government, it is largely a domestic rather than a foreign policy issue. The question is more often discussed in demographic, labor market, law enforcement, and civil rights terms than in diplomatic ones. The United States, but not Mexico, is quite aware that a substantial minority of the illegal migrants in the nation are *not* from Mexico and that the question extends well beyond this nation's relations with Mexico. In the Mexican view, the question is one of the most pressing foreign affairs issues facing the nation.

Finally, there is the often unarticulated layer of ethnicity that clouds the issue on both sides of the border; the official U.S. view is neutral on the question of ethnicity, as the U.S. immigration law has been largely free of such considerations since the 1965 Amendments to the Immigration and Nationality Act. Some of the unofficial U.S. viewpoints are not without ethnic overtones, however; some of the restrictionists are worried about the different language and cultural background (and perhaps skin color) of the migrants; some of the antirestrictionists, the Hispanics, want a more relaxed border to enlarge the size of the Hispanic community in the United States. The Mexican government (with sound historical underpinning) cannot help regarding the restrictionists as ethnocentricists, whatever considerations may be motivating them. And, when viewed from afar (or from within the Indian community), an observer might regard the entire dialogue as dealing with an essentially Indian or Mestizo population but conducted by two white governments.

Current Phenomenon

The description of the U.S.–Mexican migration question is generally a one-sided one, focusing only on movements *from* Mexico *to* the United States, whereas discussions of the movements of people across the northern border is almost always a two-sided one, as Canadians move to the United States and as Americans move to Canada. Very rarely noted in U.S.–Mexican discussions is the zeal with which the Mexican government guards its labor market from North American incursions and the difficulties faced by U.S. citizens if they seek to buy property in Mexico. One wishes that more scholarly attention were paid to this side of the coin.

Any discussion of the state of migration from Mexico to the United States must take into account the three classes of migrants recognized by U.S. law and public policy: legal immigrants, nonimmigrants, and illegal migrants.[1] U.S. policy decisions tend to be made not about Mexican migrants per se but about particular classes of migrants.

The U.S. policy on legal immigrants from Mexico, though it has varied from time to time, has been to welcome substantial numbers of such immigrants. In the last quarter of a century, for example, the United States has accepted 1,146,344 legal immigrants from Mexico, more than were admitted from any other nation in the world.[2]

Up until the 1965 Amendments to the Immigration and Nationality Act, which ended the country-of-origin quota system for the Eastern Hemisphere, no numerical limits had been placed on Mexican immigration or on that from any other Western Hemisphere nation. At that time a limit of 120,000 was placed on numerically restricted immigration from the Western Hemisphere but not on movements of certain classes of would-be immigrants who are not covered by numerical restrictions. (These exceptional cases, virtually all immediate relatives of U.S. citizens, are more likely to come from Mexico than from any other nation; in 1976, for example, a typical year, there were 18,532 exempt immigrants from Mexico among the total of 113,840 such immigrants.)

Although the 1965 Amendments created backlogs among would-be Western Hemisphere immigrants, immigration from Mexico in the ten fiscal years that followed the signature of the law totaled 538,264, compared with 419,770 in the ten previous years. Legal immigration from Mexico peaked at 71,863 in 1974.

Congress sought, in the 1976 Amendments to the Immigration and Nationality Act, to reduce legal immigration from Mexico by applying to the Western Hemisphere a 20,000-per-nation limitation (for numerically controlled immigration) that had applied since 1965 to the nations of the Eastern Hemisphere. The congressional rhetoric of the time was that it was simply applying the same set of rules to both hemispheres. Because Mexico was the only nation in the Western Hemisphere on which the new law had direct bearing, the government of Mexico and the Chicano community, understandably, regarded it as a hostile act.

What Congress sought to do, however, was soon undone by a young poverty lawyer in Chicago and the U.S. District Court judge before whom he appeared. The lawyer's client, Refugio Silva, was in the United States without the benefit of appropriate documentation; he was a would-be immigrant who had applied for a visa, apparently was eligible for it, and had been put on a waiting list. The Immigration and Naturalization Service (INS) sought to force him to leave the country until his number came up. His lawyer contended that INS had erred by counting visas issued to Cuban refugees as being within the numerical ceiling, when they should have been issued outside that ceiling. Silva, the attorney argued successfully, was one of more than 100,000 natives of the Western Hemisphere who should not have been forced to wait for their visas. Most persons in the Silva class are natives of Mexico.[3]

The *Silva* case must puzzle observers of U.S. public policy not steeped in the intricacies of the American system of three independent segments of government; where else in the world can a trial judge turn around a nation's immigration policy? Congress, of course, had no role to play in this case, and the Justice Department, which often appeals cases it loses at the district court level, did not do so.

The results of these moves and countermoves in U.S. immigration policy have produced, in the 1970s, flows of legal immigrants from Mexico shown in table 1.

Although the results of U.S. policy in recent decades have been to admit more immigrants from Mexico than from any other nation, the level of demand for visas (among those who meet the formal criteria) far exceeds even the *Silva*-enlarged supply. The numbers of persons on visa waiting lists as of January 1, 1978 are shown in table 2.

It should be noted that immigrants from Mexico are virtually all from a single class of would-be immigrants, relatives of permanent resident aliens and U.S. citizens. There are virtually no needed workers (professionals and others with labor certifications) among these immigrants, very few immigrant investors, and few refugees.[4]

Although the U.S. stance on legal immigration from Mexico has been changed by Congress twice in recent years (1965 and 1976) and by the courts, up until a minor deviation caused by the Carter White House, U.S. policy on nonimmigrant workers from Mexico has been consistent (and negative) since 1963. In that year the Congress passed, by a close margin, the final extension of Public Law 78, which permitted the admission of nonimmigrant Mexican farm workers to toil on U.S.

TABLE 1

LEGAL IMMIGRANTS FROM MEXICO

FY	No.
1970	44,821
1971	50,324
1972	64,209
1973	70,411
1974	71,863
1975	62,552
1976	58,354
1977	44,069

SOURCE: *INS Annual Reports* for the years cited, table 8.

TABLE 2
Visa Waiting Lists

Country/Region	Number Waiting
Mexico	239,647
Balance of Western Hemisphere	173,619
Eastern Hemisphere	306,113
Total	719,379

Source: Unpublished State Department data.

farms, generally in the West. The bracero program ended on December 31, 1964. In the following three years, relatively few Mexican farm workers were admitted under a provision of the Immigration Act, primarily to work in the California cannery tomato harvest. There were no temporary farm workers from Mexico working in the states from 1967 to 1977 when President Carter, reacting to an appeal from Congressman Richard White, ordered INS to admit several hundred to work in the onion and melon fields of the Presidio Valley of West Texas.

For two decades after the end of World War II, the bracero program was the major element in migration from Mexico to the United States. At its peak more than 400,000 admissions of braceros were recorded annually, with each of the workers being assigned to a specific grower (or growers' association), with the understanding that a bracero who displeased his employer would be deported. Mexican farm workers, however, were paid better than they would have been had they stayed in Mexico, and some efforts were made to regulate wages and working conditions. Eventually a coalition of the Church, the Chicanos, and organized labor caused the repeal of the bracero program on the grounds that it artificially depressed wages and working conditions for U.S. farm workers. The coalition was abetted by the introduction of cotton and tomato harvesting machines, which substantially decreased the need for stoop labor in the Southwest and thus dulled the growers' desire for braceros.

The largest, and most controversial, element in Mexican–U.S. migration is that of illegal immigration. The numbers of apprehended illegal aliens from Mexico in recent years have soared despite only minimal increases in border patrol resources. Apprehensions rose from 22,687 in 1960, when the bracero program was in full swing, to 219,254 in 1970, to 680,392 in 1975, and to 976,661 in 1978.

The phenomenon being measured here is arrests, not migration per se. Thus the numbers do not reflect either the total flow of illegal migrants (which would be reduced by double entries and increased by those who crossed the border undetected) or the illegal alien population in the United States. The persisting lack of good data on the subject reflects not only the difficulty of estimating the size of an underground population but the low priority that the U.S. government has given to this subject—a problem that could be solved by the careful expenditure of no more than a million dollars.

There appear to be four central domestic disputes about illegal immigration, which can be briefly summarized as follows:

• *Population:* Is the illegal alien population large enough to be of significance? Those who are worried about illegal aliens tend to favor larger estimates than those who are not. Thus former INS commissioner Leonard Chapman spoke of an estimated range of 4 million to 12 million and released the ill-fated Lesko report,[5] which used a narrow-based Delphi technique to arrive at an estimate of 8.3 million aliens (some 65 percent of whom were thought to be from Mexico).

Chapman's critics said that he was an alarmist and that the methodologies he used or cited were questionable. Perhaps the best—and certainly the least biased—estimate was made by Lancaster and Scheuren of the Social Security Administration (SSA); they estimated, by matching government data systems and using the capture-recapture methodology, that in April 1973 there were 3.9 million illegals in the nation between the ages of eighteen and forty-four.[6]

• *Growth of population and migration.* Another set of disputes revolves around not the size of the population and the migration flows that feed it, but their growth or lack of it. Clearly the question is one of more significance if the population is growing than if it is stationary. We have, according to one line of thought, absorbed all the illegal immigrants who are here, and if the population is stabilizing, then we do not have a serious problem. That INS apprehensions have been growing more slowly in recent years is a possible indication that the population has not been growing; that the number of Mexican nationals under the age of fifteen continues to grow (and accounts for almost 50 percent of the nation's population) is an argument used in reply.

• *Temporariness.* Still a third debate deals with the rate of turnover of the population of illegal immigrants from Mexico. (This discussion generally does not arise in connection with illegal immigrants from other nations, as it is apparent that the barriers to their crossing the border are more formidable than those experienced by natives of Mexico.) The argument goes that many Mexican natives stay in the United States only three to six months before returning to Mexico and that since this is the case the phenomenon is a nonproblem. The counterargument is that the impact of X million illegal entrants (in the labor market) is precisely the same quantitatively whether they have been in the nation for an average of three months, three years, or ten years; that is, a worker is a worker. Qualitatively, a labor force with little seniority—and with a total lack of documentation—is likely to be more passive and less skilled than a similarly illegal labor force that has been in the nation for a longer period of time.

• *Domestic impact.* The most significant debate over illegal migration revolves around the question of the impact of these migrants on the domestic economy. In recent years the debate has evolved from one that focused on illegal aliens and tax-supported programs to a more sophisticated dialogue about the role of the migrants in the labor market.

The INS under General Chapman (but not under Commissioner Castillo) contended that illegal aliens were using (and therefore abusing) tax-supported programs. Data from the North and Houstoun and *Migration Today* surveys indicate that illegal alien respondents were more likely to report paying taxes than to be using tax-supported services.[7] (Prime working-age males, the kind of aliens the INS apprehends and the kind made available for the North and Houstoun interviews, are unlikely to be using tax-supported programs even if they are citizens, a point sometimes forgotten in these discussions.) On balance it appears likely that, at this time, illegal immigrants are not major users of tax-supported programs; but it appears equally clear that it would be useful if government agencies that operate programs such as Food Stamps, Aid to Families with Dependent Children, and Unemployment Insurance would examine the impact of illegals on these programs; none has done so thus far.

The more complex debate on the domestic impact of illegal aliens revolves around their impact on the labor market. There are two prevailing schools of thought.

Wayne Cornelius and Michael Piore are the principal proponents of the view that the U.S. economy needs low-skilled, amenable workers and that, as the legal supply of such persons has been dried up by rising expectations of the domestic labor force and the cushions offered by income transfer programs, there is a strong tendency for the economy to pull such workers across borders into the United States.[8] The role now played by the illegal workers, from Mexico and elsewhere, is the role played earlier by legal immigrants, by rural people moving to the cities, and by southern blacks and Puerto Ricans moving to northern urban centers. They argue that the movement is inevitable and that its impact should be controlled within the labor market by stronger regulation of wages and working conditions and not by tighter control of the movements of persons across the border.

The opposing view is that illegal immigrants, because of their numbers and their lack of rights, tend to loosen already loose labor markets, thereby depressing wages and working conditions and impairing unions' efforts to organize workers. It can be argued that the utilization of a substantially disadvantaged labor force to subsidize the standard of living of other, more privileged elements in the society is in conflict with America's egalitarian tradition. Craig Jenkins argues, similarly, that illegal immigrants are not needed workers but that their presence ensures social control of the work force by managers of significant segments of the American economy.[9]

We will not seek to resolve these arguments here but will simply note that the policy options favored by those who regard the northward flow as inevitable are, understandably, different from those who subscribe to the social control theory; the latter are also more optimistic about the potential utility of governmental regulation than the former.

Policy Options for the U.S. and Mexico

Each nation can be viewed as having five groups of policy options available to it. To some extent the options available to each nation are not mutually inconsistent, and in all likelihood whatever postures are eventually adopted will be mixtures of policy threads along the lines of the Carter administration proposals of August 1977. The realities of the political forces operating within and between the two nations suggest that no single approach will be utilized to the exclusion of others—unless both nations continue to opt for the final alternative available to both, which is to do nothing.

The five basic U.S. options are to:

- enforce existing laws
- legalize the migrant flow
- support Mexico's economic development
- press Mexico for internal change
- do nothing

The most obvious U.S. policy option—the one used by President Eisenhower and his West Point classmate General Joseph Swing during "Operation Wetback"—is to enforce the immigration law with vigor, but this is only one of the alternatives open to the United States within the enforcement framework. The United States can choose to enforce laws now on the books with increased vigor, or it can pass new restrictive legislation. The focus of its enforcement activity can be on the immigration law (either at the border or inland or both), or it can be on the labor market. We will review these possibilities shortly.

There is no longer any possibility that a quasi-military sweep of the border, such as that used in Operation Wetback, will recur in the fore-

128

seeable future. Times have changed, issues are more complex (or are viewed as such), and no American president would adopt the simplistic posture of the Eisenhower administration. Mexico, with its oil, and the Chicano community, with its votes, are too significant to Washington for history to repeat itself.

This is not to say, however, that increased enforcement is not a potential option for the United States. The alternatives are:

• *Tighter control between the ports of entry.* The Carter administration has proposed this tactic and has made some additional resources available to the Border Patrol—the unit within INS that is most likely to secure additional resources. (It should be noted that the patrol, with two rented helicopters and some 2,000 agents for 3,100 kilometers of border, is far from a generously funded operation; the United States routinely spends much more money on the control of drugs and other contraband than it does on the control of illegal immigration.)

• *Tighter control at the ports of entry.* Though it is well known within both the INS and the illegal alien community that a major segment of the illegal traffic comes through the ports of entry—the route used by women, children, and the more prosperous or sophisticated males— few efforts have been made to strengthen the inspection function of INS. Presumably illegal alien entrances could be reduced, perhaps substantially, if immigration inspectors were given more time to inspect candidates for admission at the ports, but one of two major costs would have to be absorbed: either the lines waiting for admission (including U.S. citizens) would lengthen, or the government would have to spend more money on Spanish-speaking immigration inspectors. The federal government has shown no desire to slow the tourist traffic and has shown a preference for spending money on hardware (for example, sensors, helicopters) rather than on more inspectors. (The latter, incidentally, make minimal demands for time per inspection—they would like to have an average of 20 seconds for each applicant.)[10]

• *Tighter enforcement of immigration law in the interior.* Far more controversial than any enforcement at the border—where the government is clearly dealing with outsiders trying to get in—are efforts to enforce the immigration law inside the borders. INS raids on places of employment generally stir more journalistic sympathy for law violators than for the law enforcers. The courts have been taking a progressively dimmer view of INS inland enforcement practices, and highly effective techniques used in the past (such as street-corner and subway confrontations of aliens) have been abandoned. Given the judicial climate and the current political leadership of INS, it is unlikely that inland enforcement will be expanded in the near future.

• *Tighter enforcement of current labor market legislation.* One of the options—no matter what is or is not done to enforce the immigration law—is to enforce the labor standards laws with more vigor. The administration has taken some steps in this direction. More enforcement of the minimum wage and occupational safety laws would, of course, benefit not only U.S. workers but their illegal alien counterparts as well. Such enforcement would raise labor costs for employers accustomed to paying substandard wages who would argue that enforcement of the law might drive them out of business.

• *Enactment and enforcement of an employer sanctions law.* One of the major options—which has been supported by the House of Representatives in the past and was proposed by President Carter—is to make it illegal for U.S. employers to hire illegal aliens. The fundamental injustice that the illegal worker may be forced to leave the country (at considerable expense) for working illegally, while his employer does not even have his wrist slapped, may lead to some legislation on this subject. A continuing complication, however, is the question: "How does an employer identify an illegal alien?" Chicano organizations argue that without a work permit system "foreign-looking" people would face job discrimination; a ready answer to that valid objection would be to create a worker identification program, which, in turn, runs into objections from civil libertarians.

On balance, it appears that if the U.S. government is going to take action on the question of illegal aliens, it would involve law enforcement. The alternatives that appear to be the most likely relate to enforcement between the ports of entry and perhaps an employer sanctions bill. Mexico's sensitivities will be adversely affected by all of these alternatives, save for better enforcement of the minimum wage law.

"If you can't beat them, join them" is an old adage; the pertinent variation here would be, "If we can't beat them, have them join us." Converting illegal aliens to legal ones has a number of potential effects:

• It relieves the illegal alien of the pressure of illegality.
• It makes the individual less likely to be exploited in the U.S. labor market.
• It reduces the illegal population that INS is supposed to control.
• It tends to smooth, not irritate, U.S.–Mexican relations.

On the other hand, it has these less beneficial effects:

• It rewards the alien for past illegal activity.
• It may encourage others to follow the same path.
• As far as the environmentalists are concerned, it adds another person to the U.S. population.

The reaction of some U.S. employers to legalization is interesting; though they claim that illegals are needed workers, they do not want legalized illegals, because they will start acting like U.S. workers. Both agribusiness and the Chicano community find themselves opposed to stepped-up enforcement of the immigration law, but they disagree with each other on legalization.

There are three ways to implement legalization. The most discussed technique is the Carter administration's amnesty proposal. Illegal aliens here since January 1, 1970, would be awarded legal immigrant status: those arriving between that date and January 1, 1977, would be granted a new five year "temporary alien status." During that time they could work, pay taxes, and cross the borders, but they could not use this status to immigrate family members or to use tax-supported programs. This temporary-alien status, in short, would be a legitimization of a second-class status, defended because it would be better than the third-class status the illegals now enjoy.

Another form of legalization would be a revival of the bracero program. Mexican nationals wishing to work in the United States would apply for temporary-worker status in Mexico, and those selected would then work under governmental regulation. This approach is attractive to agribusiness and to the government of Mexico (which may not be very articulate in its support) but would cause an enormous uproar from the AFL-CIO because of its role in winning the bracero battle almost a generation ago. On no other U.S.–Mexican issue, however, can the AFL-CIO be expected to play a major role.

The third approach to legalization would be to expand Mexican legal immigration to the United States. The Carter administration proposed changing the ceiling on numerically controlled immigration from 20,000 to a joint 50,000 figure for Mexico and Canada. Because the immigration law in the past decade has been more restrictive on Canadian than on Mexican immigration, most of the 50,000 visas would go to Mexicans. Some adjustment along these lines is likely, but it will have little more than symbolic value, as the upward adjustment is unlikely to meet more than a fraction of the demand.

Supporting the economic development of Mexico, particularly in the areas that are the sources of illegal immigrants, was the stated objective of the Carter administration. Such a program of labor-intensive economic development is a long-term approach, of course, and presumably an expensive one. Although there is no ongoing direct U.S. aid to such areas in Mexico, there is a substantial World Bank–funded rural economic development program currently under way.

There are two major difficulties with this approach; the first is the lack of an AID program in Mexico (a program that Mexico does not seek and would probably refuse were it to be offered). The second, and more significant, is that there appears to be no inclination on the part of the Mexican government to shape its development programs to discourage either internal or international migration; the representatives of Mexico at the recent Brookings–El Colegio de México symposium were quite clear on this point.[11]

Just as Mexico's internal priorities would seem to preclude channeling economic development to migrant-producing areas, so the State Department's priorities preclude the fourth approach for the U.S. government: to bring pressure to bear on Mexico to smooth out its highly skewed income distribution pattern. Such a redistribution would ease some of the pressure to migrate north. It should be recalled that Mexico has no meaningful income tax on the wealthy, and no welfare, food stamps, or unemployment insurance programs for the poor; the Mexican social security program currently covers only the urban upper and middle classes. Reduction of migration is not a major item on the State Department's agenda, however; it wants the Mexicans to satisfy our appetite for oil and natural gas and not to satisfy our appetite for drugs.

The fifth option for the U.S. government is to do nothing, to maintain the status quo. Given the complex interplay of political forces within the nation, this option may well be the only one adopted for some time to come.

Mexico's cluster of five policy options can be summarized as follows:

- press the United States for migration concessions
- cooperate on labor-intensive economic development
- cooperate on migration control
- develop alternative migration targets
- do nothing

Given the strong U.S. interest in its oil, Mexico is in a good position to seek migration concessions from the United States. It can seek additional legal immigration on a permanent basis, seek amnesty for its citizens now in the states, or perhaps lobby for a temporary worker program. These Mexican options would be corollaries to the legalization options of the U.S. government.

Similarly, Mexico might seek some forms of economic development that are attractive to its own needs and, at the same time, help reduce migration. The principal thrust of the Mexican government in this area has been to propose the easing of U.S. trade barriers on Mexican products; such tariff reductions would create some additional jobs in Mexico, thereby reducing somewhat the pressures for northward migration.

A less likely option for Mexico would be to cooperate actively with the United States in law enforcement activities. Mexico, for example,

132

without interfering in the exodus of its people across the borders, could crack down on smugglers and on counterfeiters of U.S. and Mexican travel documents. There is spasmodic cooperation between some Mexican and U.S. law enforcement officials along these lines, and where it exists it can be extremely significant. Such cooperation, even on the limited basis noted here, would be unlikely unless the United States made significant concessions to Mexico.

A fourth option for Mexico, one that I have not seen discussed, would be to follow the precedent of Turkey and Korea, that is, to develop alternative nations for migration when the original host nations tighten their admissions policies. Finding Japan (in the case of Korea) and Western Europe (in the case of Turkey) no longer willing to accept their migrants, both nations turned to the oil-rich, worker-poor nations of the Middle East. Similarly, some of the former British colonies in the Caribbean have shifted their eyes from Britain to the United States and Canada, with flows of migrants moving quickly to take advantage of favorable changes in the immigration laws of those nations.

Along these lines there has been a steady increase in the relatively minor flow of immigrants from Mexico to Canada in recent years, going from 382 in 1971, for example, to 794 in 1977.[12] There has also been some movement of temporary workers to Canada. This option, of course, is a limited one.

The fifth option, and a highly attractive one to Mexico, is to preserve the status quo. Mexico is exporting unemployment (and thereby avoiding potential political unrest) and is importing remittances from its workers; this is being done on a massive scale. It is highly unlikely that any alternative scenario could be as useful to Mexico as the status quo (although the U.S. treatment of its workers causes resentment). And Mexico's fifth option has the utility of dovetailing neatly with the fifth option of the United States, which is also to do nothing.

Notes

[1] There is an interesting fourth class; that is, U.S. citizens by derivation, persons born in Mexico to U.S. citizens who subsequently claim U.S. citizenship. This is a hereditary class of nonresident U.S. citizens, who enjoy the advantages of being citizens of both nations; many of them live in Mexico but commute to work in the United States. Persons entering under this status, whether they reside in Mexico or in the United States, are excluded (presumably by oversight) from both census and INS data on immigration.

[2] Data are for fiscal years 1953 through 1977 and from table 6A of the *Annual Reports of the Immigration and Naturalization Service.*

[3] See Silva v. Levi, U.S.D.C., N.D. Ill., No. 76 C 4268.

[4] Some natives of Mexico were swept up in the exodus of refugees from Cuba.

[5] Lesko Associates, *Basic Data and Guidance Required to Implement a Major Illegal Alien Study during Fiscal Year 1976* (Washington, D.C., October 1975).

[6] Clarise Lancaster and Fritz Scheuren, "Counting the Uncountable Illegals," paper presented at the Annual Meeting of the American Statistical Association, Chicago, August 1977.

[7] David S. North and Marion F. Houstoun, *The Characteristics and Role of Illegal Aliens in the U.S. Labor Market: An Exploratory Study* (Washington, D.C.: U.S. Dept. of Labor, March 1976); and Patricia J. Elwell et al., "Haitian and Dominican Undocumented Aliens in New York City: A Preliminary Report," *Migration Today*, December 1977.

[8] Wayne A. Cornelius, *Illegal Migration to the United States: Recent Research Findings, Policy Implications, and Research Priorities* (Cambridge: Center for International Studies, MIT, May 1977); Michael Piore, "The 'New Immigration' and the Presumptions of Social Policy," paper presented at a meeting of the Industrial Relations Research Association, December 29, 1974, and subsequently condensed in the *New Republic*, February 22, 1975.

[9] Craig Jenkins, "The Demand for Immigrant Workers: Labor Scarcity or Social Control," *International Migration Review*, vol. 12, no. 4 (Winter 1978): 514–36.

[10] U.S., Department of Justice, Immigration and Naturalization Service, *Illegal Alien Study, Part 1: Fraudulent Entrants Study*, September 1976.

[11] Brookings Institution, *Structural Factors in Mexican and Caribbean Basin Migration*, proceedings of a Brookings Institution–El Colegio de México symposium, June 28–30, 1978, Washington, D.C.

[12] Ministry of Manpower and Immigration, *Immigration Statistics, Canada*, 1971 and 1977 (Ottawa), table 3.

The Illegal Alien from Mexico: Policy Choices for an Intractable Issue

Sidney Weintraub and Stanley R. Ross

More than 1 million illegal aliens were apprehended by U.S. officials in fiscal year 1977. To put this figure into some context, about 2 million people a year (not counting illegal aliens) enter the U.S. labor force. Because some persons were apprehended more than once and others never were apprehended at all, the total number of people entering the United States illegally is indeterminate. The number of apprehensions represented a 20 percent increase over the preceding year. The U.S. government believes that there are between 3 million and 5 million illegal aliens permanently living here, increasing by 300,000 to 500,000 each year, but other estimates of the numbers range from half to double these figures. Whatever the precise facts, the stream of illegal migration involves millions of people and has an important impact on the U.S. labor market, affecting both total output and the livelihood of millions of U.S. residents. Whether the economic impact of the migrants is, on balance, positive or negative, the size of the influx and the wholesale flouting of the law that it involves raise complex political, social, and foreign policy issues.

For a number of reasons, of which the most important is the permeability of our mutual border, Mexicans make up a large proportion of the total illegal migration. Thus this analysis focuses on the Mexican segment of the problem and on particular means for dealing with it. Even when this one element is in some degree isolated, the ambiguity of the evidence, the complicated mixture of personal, regional, national, and international interests, the uncertain outcome of different regulatory approaches, and the dimensions and difficulty of the overall problem facing the United States do not make for facile solutions. Given the attraction of the United States and the burgeoning populations of hemispheric neighbors, we will not be able to stanch the flow easily or painlessly.

The Carter administration acknowledged the importance of the problem when it introduced legislation aimed at curbing the flow of illegal Mexican immigrants and at the same time regularizing the status of those residing here permanently since 1970. This package of com-

135

promises, however, is virtually a dead letter. Congress not only was unwilling to act on it but has authorized establishment of a Select Commission on Immigration to report early in 1981. Delay in dealing with the problem is likely to leave us facing an increasingly intractable set of problems. Thus the issue of the illegal Mexican migration, its effects on both the United States and Mexico, and the viability of measures for dealing with it should be confronted now.

The Movement of Foreign Workers

Historically, we have encouraged workers to come to the United States in times of labor shortage and then forced them home when times were less prosperous. It is not accidental, we believe, that the current hullabaloo about illegal migrants began at a time of high unemployment in the United States. Jonathan Power, writing in the *Washington Post*, referred to temporary worker practices in the United States and to the guest worker systems of Western Europe as the policy of the lemon—first squeeze the fruit, and then throw it away.[1]

The movement of workers across the border from Mexico dates back to the demands for labor generated by the mining booms and railroad construction in the past century and by the requirements of agriculture in the present one. It was during the manpower shortages of World War I, however, that the magnitude of movement assumed significant dimensions. The northward flow continued until the depression of the 1930s when, between 1930 and 1933, over 300,000 Mexicans were repatriated to Mexico. The human tide reversed again during World War II. As a result of new manpower shortages, the bracero program was inaugurated in 1942 as a wartime measure. It was to endure much longer than anticipated.

The bracero program lasted for twenty-two years, and under its auspices some 4.5 million Mexican workers labored under contract for limited periods of time. They were concentrated on only 2 percent of U.S. farms, clustered in the Southwest and California. Mexico, in addition to insisting on additional protection for its nationals with each renegotiation, demonstrated a preference for intergovernmental agreements. By the early 1950s, it is estimated that the braceros and illegal workers in the United States were remitting more than $100 million annually. By 1952 the bracero program had been "institutionalized" and had become a "permanent" component of U.S. farm labor and of U.S.–Mexican relations. The program, however, was always the object of political skirmishes. Contemporaneous complaints and later research revealed much graft and exploitation in its implementation.

In the 1951 negotiations, Mexico advocated a government-sponsored system to oversee the contracting, which was established, and punishment of employers of illegals, which was not forthcoming. At the time, both U.S. and Mexican delegations pledged a redoubling of efforts on the part of their respective immigration authorities to prevent illegal entry. Nonetheless, a rising number of apprehensions of illegal migrants accompanied the bracero program. Apprehensions ran two to four times the number of braceros in a given year between 1948 and 1954. The advent of the post–Korean War economic slowdown brought Operation Wetback, under which a militarized border patrol rounded up and deported over a million aliens—men, women, and children—in 1954. Although 1956 was a peak for braceros, with 445,000 entering the United States, that year apprehensions had dropped to 73,000 and the Immigration and Naturalization Service (INS) could report that illegal crossing was under control. The price in violation of human rights was high.

During the 1950s, political agitation against the program increased, and the bracero arrangement would have been ended in 1961 except for Mexican advocacy for its prolongation and domestic pressure to avoid an abrupt termination. As a concession to those pressures, the Kennedy administration continued the arrangement until 1964, when it was allowed to expire. Apart from corruption and exploitation, the biggest complaint was that the bracero program continued to be accompanied by significant illegal entry. There is also evidence that those who learned the ropes as braceros—or their offspring—became the cadre for the later illegals.

It is generally accepted that Mexicans migrate to the United States because of lack of opportunity and low earnings at home compared with better work opportunities in the United States. Most illegals have no difficulty getting work in this country. At an average hourly wage of $2.34 (the figure for the Mexicans in the North and Houstoun sample taken in May–June 1975),[2] the illegals are well paid by their national standards.

Viewed from Mexico, this human movement provides the kind of escape valve that emigration has always provided, such as to the Irish coming to the United States in times of famine and Jews in times of persecution. An article in the Mexico City newspaper *Excélsior* asserted that as many as one in four Mexicans in the labor force works in the United States.[3] The remittances sent by migrants are important to the receiving families, many of them in impoverished rural Mexico, not to speak of their importance to Mexico's balance of payments.

The causes of the northward migration run deep within Mexican society. Mexico's population growth rate in the early 1970s was 3.5 percent a year, one of the highest in the world; it appears to have declined since to about 3 percent. The Latin American Demography Center estimated that Mexico's population will increase from 59 million in 1975 to 83 million in 1985 to 132 million in the year 2000. Combined

137

unemployment and underemployment now must affect at least 40 percent of the population. This figure comes from data submitted with President López Portillo's inaugural address in December 1976. The number of persons entering into Mexico's labor force each year (defined by Mexico as those reaching age twelve) is about 700,000. Despite Mexico's high economic growth rate in recent decades (2.8 percent per capita per year from 1960 to 1975), the country has been unable to absorb this level of population growth. Even if the slowed rate of population growth reported by researchers at El Colegio de México proves correct, the hundreth million Mexican is already on the way and the projection for the end of the century would be reduced only to 115 million. The labor absorption problem will be aggravated in the future because of the extreme youthfulness of the Mexican population; almost half the population is under the age of fifteen—thus the flow of people to the nearest place of reasonable opportunity, to Mexico City, to other Mexican urban centers, to the northern border, and over the border. The famous nineteenth-century Mexican statement can legitimately be reversed: poor United States, so close to Mexico.

Despite the historical fact that Mexico was the locale of the first twentieth-century nationalist social revolution, it is still a most unequal society, even by standards of other developing countries. Using data from a Bank of Mexico survey, the richest 5 percent of the population received 36 percent of total income in 1969, the richest 20 percent received 64 percent, and by contrast, the poorest 20 percent received 4 percent. Evidence from the mid-1970s from the Bank of Mexico and Mexico's Labor Ministry shows little change and, indeed, deterioration in the share of the lowest 10 and 20 percent. Mexico's average gross national product is reasonably high by world standards (over $1,000 per person per year), but a good proportion of the population does not share in this. Nor do different parts of the country share equally in schooling and health services. All these distributive inequalities are factors pushing people across the border.

Thus the migration of Mexican workers to the United States—legally or illegally—is and undoubtedly will continue to be a central factor in the relationship between the two neighbors. How the Mexican migrants are treated in the United States and how the flow is regulated will be issues of growing saliency in both U.S. domestic politics and U.S.–Mexican relations.

Economic Aspects of the Presence of Illegals

By its very nature, the dimensions of the illegal immigration into the United States—from Mexico as from elsewhere—cannot be precisely determined. The apprehension figures of the Immigration and Naturalization Service (INS) cannot tell us how many people make it for each person caught, or how many actual persons crossed the border, as many have been apprehended more than once. The best that we can do is to rely on expert judgment, which asserts that for every apprehension two or three or four get across the border scot-free. Does this mean that 1 million, 2 million, or 4 million cross each year? The differences among the numbers are significant, and the honest answer is that we do not know.

The INS lists sixty nations as the sources of illegals, with the Dominican Republic, Haiti, Jamaica, and Guatemala following Mexico as the principal source countries. About 90 percent of the illegal migrants caught by the INS are Mexicans. This high percentage is a consequence of the INS concentration of its border patrol and apprehension activities on the Mexican border and on areas where Mexicans congregate. (Despite this concentration, the number of non-Mexican Latin Americans who are apprehended each year rises.) The U.S. government believes that about 60 percent of the illegals who remain in the United States are Mexicans, although we cannot be sure this is accurate because of the lack of controls on nonimmigrants after entry into the United States.

To use the official nomenclature, more than 90 percent of the apprehended illegals are EWIs, those who enter without inspection (or without documents; hence, the term "undocumented aliens"), but there is substantial evidence that many illegals, particularly from noncontiguous countries, come here on valid visas and then overstay their permitted time. Many illegals, particularly those from Mexico, come, find jobs, and then go home, perhaps to repeat this process many times. The effects of these temporary migrants on the U.S. economic and social structure are different from the issues raised by illegal immigrants who stay permanently. (These two categories necessarily overlap, because many persons who come with the intention of staying in the United States temporarily, wind up remaining permanently.)

The fact that most of the evidence available to us is based on surveys conducted among apprehended illegal migrants creates further problems in ascertaining patterns of the whole group. It is questionable whether those illegal migrants who are apprehended are typical of those who are not and whether it is valid to describe the habits of a universe from observing the behavior of a few in captivity. The Julian Samora study of wetbacks, the David North and Marion Houstoun study of illegal aliens in the labor market, the Vic Villalpando study in its attempt to obtain a profile of the illegal aliens in San Diego County, all drew their samples (in the case of North and Houstoun, most of their sample) from detention centers.[4] It is unfair to criticize this practice, as there was no ready alternative; unapprehended illegals still in the United States do not like to talk to researchers about their habits. Unfortunately, however, as the researchers themselves mostly recognize, this does make suspect the generalizations that are derived. Villalpando's sample of 217 was all male. Fifty-three percent of those interviewed said they preferred to live in their native country, and 39 percent said they preferred to live in the United States. It is questionable whether this is valid for all illegals or even valid for those who answered the question in a detention center, because the answer almost certainly was influenced by the interviewing situation.

The apprehended Mexican illegal is usually an adult male (83 percent in U.S. fiscal year 1977), and the conventional wisdom, also questionable, has it that Mexican illegals are predominantly male.[5] North and Houstoun have pointed out that this conclusion is suspect because most of the INS enforcement staff is male and its members tend to focus on places where males congregate (such as construction sites). In addition, apprehending female illegals can be a nuisance as there are no overnight detention centers for them and they have to be lodged in jails at INS expense. There also is evidence that male enforcement officers are apprehensive about female detainees' charges of sexual molestation. The reason for the all-male sample in the Villalpando study was precisely the lack of a detention facility for females at the Chula Vista border station; the females and children were placed on buses and escorted directly across the border to Tijuana.

Another area of uncertainty relates to the amount of remittances sent home by Mexican immigrants. Official data on net unrequited transfers from the Bank of Mexico show $173 million for 1977. North and Houstoun, in their March 1976 study, estimated that $1.5 billion was a reasonable figure for annual remittances. The Mexican newspaper *Excélsior* recently estimated the figure at $3 billion. This would make it more than double the earnings from tourism.[6]

One of the most frequently cited studies about the habits of Mexican illegals is that of Wayne Cornelius, then of the Massachusetts Institute of Technology.[7] He and his colleagues conducted extended interviews of 80 residents, made a population census of 2,960 households, and searched local records in the region of Los Altos in the Mexican state of Jalisco. This particular agricultural region was chosen because of its long history of outmigration, both to other locations in Mexico and to the United States. From this sample Cornelius found that migration from this region to the United States generally has been of a temporary character and that the average length of stay in this country was about six to eight months, usually from March to early December. (The December date for returns suggests holiday visits to family during a slack agricultural period in the United States.) There were some instances of migrants remaining up to two and three years and a few even longer. About 60 percent of the migrants in Cornelius's sample worked in this country as agricultural laborers and seemed to progress into nonagricultural work as they gained experience through successive illegal entries.

A San Antonio researcher, Ron Grennes, has found that migrants from urban centers like Mexico City and Puebla tend to remain longer, even permanently.[8] Research at El Colegio de México has shown that illegals who eventually become legal immigrants come mostly from urban areas in Mexico.[9] In any event, this is a dynamic phenomenon, with more and more people apparently coming illegally across the Mexican border every year, from more and more different locations, and showing different characteristics depending on their place of origin.

Their impact on this country is seen alternatively as parasitic and productive, depending on whether the perspective is from the U.S. labor movement or the farmers and the U.S. businesses that employ the illegals. U.S. unions, led by the AFL-CIO, strongly argue that the illegal immigrants not only compete for jobs but also depress wages and working conditions for the American worker.[10] The illegal immigrants do not compete for all jobs in the United States, but certainly they must affect at least the secondary labor market (namely, less desirable jobs, such as stoop labor, household help, dishwashers, etc.). South Texas, which is one of the major areas of entry and residence for illegals from Mexico, has the three poorest standard metropolitan statistical areas in the United States (where per capita incomes are about half the national average), high unemployment, high use of food stamps and welfare assistance, and scant union activity. This cannot be unrelated to the availability of illegals who, as Labor Secretary Ray Marshall put it, work "scared and hard."

Figures from the sample in the 1976 North and Houstoun study show that 24 percent of the illegal immigrants from all sources were paid less than the minimum wage in their most recent job. The percentages were higher for domestic workers (almost two-thirds) and farm workers (one-third). The lowest wages were paid to respondents who worked in the Southwest, that is, where many of the Mexicans work. (Given the lower educational and skill levels of the Mexican as compared with illegals from other areas, it is not surprising that the average hourly wage of the Mexican workers was the lowest among the illegals.)

Illegals can be found in all kinds of jobs. Whereas those coming from areas other than Mexico and Latin America tend to enter the higher-prestige and higher-paying jobs, the Mexicans usually occupy lower-paying jobs in the secondary market. According to each of three major study samples already cited (North and Houstoun, Villalpando, and Cornelius), a majority of Mexican illegals who were apprehended worked in agriculture or other occupations requiring minimum skills. They are thus filling jobs in the United States that nationals do not want, at least not at the wages paid. Our unemployed are mainly in the cities, not in rural areas. It is also true, however, that illegals tend to go more and more to cities as they gain experience in the United States.

What would happen in the United States if the supply of illegals were cut off? This is a central question. It is clear that the illegals do presently occupy a niche in the American economy that U.S. workers are loath to fill under present working conditions and compensation. The *Wall Street Journal* made this point (in an editorial on June 18, 1976) by asserting that the supply of illegals "may well be providing the margin of survival for entire sectors of the economy," like restaurants, other small businesses, and both small- and large-scale agriculture, all of which rely heavily on unskilled labor. Evidence based on domestic demographic trends indicates that there will be a labor shortage for lower-level occupations by 1985, so that future U.S. needs for migrants (or for labor-saving techniques) are likely to be greater than now. We all take advantage of the services that illegals render. Our fruits and vegetables, for example, are cheaper than they would be if the illegals were not available for harvesting the crop. Whether we should want cheaper food under these circumstances is a separate issue, but we accept the implicit subsidy nonetheless.

Further, many researchers have contended that there is no direct evidence that large numbers of American workers have been displaced by illegal immigrants—certainly not from desirable jobs. Evidence often adduced for this view comes from two citations in the Villalpando study. The first was a program conducted in Los Angeles, in which the authorities reportedly tried to place local residents in jobs formerly held by apprehended illegals and failed because the jobs paid less than the minimum wage and the job categories were unappealing. The second was an effort to place local residents of San Diego in jobs held by illegals; the jobs were filled instead by commuters (that is, legal border crossers) from Tijuana, Mexico. On balance, then, the weight of evidence militates against equating jobs held by illegals with jobs lost by U.S. nationals.

Nonetheless, the potential upward mobility of illegals who stay in this country for some time (and evade detection by census takers and the INS) may adversely affect wages and working conditions of U.S. labor over the long term. Economic analysis would lead one to conclude that if the supply of illegals were curbed, two forces would come into play: one force, by reducing the supply, should increase the price of labor; the second, by increasing the price of labor, might lead to more use of labor-saving machinery. It is likely that some jobs would become available to U.S. workers but not to the full extent of the jobs previously held by illegals. Prices of some goods and services would increase. The U.S. anti-inflation program would suffer if the supply of illegal aliens were cut off now. The existing empirical evidence leads us to the conclusion that the truth lies somewhere in the middle: that is, some national workers are displaced or disadvantaged in terms of wages and working conditions, whereas in other cases the illegals are augmenting our labor force for the overall general benefit.

Beyond their effect on U.S. employment levels, the direct burden of the illegals on U.S. social services must also be considered. In this area, the evidence seems conclusive; most illegal workers have taxes deducted from their earnings. In the San Diego study, the interviews indicated that illegals contributed 17 percent of their wages to taxes whereas their demands on social services (police, hospitals, food stamps, welfare, burial services, education in public schools) are not great. The San Diego study is a significant one because, as the report notes, "San Diego is the most impacted area in the world by the flow of illegal aliens." San Diego accounts for 43 percent of all border apprehensions of illegals and 25 percent of apprehensions throughout the nation. Although the requests of school authorities in southern Texas for aid for their "impacted" districts suggest that the educational impact may be significant in some areas, it appears fairly clear that the cost of social services for illegals is less than their tax contribution—with one study setting the figure for social services in San Diego at $2 million a year and the tax contributions at almost $49 million.[11]

In another study, 77 percent of apprehended illegals said they had social security taxes withheld, 73 percent federal income taxes, 44 percent hospitalization insurance, and 31 percent even filed income tax returns.[12] This is contrasted with 27 percent who used hospitals, 4 percent who collected one or more weeks of unemployment insurance, 4 percent who had children in U.S. schools, 1 percent who secured food stamps, and less than 1 percent who received welfare payments.

Arguably, even if the direct costs of social services to illegals may not be high in comparison with what they contribute, there may be nonmeasurable indirect costs. That is, if illegals displace national labor and the latter must resort to welfare, food stamps, and unemployment insurance, this cost is a result of the entry of illegals. One might equally logically argue, however, that if illegals are not displacing national workers and are contributing more financially than they are receiving in social services, then the illegals are in part financing the costs of the social services for unemployed or underemployed national workers.

In sum, a thorough scrutiny of the available evidence indicates that the illegal Mexican immigrants do contribute to the U.S. economy, although they also produce social and economic dislocation here. The economic burden is greatest on those disadvantaged groups in our society with whom illegals compete directly. Perhaps the greatest burden they place on the overall American social fabric is a consequence of their illegality—both in the massive challenge posed to the U.S. government in enforcing the law curbing their entry and in possible infringements of civil liberties of U.S. residents and others resulting from enforcement measures.

The Range of Solutions to the Problem of Illegal Entrants

What means are available to us for coping with the problem of illegal Mexican immigration? The range of proposed measures is as diverse as are analyses of the problem and the interests of the various parties involved. One influential approach, presented by the *Wall Street Journal*, would have us wink at the problem and essentially "do nothing" about it, letting the flow continue to aid U.S. small businesses and large farmers.[13] Activist measures include: penalties levied against both illegal immigrants on the one hand (when caught, they are now deported or permitted to depart voluntarily) and particularly their employers on the other; the use of manpower and technology to close the border more effectively; enlarged contract labor programs for workers in both rural and urban areas; opening of the border; the application of minimum wage legislation to the aliens; special adjustment assistance for the disadvantaged in our own society who are affected adversely by the immigration; and longer-term measures for alleviating the causes of illegal immigration in the Mexican economy—on the part of both the United States and Mexico.

Regrettably, no "total" solution to the problem is in view. To look at two extreme suggestions: if illegal immigration was completely stopped, there could be an explosion in Mexico, which the United States certainly would not want; if illegal immigration is allowed to continue along its present lines, there hardly seems any reason for the United States to have immigration laws at all. The feasible policy lies somewhere between these two poles.

The Carter Administration's Proposal

President Carter's proposal on illegal immigration had two main strands: the first involved measures for cutting off the flow of illegals; and the second, stemming from humanitarian concerns, provided a form of amnesty (or, more technically, adjustment of status) for illegals who have been here for some time and have established roots. The major provisions of the legislation submitted by the administration were the following:

- It would be unlawful to hire undocumented aliens; this would be enforced by civil penalties (fines and injunctions) against employers who engage in a "pattern or practice" of such hiring.
- Persons knowingly assisting an illegal to obtain or retain a job would be subject to criminal penalties; this provision is aimed mainly at the so-called *coyotes* or *polleros* who help the illegals come to the United States.
- For those illegals who apply, their status can be adjusted to permanent residents if they have resided in the United States continuously since January 1, 1970.
- A new category of temporary resident aliens would be created for those illegals who have been in the United States continuously from January 1, 1970 until January 1, 1977; they, too, would have to register.
- The resources available to the INS to prevent illegal entry and for enforcement of the law against illegals who have entered since January 1, 1977 would be increased.[14]

The president's package was heavily influenced by the position of U.S. labor that the U.S. worker is hurt by the stream of Mexican and other immigrants into this country. It did not include contract labor programs. The amnesty provisions are essentially humanitarian actions rather than solutions to the problem of illegal immigration.[15] The most important of his legislative proposals from the viewpoint of controlling the flow of illegals were the first and the last proposals—aimed at cutting the flow through a demand-reducing approach with new sanctions on the employers of illegals, and also some effort to cut off the supply directly at the border.

If the United States so decided, it probably could close the border more tightly. It would take money, more sensing and related equipment, more personnel, but this would be a matter of resource allocation. To call this a Berlin Wall would be an exaggeration; it need not be different from entry into, say, Switzerland or the Netherlands from outside. It would not be perfect, in that many people would slip through, but it is hard to believe that, if we so wished, we could not drastically slow the process of illegal entry. There would, however, be a psychological cost in doing this.

President Carter obviously did not wish to bear the onus of ending what had always been a proud boast of the United States that we have generally open, demilitarized borders with our closest neighbors. Up to this time, it has not been clear that, as a nation, we have wanted to enforce this law, except inadequately. The INS is not a well-funded agency. A few comparisons can be revealing. In October 1976, the Metropolitan Police in the District of Columbia (with a population of 700,000) had 4,341 persons compared with 2,937 enforcement personnel for the entire INS. In fiscal year 1977, Congress authorized the employment of 1,140 policemen just to guard the buildings on Capitol Hill.[16]

In addition, the enforcement procedures have never directly punished the employers of illegals. Justice has by no means been blind in its treatment of all the parties in this system. It is against the law for a Mexican or other national seeking economic improvement to cross into the United States without documentation. It is not against the law for an employer to hire an illegal alien. Harboring an illegal alien is illegal, but under the so-called Texas proviso to the Immigration and Nationality Act, giving him employment is not considered "harboring" an illegal. One can rationalize all these provisions because employers are not intended to be law enforcers, but they also turn out to be economically convenient for some of the more powerful groups in our society. Congressman Peter Rodino of New Jersey has been introducing legislation for years to punish employers of illegals, with no result.

President Carter, however, chose to diminish the allure of crossing the border by reducing the demand for illegals through sanctions on their employers. In order to punish an employer, some basis is needed to prove that he knowingly followed a pattern or practice of hiring illegals. The simplest way to do this is through an identity card or a universal work permit. The president chose not to propose an identity card, undoubtedly influenced by the expressed concerns of Mexican-American and civil liberties groups about where this could lead. The administration's compromise proposal was a forgery-proof social security card and other documentation not yet precisely specified as evidence of legal status.

In addition to predictable opposition from many employers, this proposal aroused the ire of the Mexican-American community. On the economic aspects of the migration, the Mexican Americans are ambivalent. The kinship ties with the illegals within the Mexican-American community generate support for their entry. Because many in this community are part of an underclass of impoverished Americans, however, they may be competing for jobs with illegals. This ambivalent response was typified by the reaction of César Chávez, head of the farm workers' union, who first took a position in favor of restricting illegal immigration in order to bolster domestic farm workers' unionization and then shifted

146

position after pressure from the leaders of Mexican-American organizations.

The Mexican-American community also fears the fallout effect on themselves of a widespread campaign to enforce the ban on illegals. To use the words of the Mexican-American Legal Defense Education Fund (MALDEF),

> its adoption would unavoidably lead to widespread employment discrimination against ethnic Americans in general, and Mexican Americans in particular. Faced with a statute making it illegal to hire undocumented workers, some employers would be over-zealous in their actions, and would refuse to hire anyone whom they suspected of unlawful entry, however unfounded the suspicion and regardless of the proof of legal residence provided.[17]

Problems of Past Proposals

The Carter proposals represented a humane and courageous attempt to find a path through the welter of competing interests and opinions. That they did not constitute a successful compromise package, however, is indicated by congressional unwillingness to act on them. Their critics were vociferous and wide ranging, reflecting the intensity and divergence of the interests involved. The Carter proposals have been found wanting for ignoring the factors in the Mexican economy that impel the immigrants to seek their livelihood across the border; for harming U.S.–Mexican relations; for proposing to enact unenforceable regulations; and for a faulty assessment of the impact on the U.S. labor market. One influential school of thought criticizes the Carter approach as being too short term in perspective, contending that the flow will not cease until Mexico's economic problems, which push its people across the border, have been resolved. It is also asserted that if the exodus from rural areas in Mexico could be slowed, the migration would also be curtailed—leading to a suggestion that the United States try to "keep 'em down on the farm," or at least in rural areas.

From 1950 to 1975, the contribution of manufacturing to Mexico's gross domestic product rose from 18 to 23 percent; that of services remained relatively constant at 55 to 56 percent; and that of agriculture and livestock declined from 16 to 9 percent. This phenomenon is not unnatural for countries with high growth rates; however, it has meant an exodus from rural to urban areas and from both areas to outside of the country because of the lack of job opportunities in the urban areas. In 1950, Mexico was 57 percent rural and 43 percent urban;[18] by 1976, the figures were 37 percent rural and 63 percent urban. Mexico is beginning to tackle this problem with the aid of World Bank loans directed not only at large-scale agriculture but at smaller-scale farming. It is questionable, however, whether the exodus from rural areas can be stopped. Raúl Prebisch, the distinguished Latin American political economist, pointed out in a study in 1970 for the Inter-American Development Bank that "the exodus of agricultural workers is inevitable if the level of the rural masses is to be raised." He was discussing Latin America generally, but the same holds true for Mexico, as it did for the United States, Europe, Japan, and other countries. It would be chimerical to look toward keeping Mexicans on the farms or in rural areas as a cure for the migration problem, at least in this generation.

Mexicans sometimes assert that U.S. trade policy results in importing Mexican people instead of Mexican goods. There is something to this, as the United States does maintain import restrictions on Mexican textiles, foodstuffs, and other products, but quantitatively the current restrictions cannot really affect the employment of more than a few thousand Mexicans.

According to one argument, the incentive to emigrate must be reduced through U.S. aid to Mexican development and job creation. No one can quarrel with the thesis that it would be nice if the factors pushing Mexicans to leave did not exist or that the United States should do what it can to help Mexico develop economically to bring this about, but Keynes's famous commentary about the long run as a policy guide is most appropriate here. As he put it: "Economists set themselves too easy, too useless a task if in tempestuous seasons they can only tell us that when the storm is long past the ocean is flat again." The causative problems run deep within Mexican society and are not amenable to short-run cures.

Prescriptions for dealing with this issue must come to grips with its two-sidedness. Any policy proposal must address the impact on the U.S. economy, and on U.S. labor, of the current pattern of illegal immigration (to the extent that we know this) and what the results would be if this pattern was altered; and it must take into account the importance of the current migration pattern for Mexico and how change would affect it. President Carter's suggestions were faulty on both of these counts.

It is certain that internal instability in Mexico would have direct repercussions in the United States. Despite this, the administration's proposals were aimed at closing Mexico's escape valve without any amelioration, such as could be provided by a contract labor program. The U.S. proposals were internally directed with uncertain but potentially devastating effects on Mexico.

Mexican authorities quite naturally view the migration issue from a different perspective. To them, put bluntly, the flow of illegals is not the problem but rather the solution to Mexico's current inability to employ its rapidly expanding labor force and to the U.S. need for this labor. The Carter administration did attempt to engage Mexico in a discussion of the problem but without success. Undoubtedly, each side tends to look only at its own domestic pressures, and the Mexicans would prefer the status quo to many possible alternatives. As a result, the legislation submitted by President Carter was unilateral rather than cooperative, and it was not well received in Mexico.

Cooperation, by definition, must be more than one-sided. Mexico also has an obligation to cooperate with the United States in dealing currently with the problem of illegal migration. By all means, Mexico must treat the causes of its own unemployment and distributional problems, but the United States can help in this process, for example, by minimizing import restrictions. Further, flexibility on the U.S. part in legalizing some of the immigrant workers is probably the best means of securing Mexican aid in regulating the flow.

In its analysis of the domestic economic effects of illegal immigration, the Carter administration's proposals leaned heavily to the view that the U.S. demand for migrant Mexican labor could be met mostly from the ranks of the domestic unemployed. Administration opposition to temporary contract labor is a result primarily of labor union pressures. The Justice Department also makes another argument, that a bracero-like program involves an indentured type of employment that would weaken our free enterprise system.[19] On the contrary, we believe the entire range of the U.S. interests would be best served by a controlled contract labor program which became progressively smaller over a definite time. More importantly, such a program is valuable to the growth of the U.S. economy.

Unlike the Carter administration, we feel that the weight of the evidence demonstrates that Mexican workers add to the total product of the United States. If they were not available, the efficiency of our economy would be reduced. One way to obtain this labor in a manner that seeks also to protect U.S. labor would be via an expanded permit system for Mexican workers, for temporary work for up to six to eight months a year. (President Carter specifically rejected this idea.)[20] Legalizing some temporary workers will not keep out others (as was the case under the bracero program) unless some aspects of what the president proposed are joined with this—namely, tighter control of the border and/or fining employers for hiring migrants without temporary work visas. The advantage of an expanded labor contract program, however, is that it will legalize what is taking place in any event while giving both U.S. and Mexican authorities some basis to monitor the wages and the treatment of the workers.

How many temporary workers are needed—a hundred thousand,

half a million, more? To some extent, this could be determined by surveying the demand, both in industry and agriculture. If the labor unions consented to a contract work program (either job specific or general), the negotiation would then center on numbers, and these might be programmed to decline over time.[21] The number of permitted or legalized workers would have to be sufficiently large to constitute a significant portion of the flow of illegals. Although such a program would conjure up fears of another bracero program, accompanied by graft at the sending end and exploitation at the receiving end, these things occur now without any intervention of the authorities.

It is important to recognize that such a program, particularly if it obligated the employer to pay the minimum wage and the going fringe benefits, would have a less adverse impact on U.S. labor than the current practice, and U.S. labor could even try to unionize these temporary workers. If labor nonetheless proves adamant in its opposition to an explicit temporary labor contract program, another way to make the illegals legal would be to devise a constructively ambiguous "Mexico proviso" (on the model of the Texas proviso), making it illegal for a Mexican migrant to be in the United States without documentation unless he has a job and the employer certifies that the migrant is working. There would be civil penalties for those employers hiring more than a specified number of people (mom-and-pop shops would be exempted) who fail to render such reports. A further refinement would be that the employer must certify that the work is temporary (lasting no longer than six to eight months) and that he is paying at least the minimum wage and other usual fringe benefits and is withholding the usual taxes. This would put much of the enforcement burden on the employer, but in other respects it would have many of the same advantages and disadvantages of the expanded worker contract system. In some respects it would be simpler, because it would not imply as much tightening of the border, and in other respects more complicated in that it would leave control over the labor market to the U.S. employer and the Mexican worker without any input by U.S. labor. Our own preference is for the straightforward contract labor program.

Though a legalized temporary worker program that obligated the employer to pay the minimum wage and the going fringe benefits would affect U.S. labor less than the current system, we believe such a program should be accompanied by benefits to those U.S. workers most likely to be affected adversely. A corollary of temporary work arrangements for Mexicans is an obligation of the localities and the federal government jointly to augment training and assistance programs for affected U.S. workers.

150

Toward a Bilateral Solution

We used the word "intractable" in the title of this paper because any policy prescription entails cost. In this case the trade-offs are particularly complex. The main ones are: the damage to some U.S. workers from the present migration pattern versus the benefits for the total U.S. economy of having workers from Mexico; law enforcement (either by more effective border closure or by the use of some identification document in order to punish employers of illegal aliens) versus the threat this poses to civil liberties; or policy based on the perceived domestic political and economic consequences of our actions versus subordination of these consequences to some extent to take into account the ramifications in Mexico of what we do. Making these choices is immensely complicated by our ignorance—of the size of the problem (How many illegals are now here, and how many more come each year?) and of how the migration works in practice (Does the overwhelming majority of illegal workers go home, or does a significant proportion stay here?). Just as any prescription must, our policy suggestions have made choices among these competing interests (based on our conclusion that the availability of the Mexican workers helps our economy, that carrying out the law may require some identification of who is here legally, and that policy must be based on the perceived mutuality of U.S. and Mexican needs).

How are these choices likely to be received in the two countries? Better, we believe, than those in President Carter's program, although certainly not universally favorably. That part of organized labor in the United States that supported the administration's program probably will oppose our suggestion for more contract labor, even if on a declining basis and even if subject to U.S. minimum wage laws. Organized Mexican-American groups who opposed the employer penalty provisions of the president's program are apt to continue this opposition, but other Mexican Americans with whom illegal aliens compete for jobs might welcome either some ceiling on the number of persons admitted or minimum wage provisions on their employment. Businesses and farms that hire Mexican workers would welcome the ability to continue this practice but would oppose the enforcement of minimum wage laws that our proposal would involve. We believe that the major advantage of what we suggest is that it does not seek to cut off the supply of necessary workers abruptly but instead permits gradual adjustment to reduced numbers at the same time as an enforcement procedure is put into place.

Although we have focused on the Mexican illegal immigrant, the immigration question is obviously much broader, encompassing legal

151

permanent immigration policy and the treatment of temporary workers from other countries. A contract labor program with Mexico could (or need not) be expanded to other nearby countries; the numbers would be much smaller for us, but the escape-valve aspects would be as important to them as to Mexico. It is possible that the Select Committee on Immigration will suggest revisions in our total immigration policy, but this is some time away and nothing that we have proposed need compromise this examination.

An expanded contract labor or employer certification program might be favored by the Mexican government. President Echeverría's administration endorsed a return to a contract labor program in 1974. Mexico's ambassador to the United States recently did the same. It should also be recognized that the nature of the problem will change over the long term as Mexico further develops its economy and as demographic trends alter the supply of U.S. labor. The United States has a supportive role to play in Mexico's development process, primarily by keeping our market open for Mexican goods, but the principal task is Mexico's. Mexico has not wanted direct capital assistance from the United States, and given Mexico's apparent large oil and gas reserves, the future constraint on Mexico's development is unlikely to be a capital or foreign exchange shortage. The U.S. need for Mexican oil increases American incentives for good relations with its southern neighbor and for cooperative measures in dealing with the northward migration. It was this kind of consideration that prompted the development of the Policy Review Memorandum by the U.S. National Security Council on future U.S.–Mexican relations prior to President Carter's visit to Mexico in February 1979.

Failing effective U.S. action, the illegal alien issue is likely to escalate in intensity. Growing population pressure in Mexico and potential U.S. reactive pressure (particularly if the U.S. economy slows down) indicate a real likelihood of unilateral measures by the United States. To avoid this outcome, we believe that the need for a flexible program, limited in time, to admit Mexican immigrants legally (at the same time as employers are punished for hiring those not admitted legally) should be conveyed to the U.S. and Mexican bodies politic as soon as possible. The alternative is frustration and animosity on both sides of the border.

Notes

The research for this article was made possible by a grant from the Ewing Halsell Foundation of San Antonio, Texas.
[1] "Migrant Workers: Policy of the Lemon," April 8, 1978

[2] David S. North and Marion F. Houstoun, *The Characteristics and Role of Illegal Aliens in the U.S. Labor Market: An Exploratory Study* (Washington, D.C.: Linton and Company, 1976).

³ The figure seems high, but even a more likely figure of between 15 and 20 percent is a startling number.

⁴ Julian Samora, *Los Mojados: The Wetback Story* (Notre Dame, Ind.: University of Notre Dame Press, 1971); North and Houstoun, *Illegal Aliens*; Vic Villalpando et al., *A Study of the Socioeconomic Impact of Illegal Aliens on the County of San Diego* (San Diego: Human Resources Agency, 1977).

⁵ The data are from the INS. One example of the conventional wisdom can be found in the preliminary report of the Domestic Council Committee of the U.S. Government on Illegal Aliens, December 1976, p. 164.

⁶ North and Houstoun, *Illegal Aliens*.

⁷ Wayne Cornelius, *Mexican Migration to the United States: The View from Rural Sending Communities* (Cambridge: Massachusetts Institute of Technology, June 1976).

⁸ In Guy Poitras, ed., *Immigration and the Mexican National: Proceedings of a Conference* (San Antonio: Border Research Institute, Trinity University, 1978), pp. 47–52.

⁹ Francisco Alba, "Industrialización sustitutiva y migración internacional: el caso de México," *Foro internacional* 18, no. 3 (January–March 1978): 464–79.

¹⁰ This point, that "Illegal alien workers . . . take jobs from Americans and undermine U.S. wages and working conditions," can be found in the statement by the AFL-CIO Executive Council, August 29, 1977.

¹¹ Villalpando, *Socioeconomic Impact*. We are skeptical of the exact figures, as there is considerable anecdotal evidence that much use of services by illegal aliens escapes detection, but see no basis to disagree with the general conclusion that the financial contribution of illegals exceeds their burden on our social services.

¹² North and Houstoun, *Illegal Aliens*.

¹³ "Illegal Aliens Non-Problem," *Wall Street Journal*, editorial, June 18, 1976.

¹⁴ Some additional provisions in the president's proposal and related legislation, which may have merit in their own right but are peripheral to the main issue of what to do about illegal aliens, include: strengthening of the visa-issuing function of the State Department in order to minimize fraud; improved administration of the Fair Labor Standards Act and the Federal Farm Labor Contractor Registration Act; consolidation of the separate Mexican and Canadian immigration quotas of 20,000 each into a combined quota of 50,000.

¹⁵ As has been noted, in its adjustment-of-status proposal the administration proposed two categories: (1) to grant permanent-resident status to illegals here prior to January 1, 1970; and (2) to establish a five-year temporary-resident status for those here before January 1, 1977. The former would represent the fourth updating of the register since the country began to control and restrict immigration in 1924. The last such updating took place in 1965 and made aliens resident in the country since 1948 eligible for adjustment of status. Whereas earlier adjustments affected thousands and three such adjustments were needed to move up the date two decades, the Carter proposal advanced the date twenty-two years (1948 to 1970) and is estimated to affect millions. The thought behind the second provision is to encourage the illegals who came during the seven-year period (1970–1977) to register so that they can be counted. Attorney General Bell believed that once the number is known, a decision could be made on a more permanent solution. Many observers consider it unlikely that undocumented workers would come forth under this arrangement. News of the proposed program, however, brought about an upsurge of entries and spurred a flourishing business in forged documents to prove earlier residence.

¹⁶ David S. North, "Illegal Immigration to the United States: A Quintet of Myths," paper presented to the annual meeting of the American Political Science Association, Washington, D.C., September 1977.

¹⁷ Living in the Southwest and having many Americans of Mexican origin among our colleagues and students, we have become impressed with the emotional scars many of them bear of overt discrimination and perpetual insults, such as knowing that the border patrol will stop only cars with Hispanic-looking occupants, shove in a flashlight, and ask for documents in their search for illegals. The recent evidence of police discrimination in

cities of the Southwest against Mexican Americans is merely the newspaper-headline manifestation of a long-simmering pattern of prejudice.

[18] The arbitrary dividing line differentiating an urban and a rural locality in Mexico is 2,500 persons.

[19] U.S. Department of Justice, Office of the Attorney General, "Illegal Immigration— President's Program," April 1978.

[20] There is currently an H2 visa program permitting entry for temporary periods to meet specific employer needs. In U.S. fiscal year 1976, about 25,000 certifications were granted for temporary workers, 15,000 in activities related to agriculture and 10,000 in nonagricultural industries, services, and professions. The president specifically told representatives of the Hispanic media "that we don't intend to expand the H2 program." When, in the spring of 1977, the president overruled the Department of Labor and ordered the admission of some 800 Mexican nationals for six months to harvest melons and vegetables near Presidio, Texas, it was done as an emergency measure, and a statement was made that the action was not the harbinger of a new bracero program.

[21] We may find ten or so years hence that we will not want the number to decline, and that possibility can be looked at then.

Notes on U.S.–Mexican Trade Trends: Some Policy Alternatives

Clark W. Reynolds

The Issue

The United States and Mexico exhibit a high degree of economic interdependence involving trade, migration, finance, and technology transfers. Though it is most evident in the border regions, this interdependence has far-reaching effects and touches most businesses and households. The sensitivity of the U.S. and Mexican economies to their interconnection is heavily lopsided because more than 60 percent of Mexico's trade is with the United States, whereas only 4 to 5 percent of U.S. trade is with Mexico. This asymmetry results from an 8 to 1 differential in productivity between the two countries, plus the much larger U.S. population, which gives the United States a greater base from which to operate. The relative size and resilience of the United States tend to obscure the importance of the "silent integration" to that country, even though Mexico provides up to one-fifth of its northern neighbor's additional workers each year, and even though U.S. trade and financial systems have major linkages to the south, which, if interrupted, would raise costs and distort relative prices in the United States, leading to inflation, structural unemployment, and dislocation not only in commodity markets but, more importantly, in the "service economy" that is becoming such an important element in American life.

The main issue being addressed here is whether, in the light of recent trends in trade and financial flows between the two countries, any major changes in policy are called for at this time that might affect the progressive evolution of comparative advantage between the two countries. Ideally, such an analysis would examine the possible consequences of more or less foreign trade and investment in terms of employment, output, income, and stability on both sides of the border. These notes touch on issues that point to the need for more research in depth.

The first point to stress is the *interdependence* of flows of goods and services, labor, capital, and technology. Opening or closing one door, such as that of commodity trade, will have important repercussions on other flows, such as migration and investment. Problems of interdependency must be viewed in a common framework so as to avoid the pitfalls of partial analysis. If the United States wishes to increase its imports from Mexico, for example, this would stimulate the Mexican economy, increase employment, and reduce pressures for the emigration of Mexicans to the north. The direction is clear, but the magnitude of the linkages is uncertain. If, on the other hand, Mexico further promotes import-substituting industrialization by raising import barriers, prices would rise domestically, exports would fall, the balance of payments would weaken, and countervailing austerity policies would be required, exacerbating Mexican unemployment and emigration pressures. Yet here again the degree of sensitivity is uncertain. It is likely that the United States could counteract by attempting to close its own doors to trade and migration. It is important to extend the concept of "gains from trade" to cover all major gains (and losses) from "full exchange," defined so as to include not only trade in goods and services but also labor, capital, and technology flows as well.

The real issue is, then, what changes in trade policy might imply for each of the dimensions of full exchange between the two countries. The economic consequences have important political implications as well. Mexico's social and political stability is inherently linked to the way in which long-standing promises of social justice are fulfilled by the present leaders of business, labor, government, and education. The answer rests on practical economic performance translated into employment, income gains, and political participation for the mass of the population. The degrees of freedom for such changes depend first and foremost on the behavior of the economy. If there is no increased output to channel into wages, profits, and public revenues for education, health, welfare, housing, and other infrastructure, the promises of social justice will remain empty rhetoric. Hence those concerned with the political stability of Mexico are especially sensitive to its economic performance.

By the same token, the U.S. economy is entering a period of major structural change reflecting worldwide economic evolution. Competition is becoming much keener in the international market. Faced with the propects of stagflation, structural unemployment, and a labor force that appears to be pricing itself out of world competition, the United States is hard-pressed to find new solutions to these problems. The implications of these trends for trade policy with its nearest neighbors are crucial, because the United States, Mexico, and Canada, by their very proximity and history of interdependence, exhibit common if sometimes conflicting destinies.

156

Recent Bilateral Trade Patterns

As of 1980, Mexico became the third largest trading partner of the United States after Canada and Japan. This section deals with recent trends in trade between the United States and Mexico. Tables 1 and 2 depict commodity trade flows for selected years 1970, 1974, 1975, 1976, 1977, 1978, and 1979. The first pattern of importance is the shift in the balance of trade: the United States has maintained a traditional commodity trade surplus, which rose from $451 million (U.S.) in 1970 to a peak of $1,997 million in 1975. Following the peso devaluation in late 1976, however, there was a sharp decline in U.S. exports and an increase in U.S. imports that reduced the U.S. surplus to only $29 million (U.S.) by 1977. Mexico's 1978 overall balance-of-payments deficit of $586 million (U.S.) and the 1979 deficit of $851 million are above that of 1977 owing to more dynamic growth of the economy since 1978.

A brief analysis of sectoral trade trends shows that most of the erosion of the U.S. commodity trade surplus through 1977 came from the rapid expansion of Mexican exports of petroleum, agricultural products, and manufactured goods, which accounted for 41, 32, and 14 percent, respectively, of the 1976–1977 increase in U.S.–bound exports. During the same period, the most volatile U.S. export sector was machinery and transport equipment, and these goods, which are relatively sensitive to overall Mexican economic growth, shrank more than the next most affected sector, food and live animals, could expand. The sectoral percentage distribution of Mexican exports to the United States has shifted dramatically since 1970 and promises to continue to change as the Mexican comparative advantage evolves.

Manufactured exports taken as a group (Standard International Trade Classifications [SITC] 6, 7, and 8), for example, rose from 31 percent of all Mexican exports in 1970 to a high point of 54 percent in 1974, after which the dramatic rise of petroleum-related exports reduced them to a 1978 share of 41 percent. As Mexican petroleum industry (PEMEX) investments in the 1970s began to pay off in rising petroleum exports, the mineral fuels sector grew from a 1 percent share in 1974 to 25 percent in 1978. Crude petroleum alone accounted for 43 percent of merchandise exports in 1979 and through 1980 had reached 66 percent.[1] Although Mexican food and live animal exports had risen more than twice their 1970 level through 1977, their share in all Mexican exports to the United States had fallen from 47 percent to 22 percent in 1978. This represents a rebound, nevertheless, from a 20 percent share in 1975. Given the surge in Mexico's population and domestic demand, however, drought years of 1979 and 1980, the possibility of a

157

TABLE 1

U.S.–Mexican Trade: U.S. Imports from Mexico, Selected Years, 1970–1979
(millions of dollars)

SITC Classification	1970	% Total	1974	% Total	1975	% Total	1976	% Total	1977	% Total	1978	% Total	1979	% Total
0 Food and live animals	573.7	47.0	879.9	26.0	605.7	19.8	841.8	23.3	1,188.6	25.3	1,252.7	20.6	1,483.9	16.8
1 Beverages and tobacco	7.6	0.6	40.6	1.2	36.4	1.2	42.0	1.2	46.0	1.0	62.4	1.0	81.6	1.0
2 Raw materials excluding fuel	109.8	9.0	176.2	5.2	187.3	6.1	166.3	4.6	170.8	3.6	156.9	2.6	191.0	2.2
3 Mineral fuels, lubricants, etc.	61.3	5.0	31.1	0.9	371.0	12.1	447.2	12.4	895.2	19.1	1,516.9	24.9	3,073.9	34.9
4 Oils and fats, animal and vegetable	1.4	0.2	2.3	0.1	1.4	0.1	2.0	0.1	5.4	0.1	2.1	0.0	2.0	0.0
5 Chemicals	24.9	2.0	87.7	2.6	77.8	2.5	93.6	2.5	113.6	2.4	193.1	3.2	264.3	3.0
6 Manufactures	120.3	9.8	497.2	14.7	349.1	11.4	433.9	12.0	587.1	12.5	694.4	11.4	866.8	9.8
7 Manufacturing and transport equipment	153.7	12.6	908.9	26.8	868.3	28.3	1,021.4	28.3	1,038.4	22.1	1,415.4	23.2	1,852.5	21.0
8 Miscellaneous manufactures	99.1	8.1	597.8	17.7	389.6	12.7	394.9	11.0	431.0	9.2	556.4	9.1	710.7	8.1
9 Unclassified goods	70.5	5.7	164.4	4.9	174.3	5.8	163.5	4.5	217.7	4.6	242.5	4.0	286.6	3.2
Totals	1,222.4	100.0	3,386.1	100.0	3,065.8	100.0	3,606.3	100.0	4,693.6	100.0	6,093.9	100.0	8,813.4	100.0

SOURCE: U.S. Department of Commerce, Bureau of the Census, *U.S. General Imports*, 1970, 1974, 1975, 1976, 1977, 1978, 1979.

TABLE 2

U.S.–MEXICAN TRADE: U.S. EXPORTS TO MEXICO, SELECTED YEARS, 1970–1979
(millions of dollars)

SITC Classification	1970	% Total	1974	% Total	1975	% Total	1976	% Total	1977	% Total	1978	% Total	1979	% Total
0 Food and live animals	99.4	5.9	638.6	13.3	506.3	10.0	240.5	4.9	474.4	10.0	523.9	8.0	755.8	7.8
1 Beverages and tobacco	2.6	0.2	9.0	0.2	6.6	0.1	8.1	0.2	9.3	0.2	12.7	0.2	4.0	0.0
2 Raw materials excluding fuel	145.6	8.8	378.0	7.9	322.9	6.4	301.1	6.1	340.3	7.2	575.7	8.8	652.5	6.7
3 Mineral fuels, lubricants, etc.	66.8	3.9	174.1	3.6	218.2	4.3	181.2	3.7	149.5	3.2	177.9	2.7	220.1	2.3
4 Oils and fats, animal and vegetable	17.1	1.0	81.8	1.7	37.0	0.7	14.8	0.3	30.7	0.6	44.0	.7	39.1	0.4
5 Chemicals	170.7	10.2	489.8	10.3	503.3	9.9	529.7	10.8	554.6	11.7	673.0	10.3	1,053.0	10.9
6 Manufactures	170.7	10.2	521.2	10.9	521.0	10.3	563.0	11.5	507.4	10.7	718.4	11.0	1,209.5	12.5
7 Manufacturing and transport equipment	801.0	47.9	1,991.7	41.6	2,430.4	48.0	2,511.4	51.2	2,141.1	45.3	3,034.4	46.4	4,659.4	48.2
8 Miscellaneous manufactures	122.9	7.4	300.1	6.3	329.4	6.5	367.7	7.5	340.9	7.2	466.3	7.1	632.9	6.5
9 Unclassified goods	75.2	4.5	202.7	4.2	185.5	3.7	185.3	3.8	173.9	3.9	314.1	4.8	436.2	4.5
Totals	1,673.6	100.0	4,789.9	100.0	5,062.6	100.0	4,903.6	100.0	4,723.1	100.0	6,542.2	100.0	9,666.8	100.0

SOURCE: U.S. Department of Commerce, Bureau of the Census, *U.S. Exports*, 1970, 1974, 1975, 1976, 1977, 1978, 1979.

government embargo on sales, limited capacity to expand arable land, limited irrigation projects, and other productivity constraints, however, Mexico's agricultural sector will be hard-pressed to maintain an 11 percent share of exports in the near future (as it did in the first eight months of 1980). Mexico's agricultural imports rose rapidly in 1979–1980. Imports of grain have risen from 1.7 million metric tons (mmt) in 1976–1977 to 6 mmt in 1979–1980 and estimates of 7 to 7.5 mmt are projected for 1980–1981.[2]

Table 3 summarizes the most recent data on tourism and border transactions, which show an increasing surplus for Mexico in tourism through 1980 even as the surplus on border transactions falls. This contrasts with a decreasing surplus in tourism from the mid-1960s through 1976, because of a progressively overvalued peso and the impact of a temporary boycott on Mexican tourism in response to an anti-Zionist resolution in the United Nations during the Echeverría administration. To the net tourism surplus on service account, one should add the large and growing remittances of Mexicans working in the United States. Although these remittances go largely unrecorded in the official balance-of-payments statistics, they may well approach over $1 billion annually and are almost certainly well ahead of tourism as a net source of foreign exchange for Mexico.

Table 4 presents Mexican commodity trade as a share of total U.S. exports and imports in recent years. These statistics suggest that the deteriorating trade balance of the United States with the world in general through 1977 showed a similar trend with Mexico. Subsequently, the decline began to reverse itself as the U.S. economy slowed. The traditional commodity trade surplus of the United States has still not eroded away but nevertheless may eventually disappear as a result of the exponential growth of petroleum import costs since the mid-1970s. Commodity imports from Mexico show a small but steady increase in the share of U.S. total commodity imports to slightly over 4 percent. Meanwhile, the Mexican share of U.S. commodity exports returned to 5 percent in 1978 after falling in 1976 and 1977 during the Mexican recession.

In terms of import structure, the main increases for the United States are in chemicals and fuels at the expense of manufactures relative to its imports from the rest of the world. Mexico's comparative advantage relative to other U.S. suppliers is in the energy, petroleum, and petroleum-related sectors, despite the significant growth of *maquiladoras* (border industries, and other in-bond manufacturing), which showed a 44 percent increase in value added in 1979. On the U.S. export side, its manufactured goods fared relatively well in trade with Mexico between 1970 and 1978, especially in the mid-1970s, probably owing to

160

TABLE 3

U.S.–MEXICAN TOURISM AND BORDER TRANSACTIONS, 1978–1980
(millions of dollars)

	U.S. Revenues			−	U.S. Expenditures			=	U.S. Deficit		
	1978	1979	1980[a]		1978	1979	1980[a]		1978	1979	1980[a]
Tourism	519	692	900		1,121	1,429	1,780		602	737	880
Border transactions	752	2,517	3,450		2,364	2,982	3,760		1,612	465	310

[a] Amounts for 1980 are estimated.
SOURCE: Banco Nacional de México, *Review of the Economic Situation of Mexico*, February 1980, July 1980.

TABLE 4

U.S.–MEXICAN TRADE AS A PERCENTAGE OF TOTAL U.S. TRADE, TOTAL MEXICAN TRADE, SELECTED YEARS, 1955–1978

SITC Classification	U.S. Imports from Mexico							U.S. Exports to Mexico						
	1955[a]	1965	1970	1975	1976	1977	1978	1955[a]	1965	1970	1975	1976	1977	1978
0 Food and live animals		8.92	10.7	7.1	8.2	9.5	10.8		1.11	2.3	3.3	1.5	3.3	2.9
1 Beverages and tobacco		5.52	0.9	2.6	2.6	2.8	2.8		0.63	0.1	0.1	0.1	0.6	0.6
2 Raw materials excluding fuel		2.54	3.3	3.5	2.4	2.2	1.7		2.70	3.2	3.3	2.8	2.7	3.7
3 Mineral fuels, lubricants, etc.		1.92	2.0	1.4	1.3	2.0	3.6		5.85	4.2	4.9	4.3	3.6	4.6
4 Oils and fats, animal and vegetable		1.17	0.9	0.1	0.1	1.0	0.4		0.92	3.5	3.9	1.5	2.3	2.9

5 Chemicals		3.22	1.7	2.1	1.9	2.1	3.0		5.76	4.5	5.8	5.3	5.1	5.3
6 Manufactures		1.58	1.4	2.3	2.4	2.7	2.5		3.61	3.7	4.8	5.0	4.5	5.8
7 Manufacturing and transport equipment		0.06	1.4	3.6	3.3	2.9	3.0		4.96	4.5	5.3	5.1	4.2	5.1
8 Miscellaneous manufactures		0.57	2.0	4.2	3.3	2.9	2.9		3.45	4.8	5.8	5.6	4.7	4.6
9 Unclassified goods		4.55	5.5	7.1	6.4	8.0	6.1		3.18	5.0	5.9	6.7	5.4	6.2
All U.S.–Mexican trade	3.46	2.78	3.1	3.2	3.0	3.2	4.0	4.53	3.78	3.9	4.8	4.3	4.0	5.0
All U.S.–Canadian trade	23.35	22.62	27.8	22.9	22.0	20.0	19.0	20.37	21.70	20.7	20.1	20.8	21.2	20.0

[a] Data for this year are not comparable with SITC classification.

SOURCES: Computed from data in U.S. Department of Commerce, Bureau of the Census, *U.S. General Imports*, and U.S. Department of Commerce, Bureau of the Census, *U.S. Exports*.

temporary effects of the overvalued peso. Also, the Mexican share of U.S. food and live animal exports increased by one percentage point between 1970 and 1977, and continues to grow because of a decline in Mexican agricultural output. The general pattern indicates that U.S. trade with Mexico is not large enough to make a great impact in either direction on the American balance of payments. Even when the peso was overvalued by more than 50 percent, the relative gains in U.S. trade shares with Mexico hardly made a dent in the large and growing U.S. trade deficit.

In table 5 we see that quite the opposite holds for Mexico, as its share of commodity trade with the United States is extremely high for both imports and exports. From 1970 to 1979 Mexico imported about 63 percent of its goods from the United States. That share fell temporarily upon devaluation of the peso in 1976, and although imports declined initially, they have increased to about 70 percent as the peso exchange rate has lagged behind inflation and the Mexican economy has accelerated its growth. On the export side, the U.S. share has increased to about 70 percent, with the total value increasing significantly from 1970 (a depressed year for trade) to 1979, especially after devaluation and the new petroleum discoveries.

The recent balance-of-payments record of Mexico closely follows trends in U.S.–Mexican trade, as can be seen by comparing tables 1 and 2 with table 6. Yearly changes in the Mexican current account balance from 1974 to 1979, in millions of dollars, were −$1,179, +$644, +$1,561, −$745, and −$1,951. Changes in Mexico's merchandise trade balance with the United States in the same years were −$369, +$783, +$907, +$248, −$1,054. Much of the 1974–1975 falloff in trade with the United States was caused by weakness in exports of manufactures and agricultural products. In spite of a recovery in these areas since then, and surging petroleum exports, Mexico's chronic current account deficit has increased. As mentioned previously, the 1976 peso devaluation, followed by a period of sluggish growth in the Mexican economy in the first half of 1977, spurred a rise in exports to the United States, whereas Mexican demand for U.S. goods shrank temporarily. As the Mexican economy recovered its former pace, Mexican imports expanded dramatically and have more than offset the petroleum-led export growth.

The Mexican capital account, including errors and omissions, has also fluctuated even more. The 1976 devaluation appears to have marked a turning point. Net long-term capital inflows hit a high point in 1976 (in the private sector they peaked in 1975, as investors sensed the coming devaluation and reduced their long-term peso position), then fell in 1977 during a period of severe doubt about the Mexican economy's prospects, only to bounce back since 1978, spurred by the oil boom. Foreign pri-

TABLE 5

MEXICAN–U.S. TRADE AS A PERCENTAGE OF TOTAL MEXICAN TRADE, 1974–1979

	Mexican Merchandise Imports from the United States						Mexican Merchandise Exports to the United States					
	1974	1975	1976	1977	1978	1979	1974	1975	1976	1977	1978	1979
Trade volume (millions of dollars)	3,779	4,113	3,773	3,493	4,564	7,502	1,703	1,668	2,111	2,738	4,057	5,941
Percent of total Mexican trade	62.4	62.6	62.6	59.4	60.4	62.9	57.0	57.4	61.8	60.6	68.1	69.2

SOURCE: Mexican import-export data and percentages from the International Monetary Fund, *Direction of Trade*, 1980.

vate-sector net investment in Mexico also fell off sharply from $803 million in 1975 to $86 million in 1978, indicating a wait-and-see attitude on the part of foreign investors. Since then private-sector investment has rebounded to almost a billion dollars in 1979. Although long-term capital inflows were still falling through the first half of 1978, the short-term balance began to recover from a $1.5 billion outflow in the first six months to a net outflow of $1.1 billion for all of 1978, thanks largely to a resurgence in public-sector borrowing. As reflected in the large negative errors-and-omissions entry in table 6, capital flight reached mammoth proportions in 1976. It was cut back sharply by the 1976 devaluation and central-bank adjustments in interest rates. The 1978 data show that the outflow regained some of its former momentum in that year as a result of the failure to continue peso devaluation in the face of an inflation rate almost double that of the United States. In 1979 high domestic interest rates helped to reduce the errors-and-omission entry to $89 million, though the peso is increasingly overvalued, with inflation exceeding 25 percent in 1980.

Mexico's ties to the United States through trade are enhanced by reinforcing financial flows. When the inflation rates between the two countries diverge and the peso remains pegged as it is at present, short-term capital movements increase the instability of Mexico's balance of payments. The fact that the peso is convertible and that the two financial markets are so tightly linked makes this inevitable. Under such circumstances the degrees of freedom for monetary or fiscal policy in Mexico, designed to promote domestic stability or otherwise to reduce vulnerability to the U.S. economy, are severely limited. The lessons of history are that sooner or later peso/dollar exchange rates must adjust to reflect relative purchasing-power parities. Because Mexico's potential for output and productivity growth appears to be much better than that of the United States, however, one might expect that (in the absence of increased government restrictions on foreign investment) Mexico will sustain a net inflow of medium- and long-term capital for a reasonably long period of time, as funds seek higher real rates of return south of the border. This is likely to continue despite the unsettling character of short-term capital movements.

Basic Policy Issues

Given the preceding sketch of trade trends between the United States and Mexico, one may examine several key policy areas. The following have been of concern in recent years: illicit drug traffic, tourism, technology transfer, agricultural trade, rising petroleum exports from Mexico, the Border Industrialization Program, changing Mexican and U.S.

trade barriers, and most especially the generalized system of preferences (GSP). In this paper, discussion is limited to the last three areas. The extent of the illicit drug traffic is difficult to quantify and cannot be regarded as a sustained source of revenues for Mexico or as a reasonable element in the discussion of trade policy between the economies. Tourism has great potential but is not likely to depend on major U.S.–Mexican policy decisions, except perhaps those concerning transportation, such as the effect of the Civil Aeronautics Board's approval of airfare reductions on Mexican airline development and infrastructure investment. The conditions of technology trade are of immense importance to the future growth of Mexico and warrant a study in themselves, though this topic bears some relation to that of border industries. Agricultural trade policy will be treated in the section on general trade barriers.

U.S. Trade Barriers and the GSP

Not surprisingly, U.S. labor has joined with management to favor protection for those U.S. industries threatened by lower-cost Mexican imports, because it is believed that U.S. jobs and profits would be lost. Though U.S. consumers would suffer from higher prices through protection, consumers tend not to be well represented in the political process. On January 1, 1976, the United States granted special trade preferences to less developed countries as a class (with some exceptions) under its own version of the generalized system of preferences. Under GSP the United States allows duty-free entry of 2,734 commodities. Goods excluded include primary petroleum products, autos, watches, clocks, textiles, electronic equipment, glass, china, bicycles, and a number of other commodities, many of which can be exported by Mexico. At present about 1,000 Mexican products benefit from U.S. GSP. There are limits, however, because GSP benefits apply only if imports of a given product are less than $34 million (U.S.) in the first year, with this limit rising each year. Also, the exporting country's share must be less than half of the total U.S. imports of that product, and at least 35 percent of production costs must be incurred in the exporting country. The restrictiveness of these rules plus misunderstanding and unfamiliarity with market opportunities under GSP have somewhat limited Mexican exploitation of the program, though its total benefits for 1977 were estimated at $368 million (8 percent of Mexican exports).[3] There is reason to believe that a relaxation of the restrictions in GSP would significantly increase Mexico's trade benefits (though benefits should be measured in net terms deducting the opportunity costs of inputs rather than in gross terms as above).

The U.S.–Mexican Trade Agreement, which took effect on March

TABLE 6

BALANCE OF PAYMENTS OF MEXICO, 1974–1979
(millions of dollars)

Item	1974	1975	1976	1977	1978	1979
Deficit in current account	−2,558.1	−3,692.9	−3,044.3	−1,779.7	−2,342.3	−4,245.5
Income	6,342.5	6,305.4	7,231.2	8,009.7	11,925.7	16,403.4
Export of merchandise	2,850.0	2,861.0	3,315.8	4,092.9	6,217.5	8,913.3
Processing services, *maquiladoras*	443.5	454.4	520.1	502.7	714.3	1,027.2
Uncoined silver and gold	148.9	145.7	160.3	185.3	243.0	509.7
Transportation	78.1	88.7	189.8	216.8	251.3	322.4
Tourism	842.0	800.1	835.6	863.3	1,121.0	1,429.1
Border transactions	1,372.9	1,541.6	1,609.7	1,453.8	2,363.5	2,981.8
Investment income[a]			98.2	150.2	246.6	333.3
Other services	607.1	413.8	332.0	350.7	543.0	640.1
Transfers[a]			169.7	194.1	225.6	246.7
Outgo (−)	8,900.6	9,998.4	10,275.6	9,789.4	14,268.0	20,649.9
Import of merchandise	6,056.7	6,580.2	6,029.6	5,487.5	8,143.7	12,097.2
Uncoined gold[a]			41.7	30.9	73.9	157.5
Transportation	96.8	134.1	232.2	218.0	357.8	512.9
Tourism	334.8	399.4	382.9	326.7	519.0	692.3
Border transactions	819.2	957.7	1,051.5	1,059.9	751.5	2,516.6

Investment-related outgo	1,222.2	1,483.5	2,017.0	2,185.8	2,773.9	3,881.2
Profits remitted on foreign investment	633.7	632.6	751.0	643.5	750.9	986.8
Public-sector interest	588.5	850.9	1,265.9	1,542.3	2,023.1	2,894.4
Other services	370.9	443.5	504.0	459.8	620.5	763.4
Transfers[a]			16.7	20.9	27.7	28.7
Capital account (net)	2,730.8	4,318.0	5,307.8	2,462.3	3,223.8	4,554.7
Long-term capital (net)	2,730.8	4,318.0	4,594.8	3,987.4	4,357.5	4,094.9
Public sector (net)	2,104.3	3,514.8	4,207.0	3,901.1	4,063.2	3,146.7
Private sector (net)	626.6	803.2	387.8	86.3	294.3	948.2
Short-term capital (net)[b]			713.0	−1,525.1	−1,133.7	459.7
Liabilities (net)			1,456.6	−1,231.0	−670.9	1,204.6
Public sector (net)			878.0	−949.7	−1,489.4	205.5
Private sector (net)			578.6	−281.3	818.5	399.1
Assets (net)			−743.5	−294.1	−462.8	−744.9
Special Drawing Rights						70.0
Errors and omissions (net)	−135.8	−460.0	−2,596.6	−212.0	−659.0	−89.3
Variation in Banco de México reserves	36.9	165.1	−333.1	470.7	222.5	288.9

NOTE: The minus (−) means outgo of currency. Amounts for 1977 and 1978 are preliminary. Special Drawing Rights evidenced no change, so were not included.

a Short-term capital balances for 1974, 1975 included in "Errors and omissions."
b 1974 and 1975 balances included under "Other services."

SOURCES: Banco Nacional de México, *Informe anual*, 1975, 1976, 1977, and *Review of the Economic Situation of Mexico*, February 1980.

1, 1978, gave Mexico most-favored-nation status and provided import duty restrictions on many goods for which Mexico has an actual or potential comparative advantage, including fruits and vegetables, canned foods, handicrafts, petroleum, sulfur, shrimp, and auto engines and transmissions. Data are not yet available on the possible benefits to either country from this agreement. The limits placed on GSP benefits are criticized by Mexican exporters, many of whom lost their 1978 preferences by exceeding the 1977 limits. The outright exclusion of textiles and electronic equipment in the GSP agreement was another drawback. U.S. interests (such as the cotton lobby) have blocked further liberalization for now, not only vis-à-vis Mexico but worldwide. A movement took place after GSP to urge greater reciprocity from middle-income developing countries such as Mexico in exchange for continuing trade concessions from the industrial countries. Under López Portillo, Mexico made initial overtures to join the General Agreement on Tariffs and Trade (GATT), and a tentative agreement was reached that Mexico elected not to ratify. In March 1979 President López Portillo formally declared that for the time being Mexico would stay out of GATT. Given the special role that oil export policy has had in Mexico's bilateral trade negotiations since 1978, this strategy appears to make sense, notwithstanding some chagrin in U.S. official circles at the end of the Carter administration.

Several options should be considered in solving the problems posed by trade barriers.

Option 1: Continue the status quo and avoid retaliation for Mexico's refusal to join GATT. Mexico has considerable benefits yet to be realized from trade with the United States. Against this are perceived costs to the United States from illegal immigration as the large increase in supply of Mexican workers outstrips modest employment gains resulting from the existing GSP and Mexican Trade Agreement measures. Still there is a strong apparent demand for low-cost Mexican labor in important sectors and regions of the U.S. economy. For the United States, option 1 would probably be the most feasible politically and economically, at least in the very short run. But trade and immigration policy will have to be reevaluated soon.

Option 2: Raise the GSP limits. Politically this is very difficult, especially because of the U.S. recession. Strong pressure groups would oppose such an approach, since the limits would extend to all qualifying less developed countries (LDCs), opening the door to much larger imports to the United States. The benefits to Mexico would probably be limited relative to the perceived costs to U.S. competitors. On the other hand, making a special exception for Mexico to the GSP limits would set a precedent from which other LDCs such as Brazil might wish to profit. On the positive side an exception for Mexico could keep increases in U.S. imports to manageable proportions while allowing Mexico to benefit from an expanded international market. The European Economic Community takes advantage of options of the GATT for its regional trading groups, and the United States might well do likewise with respect to its close neighbors.

Option 3: Continue negotiations to reduce bilateral trade barriers further. This is indeed feasible for both Mexico and the United States, especially if Mexico remains dedicated to improving the efficiency of its national enterprise.

Mexican Trade Barriers

Mexico's major trade restrictions primarily reflect post–World War II policies favoring import-substituting industrialization. By erecting protective barriers around selected industries and granting them subsidies and tax benefits, the Mexican government has created an antiexport bias within its industrial sector, allowing firms to price at noncompetitive levels by the standards of the world market.

At present the government is involved in a program to dismantle its system of import permits, replacing them with outright tariff protection. Though this program is proceeding on schedule,[4] there has been little news about the future implementation of more extreme measures proposed by President López Portillo that would have scrapped tariffs as well by 1982. In the 1978 trade agreement, however, Mexico did grant U.S. exporters easier entry for grains, powdered milk, processed foods, and industrial goods not presently produced domestically. The importation of technology, subjected to severe restrictions by a 1973 Law of Technology Transfer, has been liberalized somewhat by recent measures aimed at attracting foreign direct investment. Mexican industry imported some $400 million in technology in 1977 (though total fees and royalty payments fell from $86 million in 1976 to $75 million in 1977).

There are two options for dealing with problems arising from Mexican trade barriers.

Option 1: Maintain the status quo with respect to foreign trade and investment barriers. This may be acceptable in the short run, satisfying the interests of labor and management in protected industries, reducing tendencies toward the denationalization of Mexican enterprises, and relieving the United States of the need to make matching reductions in its own trade barriers. On the other hand, preserving the status quo

171

would perpetuate the anti-export bias of much of Mexican industry, thereby limiting that country's trade efficiency and reducing its potential for penetrating world markets. More seriously, in the short run, this option would continue to inflict high costs on the agricultural sector of Mexico, which is denied imported technology in favor of higher-cost Mexican inputs. Agricultural stagnation is reflected in outmigration from the rural areas to overcrowded Mexican cities and to the United States. This option would, however, increase markets for U.S. commodity exports such as grains by keeping agricultural production costs high.

Option 2: Bargain for mutual tariff reductions. This would involve costs to Mexican industries and to wasteful, less efficient U.S. firms, though economies of scale from increased markets could be especially beneficial to Mexico, where the domestic market is limited. Importers on both sides would gain. U.S. grain exporters might lose in the short run as total Mexican agricultural output increased, reflecting declining input costs. But access by producers to the U.S. market could increase bilateral agricultural trade along the lines of comparative advantage so that Mexico would export high-unit-value cash crops that are more labor intensive, and import capital and land-intensive crops such as wheat. Gains from trade to labor-abundant Mexico could help to abate the illegal immigration problem. Even if such bargaining made only token progress, it would provide a forum for the discussion of more wide-ranging proposals on bilateral trade in the future.

Border Industrialization Program

The Border Industrialization Program was set up in 1966 as an attempt to offset some of the unemployment caused by the U.S. decision to end the bracero program two years earlier. It allows U.S. companies to set up Mexican plants near the border to process raw materials from the United States. The inputs were admitted duty free provided that their output was reexported to the United States. The U.S. Customs Code allowed reimportation to occur subject to duties assessed only on Mexican value added.

The program had grown to involve over 440 plants as of June 1978 and has extended beyond the border region, where 37 plants are located. Employing over 103,000 Mexican workers in 1978, these plants reexported a Mexican value added of about $460 million worth of goods to the United States in the first half of 1979 and $574 million in the first six months of 1980.[5] U.S. labor organizations criticize the program for allegedly exporting U.S. jobs. This is an open question, as a study made by the Flagstaff Institute indicates that border processing plants in Mexico were directly responsible for the creation of 40,000 jobs in the United

172

States in 1974, 39,000 jobs in 1975, and 48,000 jobs in 1976. Indirect job creation in the United States during those respective years numbered 129,000, 125,000, and 154,000.[6] Some Mexicans have criticized the program for increasing Mexican dependence on U.S. economic fluctuations and for employing women at lower wages (workers receive at least the legal minimum wage) instead of alleviating male unemployment. U.S. business and Mexican labor generally support the program, however, as does the Mexican government.

Table 7 summarizes recent data on the program, which has expanded considerably since 1978. The following are three options for dealing with problems arising from border industrialization.

Option 1: Increase duties on in-bond program's reexports to the United States by repealing the relevant U.S. Customs Code items (806.30 and 807.00). This could well reduce the Border Industrialization Program by 75 percent, wiping out nearly all of the apparel plants and over half of the electronics firms. Because these are highly competitive operations, they would probably relocate in Asia, where a smaller proportion of U.S. components would be demanded, or in other parts of Latin America where wage costs are considerably lower than those in northern Mexico. According to these estimates, a multiple of U.S. jobs would be lost together with those of over 100,000 Mexicans.[7] Prices for goods produced in *maquiladoras* (in-bond industries) might rise somewhat in the United States; pressures for illegal immigration could increase; and a negative multiplier action would almost certainly magnify the cost to Mexico several times in terms of income and jobs. Such an action would seriously affect bilateral relations.

Option 2: Liberalize the U.S. Customs Code still further, eliminating all U.S. entry duties and encouraging more U.S. firms to open plants along the border. This would lower the prices of U.S. goods; employ more Mexicans, part of whose income would be spent on imports from the United States; and expand jobs for Americans in complementary activities while almost certainly reducing employment in competing activities. Such firms could also export their production to the Latin American Free Trade Area at tariffs below those facing U.S. exports, thereby increasing both U.S. and Mexican trade.[8] Employing Mexican workers, mostly women aged seventeen to twenty-three, would tend to reduce fertility rates, offsetting population pressures in the border region, although migration from other regions to the border would probably increase.

Option 3: Liberalize the U.S. Customs Code, eliminating all U.S. reentry duties for new in-bond plants but focusing particularly on those located outside of the border area. This would have the same effect as option 2, except that the United States would receive *less* income stim-

TABLE 7

MEXICO: IN-BOND (PROCESSING) EXPORT INDUSTRY, 1973–1980

Item	1973	1974	1975	1976	1977	1978	1979	1980
Number of plants	257	455	454	448	448	441	540	635
Personnel employed (average)	64,330	75,977	67,214	74,496	78,433	103,000	111,000	130,000
Value added[a] (millions of dollars)	278	443	454	520	503	713	1,025	1,350 (est.)
Wages, salaries and benefits (millions of pesos)	1,443	2,433	2,430	3,321	4,558	2,720	N.A.	N.A.
Raw materials imported	349	555	684	750	789	536	N.A.	N.A.

N.A. = not available.

[a] Includes the value of national inputs incorporated into the merchandise exported.

SOURCE: Prepared by the Economic Consultative Staff of Bancomer, with data from the Bureau of Statistics, Secretariat of Planning and Budgeting; Banco Nacional de México, *Review of the Economic Situation of Mexico*, July 1980, December 1980.

ulation from Mexican expenditures on border transactions in the United States and would conversely experience less potential immigration pressure from those who would otherwise have relocated on the border in search of jobs. Economic benefits would be more widely distributed in Mexico, and nonborder plants might save through lower costs to the extent that labor and other inputs tend to be higher-priced in the border area. This is the most reasonable option given long-run U.S. and Mexican policy objectives. The border region is already the most dynamic area of both countries, and its momentum will increase under the present customs code while a selective liberalization for the nonborder areas of Mexico would spread the benefits to both countries.

Implications

The main problem facing Mexico is that 40 percent or more of its labor force is unemployed or earns one-eighth or less of North American wages. This is not only a Mexican problem, because the pressures it creates also lead to frictions and anxieties in the United States, not only through illegal migration but also from the fear of low-cost imports that compete with the products of U.S. firms. Every time a U.S. trade barrier is removed, new Mexican commodities flood in, and every time Mexico lowers its barriers, U.S. investment makes additional inroads on the ownership of productive wealth in that country. Lagging interest rates, increased exchange risk, and political uncertainty all have led to short-term capital outflows from Mexico while devaluation of the peso, rising peso interest rates, and increased political stability cause reverse flows as we have seen. These short-term capital movements have severe destabilizing consequences for the smaller partner. In the longer run, however, net capital flows into Mexico are certain to continue as long as the two countries remain so far apart in the ratio of capital to labor and have such disparities in the rates of return on investment. The response of investment to inequalities in wealth leads to increased inequality in power, something of concern to the Mexican authorities.

Can trade policies alleviate some of the problems of underemployment and poverty in Mexico without flooding the United States with immigrants, increasing unemployment, and depressing wages? This is the fundamental question. The previous discussion indicates that although the economies of the two countries are closely interwoven, the share of U.S. trade from Mexico, although growing, is still quite small, amounting to less than 1 percent of the U.S. gross domestic product. This means that there is ample scope for an upward adjustment of trade flows without a serious negative impact on the U.S. economy. And even a small upward adjustment would have a considerable benefit for Mexico, given its already high trade shares with the United States. During the past decade, the Border Industrialization Program has grown to provide well over 100,000 direct jobs, only one-eighth of the annual growth in Mexico's supply of labor, though the job multiplier was probably significant. The fact that world trade and employment have grown apace suggests that gains from trade include increased employment notwithstanding the shift in jobs that must take place from lagging to leading sectors. The dislocation costs and adjustment problems that are certain to arise as the United States responds to changing international comparative advantage will be difficult to resolve without a major public policy effort, however. This means that a program to facilitate job and capital relocation must underlie any major new effort from the U.S. side for freer trade with Mexico if it is to be politically acceptable.

It is imperative that those involved in the decision-making process see the big picture, namely the vulnerability of the U.S. economy to changes in world markets that reflect the growth and comparative advantage of the developing countries. The situation will never be as it was, and Mexico's unique position offers a chance for the United States, through production sharing and a controlled temporary migration program, to stay in the front ranks of trade, investment, and technological progress. Representatives of business, labor, and consumers and the informed public in both countries should be called upon to work together in a common effort, consistent with their respective desires for autonomy, social welfare, and national security.

Neither nationalism nor narrow considerations of national security are contradictory to a major effort to provide the means whereby workers throughout Mexico can begin to earn wages somewhere in the neighborhood of those paid north of the border. It is true that the recent history of Mexico has been one in which a small share of the population, mislabeled the "middle class," has enjoyed elite incomes up to and surpassing U.S. levels. They are the lucky few whose education, family background, and talents have allowed them a competitive advantage in a tight market for skills over the majority of their fellow citizens, who have little education or access to opportunity, yet whose expenditure of energy and intrinsic abilities may be as great or greater than that of the "middle-class" elite. A radical attempt to equalize incomes in Mexico, however appealing it may be to moralizers north and south, would at best move incomes in that nation to an average of about one-eighth of those in the United States, further fueling the fires of resentment, hostility, and potential conflict between the two countries. What is needed instead is to find a way by which the enlightened guidance of economic forces can rapidly open the door to new opportunities for income and productivity gains, by making the *value* of Mexican labor comparable with the human energy it reflects and by giving Mexican workers a stake in the capital stock of the country.

Economists have traditionally evoked the "factor price equalization theorem" to argue that with free trade, subject to a number of strong assumptions about free competition and other ideal market conditions, the process of exchange will equalize real wages between trading partners. The United States and Mexico, however, have had substantial trade interaction since independence, and relative wage differentials remain as wide as ever, though along the frontier they are narrower (as they always have been, ever since the time when much of the Sunbelt belonged to Mexico). There is no need to puzzle over this apparent anomaly, nor do trade and migration barriers that presently exist provide an explanation. The main reason for lack of convergence in wages is that a large and growing share of employment in both countries is in the so-called nontradable or service sector. Services and other tertiary activities employ four out of ten workers in both countries, and the employment share of both is growing. Yet these activities largely produce "nontradables," except to the extent that Mexican tourism can be "exported" to visiting Americans or that Americans can enjoy lower-cost personal services at home through the immigration of Mexican workers.

It is in this essentially "nontradable" area as well as in rapid growth of the Mexican economy that the answer lies for the absorption of Mexico's underemployed labor, a process that could allow real wages to approach U.S. levels. But this means at least temporary migration of Mexican labor to the United States to take jobs in the "nontradable" sector, and the migration of skilled labor and managers to Mexico to permit a rapid expansion of its economic base. Such an exchange will not be easy for either country in social and political terms. The implication of further exchange in services is that U.S. service workers would have their incomes grow at a slower rate (or perhaps even decline after taxes and inflation). Immigration of skilled labor to Mexico would cut into the privileges of its own elite. It is here that considerations of trade and migration policy must be linked with those of welfare for competing groups in both countries. At stake is the elimination of poverty, political stability, and broader general economic gains north and south. Only through a greater degree of exchange, which includes services and therefore requires a legalized flow of labor in both directions, as well as goods and capital between the two countries, can some degree of factor price equalization occur within the foreseeable future except perhaps through erosion of real wages in the United States that would be the consequence of an attempted "closed door" policy.

Because Mexico's high fertility rate is now beginning to decline, there is hope that its supply push of labor will be reduced by the year 2000, but for the next two decades the tidal wave of workers from its earlier population explosion will continue to flow. During that period, the lack of increased exchange will widen income gaps within Mexico and between the two countries. Although oil may help Mexico to expand employment opportunities and real wages, much more than oil exports alone is required of both countries in the immediate future. The coordination of trade, migration, and investment policies will require the highest level of mutual understanding and commitment to collective action. And only in such circumstances can both countries be expected to prosper.

Notes

The author acknowledges the assistance of John Macgregor and Don Bovee in the preparation of this paper.

[1] John Christman, "The Economy in Review," *Mex-Am Review* (August 1978), p. 22; U.S. Embassy, Mexico City, *Foreign Economy Trends (FET)*, 1980-052.

[2] U.S. Department of Agriculture, *Foreign Agriculture*, October 1980.

[3] Mark Fazlollah, "Mexico and GSP," *Mex-Am Review* (August 1978), p. 6. The July 1978 supplement to U.S. Department of Agriculture, *Foreign Agriculture*, notes that of $92.9 million of Mexico's GSP-eligible agricultural exports to the United States in 1977 (6.2 percent of all U.S. GSP-eligible agricultural imports), $47.6 million were admitted duty free and $45.3 million were imported with reduced duties. Mexican agricultural exports totaling $32.4 million were removed from GSP eligibility because of lack of "competitive need" (GSP limits having been exceeded). These included grain sorghum, cucumbers, okra, radishes, brussels sprouts, broccoli, cauliflower, chickpeas, miscellaneous salt-pickled vegetables, mangoes, cantaloupes, processed parsley, some vegetable oils, some types of hair, processed chicle, and processed straw and fibrous vegetable substances.

[4] *Commerce America,* July 31, 1978.

[5] Banco Nacional de México, *Review of the Economic Situation of Mexico*, vol. 56, no. 656 (July 1980), p. 199. Employment estimates were as high as 130,000 in 1980.

[6] *Journal of the Flagstaff Institute*, vol. 2, no. 2 (July 1978).

[7] Banco Nacional de México, *Review of the Economic Situation of Mexico*, March 1978.

[8] "Border Industries Far from the Border," *Mex-Am Review* (February 1978), p. 13.

U.S.–Mexican Trade: Situation and Outlook

Sidney Weintraub

During about the past fifty years, Mexico has developed its industry mostly by looking inward. A pioneering study of Mexican industrialization policy as it developed in the 1940s stressed the impetus for investment that came during World War II for domestic production of goods not easily available from abroad, coupled with insistence on protection by the Mexican government against the time foreign production would resume, particularly in the United States.[1] By the 1950s, the pattern of industrialization was one of conscious import substitution, to manufacture in Mexico what could be made there and then provide almost absolute protection against import competition. By November 1976, when Mexico began a process of import liberalization, about 85 percent of all products required permits before they could be imported.[2] Mexico was not unique in its import substitution policies; other less developed countries, particularly in Latin America, followed similar practices.

These policies had several consequences. Annual average growth in manufacturing was more than 7 percent between 1950 and 1975. Manufacturing accounted for 17 percent of gross domestic product (GDP) in 1950 and grew to 23 percent in 1975.[3] The subsidization of industry inherent in this policy had its cost in other sectors of the economy, however. The primary sector (agriculture, forestry, and fishing) grew by only 3.6 percent a year over this period (slowing to much less than that since 1965), and its share of GDP declined from 19 percent in 1950 to 9.5 percent in 1975.

Mexico permitted the import of most capital goods used for investment free of duty. This was coupled with what was deemed to be a humane social policy of setting minimum wages and providing generous social security and other welfare coverage. This combination meant that capital costs were pushed down and labor costs were pushed up, thereby encouraging capital intensity in industry. One study has shown that for each million dollars of output in manufacturing, Mexico used 101.3 workers in 1970, whereas South Korea used 227.8 (in 1969). Worker remuneration was more than $1,500 per year in Mexico and a third of that in Korea.[4] This policy contributed to overt unemployment and underemployment, which together now affect an estimated 50 percent of Mexico's economically active population.

The foregoing general picture is a necessary backdrop to an understanding of the debate that has been taking place in Mexico in recent years regarding its future trade policy. An industrial structure has been established but has been able to thrive only behind protective walls and generally has not been competitive in export markets. The agricultural sector was weakened. The Mexican economy has not been able to provide enough jobs for a labor force that will continue to grow rapidly because of annual population growth rates of around 3 percent, a population of which almost half consists of persons under fifteen years of age and one in which women have not yet entered the labor force in great numbers. The Mexican development model aimed for high overall growth rates in the hope that this would translate over time into some reasonable distribution of the fruits of economic growth and into enough jobs to meet the demand. The overall growth was achieved, but not the rest.

I intend to do three things in this paper: (1) explain the policy framework and show the actual content of Mexico's trade; (2) analyze the options open to Mexico for its future trade policy; (3) relate these options to U.S. interests in its relations with Mexico.

Mexico's Trade Policy and Content

Tables 1 through 6 (see appendix to this paper) provide summary data on Mexico's trade with the world and separately with the United States.[5] Table 7 adds to the trade data to show the other elements in Mexico's balance of payments. The pattern of the balance of payments has been that Mexico has had a trade deficit, one that grew dramatically during the six-year term of President Luis Echeverría, subsided as Mexico entered into a stabilization program in 1977, and then rose again in 1978 and 1979 because of the recovery in Mexican growth. The trade deficit was financed by large capital inflows. It is a reasonable statement to make that Mexico's economic growth was financed by a combination of internal and external savings, and the result was a large external public debt. At the end of 1980, just the public-sector portion of Mexico's external debt was more than $33 billion.[6] The interest on Mexico's public external debt was approximately $3 billion in 1979.[7]

Mexico's import substitution policy aimed at producing internally what could be produced, generally consumer goods, with the result that consumer goods imports have been kept to a minimum. Even the modest percentage of consumer goods imports out of total imports (about 5

180

percent in 1978 and 6 percent in 1979) is as large as it is because of foodstuff imports, which make up more than half of what are labeled consumer goods in table 1. Most imports consist of raw materials and intermediate goods for further processing in Mexico and capital goods for Mexico's transformation industries. When imports had to be cut in 1977 under the stabilization program, all the reductions came in these two categories, which in turn meant that industrial production had to suffer.

Mexico's exports were fairly equally divided until 1978 among extractive industries, manufacturing, and agriculture. This is deceptive, however, unless one looks behind the figures given in table 2. About two-thirds of Mexican exports of manufactures to the United States take place because of special provisions in the U.S. law. Thus, in 1979, out of $3.7 billion worth of exports of manufactures to the United States, more than $540 million came under the U.S. generalized system of preferences and $2.5 billion under sections 806.30 and 807.00 of the U.S. tariff schedule.[8] The evidence is that Mexican industry is generally not competitive. It has been heavily protected in the home market and has succeeded in export markets largely because of special regimes, such as those in the United States, or because of preferential treatment received in the markets of other members of the Latin American Free Trade Association, or because Mexican regulations force exports of automobiles and parts dollar for dollar for any increase in imports by the foreign automobile companies producing in Mexico, or because of export subsidies.

Another significant aspect of Mexico's exports is the growing importance of petroleum. The increases in the value of exports from extractive industries since 1975 shown in table 2 are mostly the result of increased exports of petroleum and petroleum products. This will be even more significant in the future. Official plans now call for Mexican crude and condensate production to grow from about 1.5 million barrels a day in 1978 to 2.7 million barrels a day in 1981 and then continue to grow at a modest rate in the 1980s. Exports are projected to reach a platform in 1982 of 1.1 million barrels a day of crude and 0.2 million of derivatives. These are conservative estimates of growth. Mexico's new industrial development plan projects export earnings of about $8.5 billion in 1982 (current dollars) from petroleum compared with $1.8 billion in 1978.[9] Despite this substantial increase in crude petroleum exports, the industrial development plan projects a continuing and even growing deficit in the current account of Mexico's balance of payments in the 1980s because of growing imports.

Tables 3 and 4 show the dominance of the United States in total Mexican trade. In recent years, the United States has taken about 65 percent of Mexico's exports and provided about the same percentage of Mexico's imports. By contrast, all other markets for Mexican exports are small, although Western Europe does provide some 20 percent of Mexico's imports. Japan also is growing as a source of goods. Tables 5 and 6 show the contrast between the importance of the United States to Mexico and of Mexico to the United States. Although Mexico is an important market for U.S. goods, it took only about 5 percent of the total in 1979. Mexico provided about 4 percent of the value of U.S. imports that year. One perennial objective of Mexican policy is to diversify its markets. As table 3 shows, this has not been accomplished in recent years. It is likely that trade between Mexico and the United States in both directions will increase in the future at greater rates than in the past because of the growth of Mexican petroleum exports and the ability this will provide Mexico to increase its imports without excessive reliance on further buildup of external debt.

It already has been noted that Mexican commercial policy has relied on quantitative restrictions (import licensing) as the primary instrument of protection. The policy began to shift in late 1976, at about the time Mexico went through its worst financial crisis since World War II and was forced to seek help from the International Monetary Fund. Both before this help was granted and since, thousands of individual items have been freed from the import licensing requirement and made subject to tariff protection instead. In time, these tariffs may come down. Indeed, the logic of a tariff is to provide some price protection to domestic producers but not absolute protection. One of the major recommendations made by a study group from the World Bank was that Mexico should aim in several years to have a tariff structure averaging 10 to 15 percent for manufactures, with some tariffs of 20 to 25 percent for sectors with much underdeveloped potential.[10] A necessary accompaniment to this recommendation for moderate and relatively uniform protective tariffs is that Mexico should not allow its exchange rate to become overvalued, as happened during the 1970s until devaluation in September 1976. There is some evidence that Mexico's exchange rate may again be becoming overvalued because prices in Mexico have been increasing more rapidly than in the United States. Because of the dominance of the United States in Mexican trade, the crucial exchange-rate relationship for Mexico is that between the peso and dollar.

One final aspect of the U.S.–Mexican trade relationship is worth citing, namely, the extent of U.S. protectionism against Mexican products. On various occasions, Mexicans have linked the solution of the problem of undocumented workers with improved trade relations with the United States, leaving the implication that much of the problem is caused by U.S. protectionism.[11] The kinds of problems cited by the

Mexicans are the tariff structure of the United States, in which tariffs are higher the more value is added to a product (this is typical of the tariff structures of most countries, including Mexico to the extent that it has relied on tariffs), and some specific U.S. restrictions.[12]

U.S. tariffs do increase as value is added. Raw materials generally enter free of duty, and tariffs are higher for most finished goods than for intermediate goods. To adduce this as a major cause of Mexico's trade deficit with the United States, however, is overstatement because other countries overcome this escalation. In addition, to the extent that the problem did exist before, it will be diminished as the lower tariffs agreed to in the multilateral trade negotiations are put into effect.[13]

U.S. protectionism has been significant in limiting imports from Mexico of textiles and apparel and potentially important in restricting Mexican exports of tomatoes and other winter vegetables. U.S. imports of cotton, wool, and man-made fibers, textiles, and apparel are controlled under an agreement dated February 26, 1979, whose general purpose is to limit the increase in these exports to about 5 to 6 percent a year.[14] The agreement lists many specific categories with specific limitations, but, more significantly, it sets up a consultative mechanism when imports of particular categories seem to be growing too rapidly. As this is written, these are the only protectionist quantitative restrictions the United States imposes against Mexican products. The agreement is comparable to the dozen and a half similar agreements the United States has with individual countries under the umbrella of the multilateral multifiber agreement. The agreement clearly restricts Mexican exports. If all such restrictive bilateral agreements were eliminated, however, it is not clear that Mexico would be a major beneficiary. Other countries, with lower wage rates and equally or more efficient industries, would probably benefit more than Mexico.

Mexicans often assert that the United States is a difficult partner with which to do business because export success breeds U.S. protectionism.[15] The textile and apparel trade is an example of this but not one unique to U.S.–Mexican trade relations because worldwide trade in these products is controlled. A better and more pinpointed example is the harassment to which Mexican exporters of tomatoes and other winter vegetables have been subjected over the last decade or more.

Looking only at tomatoes, we see that Mexico in 1978 exported $161 million worth and $154 million in 1979. The figures are higher if other winter vegetables, such as peppers, cucumbers, eggplant, and squash, are included. As the export value shows, this is not a trivial issue for Mexico; in addition to the earnings, about 100,000 persons reportedly are employed in the growing of these products, all of which takes place in and around the city of Culiacán in the Mexican state of

Sinaloa. Over the years, the Mexicans have had to contend with marketing orders issued by the U.S. Department of Agriculture complicating the export of these products, expensive border-crossing arrangements, hearings called by Florida legislators in the U.S. Congress ostensibly based on inspection standards for Mexican vegetables but going well beyond this into potential restrictions of imports from Mexico, proposed legislation affecting the packaging of these products introduced into the U.S. Congress, and most recently, an antidumping petition introduced by Florida growers seeking to make the case that many individual shipments of these perishable commodities are made below cost of production and should be subject to an antidumping duty. This petition was withdrawn at the eleventh hour in July 1979, just before the U.S. Treasury was to make a finding on the dumping charge, to permit time for government-to-government negotiations to regulate (restrict) Mexican exports. The Treasury later denied the antidumping petition.

One can summarize the current state of trade between the two countries by noting that its level is substantial in both directions. U.S. exports to Mexico are larger than to any other developing country and imports exceed those from any other developing country save large oil exporters, such as Saudi Arabia (although the values are modest compared to U.S. trade with Canada). For Mexico, the United States is overwhelmingly the predominant trading partner. The trade is apt to grow at an accelerating rate in both directions in the near future as Mexico increases its oil exports and increases its imports to meet its development objectives. Mexico's import restrictions are extensive, although they are in the process of being changed from quantitative limits and prohibitions to tariffs. U.S. restrictions against imports from Mexico, although troublesome for some products, have not prevented the growth of Mexico's textile and apparel industry and have permitted exporters of fresh tomatoes from Mexico to capture about half of the fresh winter tomato market.

Options for Mexico's Future Trade Policy

A significant debate took place last year in Mexico on future trade policy. It took the outward form of an institutional debate as to whether Mexico should join the General Agreement on Tariffs and Trade (GATT) or continue to remain outside (as Mexico ultimately chose to do). The institutional issue was merely a proxy for the substantive choices open to Mexico, however.

Mexico entered into the multilateral trade negotiations with a view to acceding to the GATT depending on the negotiating outcome and on Mexico's assessment of the flexibility it would have as a developing country to carry out its development program. Though the GATT does permit greater leeway to developing country members than to the developed industrial countries, the GATT system does favor tariff or price techniques of protection over quantitative restrictions. In addition, if Mexico were to accede to the GATT, it would be expected to offer some concessions, even if not fully equivalent, in return for the concessions it received. Until now, Mexico has been a classic free rider, obtaining the benefits of most-favored-nation treatment from concessions granted by others without being asked to provide anything in return.

The opposition in Mexico to GATT accession involves a left-right alliance. On the left are many Mexican economists, particularly those affiliated with the Colegio Nacional de Economistas, who argue that Mexico could not get adequate special treatment to pursue its own plans if it joined the GATT. These persons argue that Mexico could apply

Appendix: Tables 1–7

TABLE 1

MEXICO'S MERCHANDISE IMPORTS, BY TYPE OF PRODUCT, 1975–1979

	1975	1976	1977	1978	1979[a]
	In Millions of Dollars				
Consumer goods	600	311	417	427	678
Intermediate goods	2,903	2,706	2,537	5,316	7,412
Capital goods	2,391	2,510	2,087	1,981	3,407
Other	686	503	849	[b]	[b]
Freight and insurance	[c]	[c]	[c]	419	600
(C.I.F.) Total	6,580	6,030	5,890	8,144	12,097
Commercial value	[c]	[c]	[c]	7,725	11,497
	In Percentages				
Consumer goods	9.1	5.1	7.1	5.2	5.6
Intermediate goods	44.1	44.9	43.1	65.3	61.3
Capital goods	36.3	41.6	35.4	24.3	28.2
Other	10.4	8.3	14.4	[b]	[b]
Freight and insurance	[c]	[c]	[c]	5.1	5.0
Total	100.0	100.0	100.0	100.0	100.0

NOTE: Detail may not add to totals because of rounding.
[a] Preliminary data.
[b] Subsumed under different categories.
[c] Not separately listed in official statistics.
SOURCE: Banco de México, *Indicadores económicos,* December 1977, December 1978 issues, pp. 76–79 in each; December 1979, pp. 68–71; and February 1980, pp. 68–69.

those aspects of GATT that suited it if it stayed out, without being under any obligation to follow those procedures it opposed.[16] The policy advocated in the Colegio Nacional paper would constitute continuation of past Mexican trade policy but without past errors. On the right, also opposing Mexican accession, are many businessmen who fear loss of protection they now enjoy. Those on the left who in the past opposed the oligopoly profits Mexico's protectionism gave to many of Mexico's businessmen found themselves in the unenviable position of defending a policy that would continue these profits.

Mexico has three broad options (each with many variants) for its future trade policy.

1. Mexico might continue absolute or near-absolute protection of domestic industries (and agriculture). It could not return precisely to the status quo ante because too many items have been freed from import licensing since 1976, but tariff levels could be kept high and import licenses could be retained for those industries where import competition might bite. This would seem to be the policy the anti-GATT forces advocate.

The danger of this policy is that its consequences would be no

TABLE 2

MEXICO'S MERCHANDISE EXPORTS, BY TYPE OF PRODUCT, 1975–1979

	1975	1976	1977	1978	1979[a]
	In Millions of Dollars				
Agriculture and livestock	815	1,186	1,439	1,503	1,778
Extractive industries	738	835	1,288	1,988	4,104
Manufactures	1,187	1,191	1,611	2,726	3,031
Nonclassified	122	104	80	[b]	[b]
Total	2,861	3,316	4,418	6,217	8,913
	In Percentages				
Agriculture and livestock	28.5	35.8	32.6	24.2	20.0
Extractive industries	25.8	25.2	29.2	32.0	46.0
Manufactures	41.5	36.0	36.5	43.8	34.0
Nonclassified	4.3	3.0	1.8	[b]	[b]
Total	100.0	100.0	100.0	100.0	100.0

NOTE: Detail may not add to totals because of rounding.
[a] Preliminary data.
[b] Subsumed under other categories.
SOURCE: Banco de México, *Indicadores económicos*, December 1977 and December 1978 issues, pp. 70–75 in each; December 1979, pp. 72–77; and February 1980, pp. 70–72.

different in the future from what the comparable policy achieved in the past. This is not necessarily foreordained, as protectionism does not necessarily involve capital intensity, but it is rare among developing countries that excessive protectionism leads to efficiency. If protectionism did result in general noncompetitiveness of Mexican industry, this would mean that Mexican industry would continue to have to look inward and export through subsidizing the inefficient.

2. A more likely outcome is substantial liberalization of Mexico's trade (that is, almost complete replacement of quantitative restrictions by tariffs), coupled with a slow process of reducing the protective level

TABLE 3

MEXICO'S MERCHANDISE EXPORTS, BY COUNTRY AND AREA, 1975–1979

	1975	1976	1977	1978	1979[a]
	In Millions of Dollars				
United States	1,614	1,854	2,399	4,411	6,147
Canada	43	48	44	61	74
Europe	333	367	397	572	1,098
South America	268	315	371	381	419
Caribbean and Central America	214	191	215	240	271
Other including:	233	214	224	552	905
Israel	44	65	70	106	299
Japan	109	100	82	171	248
People's Republic of China	25	9	17	123	129
Total	2,705	2,989	3,650	6,217	8,914
	In Percentages				
United States	59.7	62.0	65.7	70.9	68.9
Canada	1.6	1.6	1.2	1.0	0.8
Europe	12.3	12.3	10.9	9.2	12.3
South America	9.9	10.5	10.2	6.1	4.7
Caribbean and Central America	7.9	6.4	5.9	3.9	3.0
Other including:	8.6	7.2	6.1	8.9	10.2
Israel	1.6	2.2	1.9	1.7	3.3
Japan	4.0	3.3	2.2	2.8	2.8
People's Republic of China	0.9	0.3	0.4	2.0	1.4
Total	100.0	100.0	100.0	100.0	100.0

NOTE: Detail may not add to totals because of rounding.
[a] Preliminary data.
SOURCE: Banco de México, *Indicadores económicos*, December 1977 and 1978, pp. 66–69; February 1980, p. 67.

of Mexican tariffs. This policy is compatible with retaining absolute protection for those industries considered indispensable. The logic of this policy is that it would force Mexican industrialists to look outward, although just how much would depend on the level of the remaining tariff protection. Mexico's adherence to the GATT would not assure this outcome, but it would indicate that the supporters of greater trade liberalization have prevailed, at least for now.

One of the unspoken aspects of the liberalization cum GATT debate

TABLE 4

MEXICO'S MERCHANDISE IMPORTS, BY COUNTRY AND AREA, 1975–1979

	1975	1976	1977	1978	1979[a]
	In Millions of Dollars				
United States	4,108	3,765	3,485	5,023	7,637
Canada	146	141	166	162	197
Europe	1,377	1,275	1,131	1,768	2,508
South America	412	245	244	346	576
Caribbean and Central America	102	163	73	64	123
Other including:	433	441	390	780	1,056
Israel	2	0.5	0.5	1	4
Japan	298	306	295	590	787
People's Republic of China	9	9	9	24	43
Total	6,580	6,030	5,489	8,143	12,097
	In Percentages				
United States	62.4	62.4	63.5	61.7	63.1
Canada	2.2	2.3	3.0	2.0	1.6
Europe	20.9	21.1	20.6	21.7	20.7
South America	6.3	4.1	4.4	4.2	4.8
Caribbean and Central America	1.6	2.7	1.3	0.8	1.0
Other including:[b]	6.6	7.3	7.1	9.6	8.7
Israel	c	c	c	c	c
Japan	4.5	5.0	5.3	7.2	6.5
People's Republic of China	c	c	c	c	c
Total	100.0	100.0	100.0	100.0	100.0

NOTE: Detail may not add to totals because of rounding.
[a] Preliminary data.
[b] In the years shown, Japan generally has accounted for 75 percent of the "Other" category.
[c] Less than 0.5 percent.
SOURCE: Banco de México, *Indicadores económicos*, December 1977 and December 1978, pp. 66–69, and February 1980, p. 66.

is the extent of future Mexican–U.S. economic integration. The protectionists tend to want to limit this integration out of concern that the greater the integration, the more dependent Mexico will be. Yet the two countries are each other's natural markets, as current trade statistics demonstrate, in some cases competitive and in others complementary. There is every reason to expect economic interaction between Mexico and the United States to flourish just as U.S.–Canadian economic interaction has flourished, unless either country takes actions to prevent it. This would imply a good deal of mutual dependence. Much of the opposition in Mexico to trade liberalization is based on the desire to escape this dependence.

3. Finally, an option that Mexico might choose is to accept the inevitable growth of integration between its economy and that of the United States and plan for a larger free-trade area encompassing both countries, or North America as a whole. This conception would look to sectoral arrangements, or to free trade generally, to be achieved gradually over an extended period, say, by the end of the century.[17]

TABLE 5

U.S. EXPORTS TO MEXICO, BY MAJOR COMMODITY CATEGORIES, 1975–1979

	1975	1976	1977	1978	1979
	In Millions of Dollars				
Food and beverages[a]	509	285	580	786	760
Industrial supplies[b]	1,556	1,497	1,436	1,878	2,369
Capital goods[c]	1,913	2,007	1,679	2,452	5,431
Consumer goods[d]	893	927	868	1,174	666
Other[e]	270	274	259	391	436
Total	5,160	4,990	4,822	6,681	9,667
As percentage of total U.S. exports	4.8	4.3	4.0	4.6	5.4

NOTE: Because this table is based on data from the U.S. Bureau of the Census, the figures differ from Mexican trade data. Detail may not add to totals because of rounding.
[a] Schedule E codes 0 and 1.
[b] Schedule E codes 2–5 and 671–677 and 681–691.
[c] Schedule E codes 6 and 7 less 671–677, 681–691, 781, 785, 793, and 799.
[d] Schedule E code 8 and 781, 785, 793, and 799.
[e] Schedule E code 9.
SOURCE: Overseas Business Reports, "United States Trade with Major Trading Partners, 1972–1978," Department of Commerce, International Trade Administration, May 1980, pp. 33–35 for 1976–1978; and Department of Commerce, "U.S. Exports of Domestic Merchandise," calendar year 1979, pp. 3-179–3-190, for 1979.

This could encompass an energy common market in North America, as many have advocated, or not. The merit to this option is that it would provide certainty to investors and planners about the future direction of trade in both countries, or in North America as a whole, and reduce the probability of protectionism by any one country as the markets became more integrated.

This is not a likely outcome. The economic opposition would argue that free trade between the two countries would polarize development, putting high-technology industry in the United States or Canada because of the infrastructure that already exists and leaving Mexico with simple industry that relies on cheap labor. This might or might not be the outcome some twenty-five years from now, but this would be Mexico's economic concern.[18] The more pervasive opposition to this option will be political. If straightforward trade liberalization is being opposed by many in Mexico because of the fear that this will lead to greater economic integration with the United States (and to greater dependency in the process), then it is evident that consciously seeking to promote integration would be opposed even more.

TABLE 6

U.S. IMPORTS FROM MEXICO, BY MAJOR COMMODITY CATEGORIES, 1975–1979

	1975	1976	1977	1978	1979
	In Millions of Dollars				
Food and beverages[a]	647	887	1,237	1,309	1,566
Industrial supplies[b]	928	1,065	1,646	2,499	3,942
Capital goods[c]	704	781	749	1,162	2,124
Consumer goods[d]	599	700	833	880	895
Other[e]	182	165	220	244	287
Total	3,060	3,598	4,685	6,094	8,813
As percentage of total U.S. imports	3.2	3.0	3.2	3.5	4.3

NOTE: Because this table is based on data from the U.S. Bureau of the Census, the figures differ from Mexican trade data. Detail may not add to totals because of rounding.
[a] Schedule A codes 0 and 1.
[b] Schedule A codes 2–5 and 671–677 and 681–691.
[c] Schedule A codes 6 and 7 less 671–677, 681–691, 781, 785, 788, 793, and 799.
[d] Schedule A codes 8 and 781, 785, 788, 793, and 799.
[e] Schedule A code 9.
SOURCE: See table 5, for 1976–1978; and Department of Commerce, "U.S. General Imports," pp. 3-149–3-152, for 1979.

This should not be an unthinkable option, however. Mexican industrialization could be planned with considerations of scale in mind and with some assurance that export success will not bring import restrictions in the United States. Over time, Mexican wage rates might increase sufficiently to remove this element of competitiveness from location in Mexico for sale to a larger market, but by then this should no longer matter. For the United States, a larger North American free-trade area would be important not to increase the scale of industries but as a way of combining complementary factors of production more efficiently. For all parties, a long transition period would permit time for adjustment. At any rate, movement toward sectoral or general free trade is a viable option—a politically and economically difficult one and for that reason an unlikely one.

The U.S. Stake in the Mexican Choice

U.S. national interests in Mexico include the following:

- economic stability
- reasonable prosperity, as this enlarges the market for U.S. goods
- progress in reducing unemployment and underemployment in Mexico, as this presumably would reduce the pressure to emigrate to the United States
- maximum feasible development of Mexico's energy resources, as this reduces world supply pressure

TABLE 7

SUMMARY OF MEXICO'S BALANCE OF PAYMENTS, 1975–1979
(millions of dollars)

	1975	1976	1977	1978	1979[a]
Trade balance	−3,719	−2,716	−1,471	−1,926	−3,184
Balance on goods and services	−3,693	−3,069	−1,623	−2,342	−4,247
Capital balance	4,318	5,202	2,229	3,224	4,555
Errors and omissions	−460	−2,452	−101	−659	−89
Changes in reserves	165	−321	504	223	289

NOTE: Different institutions use different techniques for calculating the elements of the balance of payments. Had I used the data in the IMF's *International Financial Statistics*, the merchandise deficit would show up smaller and the other balances sometimes smaller and sometimes larger. The trends would look the same.
[a] Preliminary data.
SOURCE: Banco de México, *Indicadores económicos*, December 1977, December 1978, December 1979, and February 1980, pp. 64–65 in each issue.

• freedom of legal movement across the border because of the cultural and social interaction between the people of the two borderlands.

Mexico's decisions on trade policy, and on the industrial and agricultural policies that lie behind trade policy, will affect all of these interests. In turn, of course, U.S. trade policy will affect Mexican interests.

Trade relations between the two countries would obviously be close and would call for much adjustment on both sides, if there were a gradual movement toward greater integration, either sectorally or across the board. This would not be uniformly welcome in the United States, because there would be losers, such as the producers and workers in labor-intensive industries and agriculture (if agriculture were included) and possibly in industries in which Mexico enjoys other advantages (such as more modern facilities to produce steel and availability of feedstocks for petrochemicals). An agreement looking to a gradual movement toward free trade, partially or fully, would signify that Mexico is prepared to overcome political objections that would exist to such a step. As already indicated, this is an unlikely outcome.

A substantial liberalization of Mexican trade also would result in a further deepening of economic relations between the two countries, however, perhaps in time approaching those that exist between Canada and the United States.

It is hard to envisage Mexico returning completely to the policy of protectionism that existed until 1976, but a distinctly protectionist trade policy is possible. Even such a policy, however, is unlikely to slow the process of extensive economic integration between the two countries although it could change the composition of products in their bilateral trade.

Let me conclude with the following three points: (1) The United States does have a stake in the trade policy choices Mexico makes and therefore has a right to express an opinion. Diplomacy may require that opinions come from private rather than from official sources. (2) The worst choice from the U.S. viewpoint would be for Mexico to revert to absolute protectionism because it probably would not work to absorb needed amounts of labor. Mexico is also sufficiently advanced to have lost any justification to be a free rider in the international trading system. (3) The United States need not have an opinion as between liberalization and deliberate steps toward trade integration, because each alternative has uncertain costs and benefits for each country; however, the issue of deliberate integration over time, involving just Mexico and the United States or including Canada as well, merits debate and analysis in all the potentially affected countries.

192

Notes

[1] Sanford A. Mosk, *Industrial Revolution in Mexico* (Berkeley: University of California Press, 1950), p.21.

[2] A. Nowicki et al., *Mexico, Manufacturing Sector: Situation, Prospects, and Policies* (Washington, D.C.: World Bank, March 1979), p.16.

[3] GDP data are from Banco de México, *Información económica: producto interno bruto y gasto, cuaderno 1960–1977,* August 1978.

[4] Susumu Watanabe, "Constraints on Labour-Intensive Export Industries in Mexico," *International Labour Review* 109 (January 1974): 23–45.

[5] Mexican sources were used for showing Mexican trade with the world and U.S. sources for the bilateral trade between the United States and Mexico. The two sets of data often show different figures. The differences do not alter the general trends that will be described here, however.

[6] Banco de México, *Informe anual,* 1980, p. 92.

[7] World Bank, *World Debt Tables* (Washington, D.C., 1980).

[8] Items that enter under the U.S. system of preferences pay no duty. Under sections 806.30 and 807.00, the U.S. duty is paid only on the value added in Mexico and not on the raw materials and other inputs sent from the United States to Mexico for further processing.

[9] Secretariá de Patrimonio y Fomento Industrial, *Plan Nacional de Desarrollo Industrial, 1979–82* (1979), p. 79. Petroleum exports were $9.4 billion in 1980.

[10] Nowicki, *Mexico,* p. 23.

[11] David F. Ronfeldt and Caesar D. Sereseres, "Treating the Alien(ation) in U.S.–Mexico Relations," Rand Paper series, August 1978, cites López Portillo to this effect (p. 22).

[12] The complaint about tariff escalation as value is added was included at Mexican insistence in the joint communiqué of February 16, 1979, following President Carter's visit to Mexico. López Portillo is cited as requesting the United States to do what is necessary to permit "an increase in the export of Mexican merchandise, particularly those of higher value-added which would benefit both countries." U.S., Department of State, *Bulletin* 79, no. 2024 (March 1979): 60.

[13] The publication "Results of the U.S. Tariff Negotiations with Other Major Developed Countries in the Multilateral Trade Negotiations," Office of the Special Representative for Trade Negotiations (Washington, D.C., June 21, 1979), shows average U.S. tariff levels at 6.1 percent before the trade negotiations and 4.2 percent when the results of the negotiations are fully in effect (p. 4). Though an "average" tariff level can obscure many high tariffs, there is no convincing evidence that tariff escalation has been a major reason for Mexico's general noncompetitiveness in the export of manufactures to the United States.

[14] To give just recent data, U.S. imports of clothing from Mexico were $167 million in 1977 and $204 million in 1978.

[15] An excellent citation on this point was made by Miguel M. Blasquez of the U.S.–Mexican Chamber of Commerce in a speech in Chicago: "Mexican exporters worry every time the U.S. Congress meets." *Washington Letter* of the U.S.–Mexican Chamber of Commerce, November 1977, p. 5.

[16] The position of the Colegio Nacional de Economistas was made known in a letter and broadside dated May 23, 1979, to President López Portillo, entitled "Policy Alternative to Protectionism and to Adhesion by Mexico to the GATT." The free-rider position is stated explicitly in this document when it is argued that Mexico should follow a GATT policy similar to its policy of following OPEC prices without joining OPEC.

[17] There is a technical difference between a free-trade area and a customs union in that the latter implies a common external tariff for all the members and the former does not. Because the U.S. tariff level is much lower than that of Mexico, a customs union between

the two would require either a drastic reduction in Mexico's tariffs or a large increase in the U.S. tariff level or some combination, none of which is practical. For this reason it seems more sensible to speculate about a free-trade area.

[18] This tendency toward polarization is being belied in Ireland since its adherence to the European Economic Community. Greece hopes that joining the EEC will stimulate its industrialization.

U.S.-Mexican Oil and Gas Relations: A Special Relationship?

Henry R. Nau

Since the energy crisis in 1973, relations between the United States and Mexico have acquired a new dimension. Oil and gas issues are now fundamental to these relations, and how these issues are handled will have a critical impact on the older and broader political relationships between these two countries.

The new dimension derives from continuing U.S. requirements for oil and gas imports through the 1980s and from Mexico's recent willingness and ability to produce and to export oil and gas, particularly oil, far beyond what analysts expected in the mid-1970s. Despite two energy crises, the United States continues to import sizable amounts of foreign oil, particularly from potentially unfriendly Arab states. The United States also imports natural gas. Prior to the decision in 1978 to decontrol natural gas prices by 1985, the United States stood on the verge of importing vast additional amounts of gas in liquefied form from the same countries that monopolize world oil supplies, namely members of the Organization of Petroleum Exporting Countries (OPEC) such as Indonesia, Iran, and Algeria. Mexico, on the other hand, has emerged rather rapidly from being a net importer of energy in 1975 to being a major exporter of oil and gas in 1980, particularly to the United States, where it now ranks third among oil exporters to the United States. Mexico's production and export potential is even more astonishing, ranking, in the estimates of some experts, with that of principal OPEC producers such as Saudi Arabia or Iran before the fall of the shah.

The energy patterns and policies of the United States and Mexico are rooted in domestic politics and represent only one aspect of a complex set of foreign policy relationships between the two countries. Nevertheless, the accelerated development of Mexican oil and gas since 1976 and the export of much of this oil and some, albeit small amounts, of this gas to the United States continue to encourage speculation of a "Northern Connection" involving substantial Mexican oil and gas exports to the United States.[1] This connection, it is argued, could result in significant benefits for both countries. The United States would obtain a relatively more secure source of foreign oil and gas to replace insecure

Arab OPEC sources, and Mexico would obtain the maximum economic and political returns from its energy resources, both because exports to the U.S. market are the most profitable (since transportation costs are low) and because energy gives Mexico an unprecedented source of political leverage in dealing with its historically dominant northern neighbor.

The possibilities suggested by a Northern Connection have been analyzed from a number of different perspectives.[2] In this essay, I look at these possibilities as alternatives, seeking to refrain from arguing a preference. A prevalent view in 1976 was that Mexico, despite its plans for increased production of oil and gas, would not meet its goals. That view in retrospect proved wrong. In the summer of 1980, Mexico met its original goal of producing 2.25 million barrels per day (mbd) of oil by 1982 and announced a new goal of 2.75 mbd to be achieved by early 1981. On the other hand, the United States fell short of oil import requirements projected in the mid-1970s. From 1973 to 1977, U.S. imports jumped from 36 to almost 50 percent of total domestic consumption. That trend was projected to continue into the 1980s. In the first half of 1980, however, under the impact of substantial OPEC price increases in 1979 and a domestic recession, the United States reduced imports to 41 percent of total consumption. U.S. reductions in the second half of 1980 were even more substantial.

Such changes in U.S. and Mexican policy behavior are difficult, if not impossible, to predict. Thus, for the future, it may be more useful to consider a range of possibilities in U.S.–Mexican energy relations than to predict a favored outcome. The following outlines the dimensions and considerations of a number of U.S.–Mexican relationships. It takes into account but does not elaborate broader foreign policy aspects of these relationships, which are covered elsewhere in this volume.[3] Most important, it does not argue for or against a special relationship in energy or any other area, but rather looks analytically at the facts and figures within which such arguments will have to be made.

Magnitude of a Northern Connection

The significance of a Northern Connection depends in part on its potential magnitude. What are some reasonable estimates for Mexican oil and gas production and export and for U.S. import requirements? Few activities are more hazardous than trying to estimate and to relate the geological, engineering, economic, and, most important, political and social factors that figure into estimates of future production and consumption of energy. Nevertheless, let us begin with the situation as it existed both before the Iranian and related OPEC crises of 1978–1979 and in the circumstances of late 1980 with the Iranian-Iraqi war still in progress and a third world oil price crisis pending.

In 1977, the United States imported 8.7 million barrels of petroleum (crude and refined) per day or 47 percent of total petroleum consumption. These figures were up from 6.3 mbd or 36 percent in 1973. Moreover, petroleum imports (both direct and indirect) from potentially unfriendly Arab sources (namely, OPEC states that embargoed the United States in 1973) totaled 3.6 mbd in 1977 or 41 percent of total imports, as against 1.4 mbd in 1973 or 22 percent of the total. Thus, U.S. dependence on insecure Arab oil grew from 1973 to 1977 at a rate of about 0.5 mbd per year.

By late 1980, U.S. imports had dropped below 7 mbd with about 40 percent still coming from insecure Arab sources. It is disputed whether this turnaround was due primarily to higher prices from the 1978–1979 crisis or to the related recession in the U.S. economy. U.S. imports from insecure Arab sources, however, still amounted to 2.8 mbd or twice the 1973 figure, an increase over seven years of 0.2 mbd per year.

Meanwhile, Mexico's crude oil production grew from 1977 to 1979 at an average rate of 0.35 mbd per year, from 0.8 mbd in 1977 to 1.9 mbd at the end of 1979. Roughly half of this production is exported, and until 1980, 85 percent of these exports went to the United States. This means that from 1977 to 1979, the United States imported Mexican oil at an average rate of increase of about 0.15 mbd per year (0.5 × 0.35 mbd × 0.85), or approximately 30 percent of the annual increase of U.S. dependence on insecure Arab sources from 1973 to 1977 and 75 percent of this increase from 1973 to 1980. Thus, as U.S. dependence on Arab oil slows, which seems to have been the case since 1977, Mexican oil becomes an increasingly important potential substitute for Arab oil.[4]

Going beyond 1980 introduces much greater uncertainty into the calculations. Estimates of Mexican oil production in the period from 1985 to 1990 range from a low of 3.0 mbd in 1988 to a high of 7.2 mbd in 1990 (latter assumes an annual production increase of 0.5 mbd, or somewhat higher than the rate prevailing from 1977 to 1980).[5] If Mexico continues to discover new reserves, daily production of oil and gas could reach as high as 12 mbd (assumes 100 billion barrels [bb] in reserves and a 20:1 reserve/production ratio). At the lower end of these estimates, oil exports might be only slightly greater than in 1980, around 1.5–2.0 mbd; at the upper end, oil exports could range as high as 5 mbd or more. If the United States imports a total of 10–14 mbd of oil by 1985–1990—which, since 1979, has been considered an upper limit—

Mexican oil exports, if shipped predominantly to the United States, could equal 40 percent or more of U.S. total imports, entirely displacing present levels of imports from potentially unfriendly Arab sources.

Mexican gas production and exports are related to oil, because the two are associated in the largest Mexican fields. Plans in 1977 called for gas exports to the United States of 0.8 trillion cubic feet (tcf) per year by 1982. A dispute over prices subsequently reduced this amount to 0.11 tcf in 1980 (see note 1). Nevertheless, the potential involved here equals the amount of gas expected from Alaskan fields by 1985 and represents about 4 percent of current gas consumption in the United States, which has not grown but declined since 1972. Moreover, if oil and hence gas were to be produced in Mexico at maximum rates, gas exports to the United States by 1985–1990 could total 2.0–2.5 tcf or 10–12 percent of U.S. consumption, assuming the latter remained constant. While this prospect is unlikely, the amount involved would exactly offset the imports of liquefied natural gas projected for this period from projects under construction in Algeria, Indonesia, and Iran. Once again, Mexican exports could play a significant role in reducing (or in this case, preventing) U.S. dependence on insecure Arab energy sources.

The Issues

None of these projections may prove to be correct, because all such projections depend heavily on decisions taken between now and 1985–1990 by the U.S. and Mexican governments, as well as by other actors in U.S.–Mexican energy relations such as the major international oil companies. Yet the above discussion suggests that the magnitude and potential significance of a Northern Connection are sufficient to require a careful examination of the issues and options each government will face in making energy decisions over the next decade. From the U.S. point of view, the issues can be formulated in three questions:[6]

1. What supplies of oil and gas does the United States require by the mid-to-late 1980s, given the desired mix of energy sources in U.S. consumption (oil and gas, coal, nuclear, solar, etc.) and the estimated domestic and world supplies to meet these needs?

2. What is the prospect that Mexico can achieve production and export levels sufficient to meet important U.S. energy needs?

3. How important is Mexico compared with other suppliers as a source of U.S. energy imports, and what price is the United States willing to pay in energy and/or other areas for a special relationship with Mexico?

U.S. Needs

Oil and gas currently supply three-quarters of U.S. energy needs, up from somewhat more than one-half in 1950. The share of gas increased steadily from 18 percent in 1950 to 33 percent in 1971, whereas the share of oil remained relatively constant after 1955 at about 44 percent. After 1972 the share of gas fell back to 26 percent, and the share of oil increased to 49 percent. The shift from gas to oil, together with the decline in domestic oil production, exacerbated U.S. requirements for oil imports. Since 1977, domestic oil production has increased slightly because of Alaskan supplies, and further but unknown additions to oil and gas supplies are anticipated as a result of the energy price increases in 1978–1979, the decontrol of oil prices in early 1981, and the gradual decontrol of gas prices by 1985.

Given this situation, two broad reactions have characterized the U.S. policy debate on energy. Each of these reactions entails a different evaluation of the need for Mexican oil and gas.

Future Oil and Gas Shortage. The first view, which characterized the Carter administration's energy plan in 1977, holds that domestic oil and gas supplies are physically limited and that world supplies will also peak and begin to decline in the mid-1980s. Under these circumstances, it is felt, there is little reason to encourage further oil and gas production, which will only hasten the day when supplies will be exhausted. The need is to shift out of oil and gas into alternative energy sources. Proponents of this point of view divide further into two schools, one favoring hard options as alternatives to oil and gas (coal, nuclear power), another preferring soft options (solar, geothermal, wind, etc.). To encourage development of these alternatives, however, both schools favor sustained and perhaps even gradually increasing world oil and gas prices, as the price of alternatives continues to stay above oil and gas price levels. Both schools also favor heavy investments in research and development of new energy sources as well as in new conservation measures. They differ primarily on the environmental costs of developing hard versus soft sources of energy.

Carter's energy plan in 1977 implemented this perspective. It sought to raise domestic oil prices while taxing profits (as no substantial new production was expected), to increase domestic gas prices for low-priority users while continuing to control such prices for high-priority users (the assumption being that there was not enough gas for both), and to increase outlays for new alternatives, including synthetic fuels and conservation measures (reflecting again the assumption of limited production possibilities).

199

Not surprisingly from this point of view, Mexican oil and gas supplies did not register as a major factor for dealing with future U.S. energy needs.[7] At best, Mexican gas might help to meet short-term gas requirements. Even then, the price of this gas became an important issue. Some considerations were:

• Could the United States pay a higher price for gas to a foreign producer than it was willing to pay to domestic producers under price controls prevailing in the United States in 1977? Moreover, for pipeline gas, is any price above the U.S. domestic price justifiable in economic terms when Mexico has no other market for this gas (and liquefaction involves considerably higher costs and lower profits)? Finally, could the United States afford to set a precedent in pricing Mexican gas imports that links this price with world oil prices and future world oil price increases, as the Mexican government desired?

• Could the United States pay a higher price for Mexican gas than it was paying for equivalent pipeline gas from Canada? Moreover, would Mexican gas imports reduce the need for Alaskan gas (assuming there was insufficient requirement for both), unraveling all the effort that has gone into the development of the Alaskan gas pipeline project?

• Could the United States continue to support roll-in pricing of larger and larger amounts of high-priced foreign gas, including liquefied natural gas where higher prices are justified to some extent by higher costs, when the eventual burden of these higher prices might fall on the same high-priority users of gas for whom prices were to remain controlled (assuming low-priority users were driven out of gas, as the National Energy Plan I envisioned)?

Nor, according to this view, did the prospect of Mexican oil production (which is associated with gas) and export to the United States justify a higher price for Mexican gas. Mexican oil might be useful in the near term to soften the impact of eventual oil shortages in the 1980s, but to do so, it would not necessarily have to be exported to the United States. It would add to world oil supplies and moderate future world oil price increases wherever it might be exported. And, fundamentally, neither Mexican oil nor gas could change the basic supply picture of physical depletion of world oil and gas resources. Moreover, since oil and gas imports would eventually decline anyway, security of supply was not a long-term problem. In the interim, security requirements could be adequately covered by the consumer country emergency oil-sharing plan administered by the International Energy Agency and by a shift of U.S. diplomacy in the Middle East toward greater evenhandedness between Israel and the Arab states, thereby reducing the probability of another Arab oil embargo.

Adequate Oil and Gas Supplies. A second view of U.S. energy needs embraces some aspects of administration policy under Presidents Nixon and Ford and beliefs strongly espoused by Governor Reagan in his successful campaign for the American presidency in 1980. This view rejects the notion that oil and gas supplies are physically limited. It holds that domestic oil and gas production is limited in considerable part by continuing domestic price controls, whereas world oil and gas supplies are adequate and, under the stimulus of higher prices and expanded exploration, are likely to increase for some time to come. It is noted, for example, that gradual decontrol of domestic gas prices in the United States begun in October 1978 brought about an immediate gas surplus of some 1 tcf, or 5 percent of U.S. consumption. This surplus permitted some shift back to gas from oil and reduced the strain on oil use and oil imports that characterized the period from 1973 to 1977. Moreover, prior to the Iranian crisis of 1978–1979, world oil supplies were in surplus. The *Petroleum Economist* reported in October 1978 that "there is, in academic and certain government circles, a growing suspicion about the concept of an impending oil shortage; a feeling that world energy may be facing a deluge, not a drought." Alaskan, Mexican, North Sea, and potentially Chinese oil, as well as oil from developing areas, were seen as contributing to this deluge. Admittedly, the Iranian crisis and then the Iranian–Iraqi war in September 1980 added new uncertainties to the market situation. But the obstacles to increased production, it was pointed out, were not geological or even economic but political. Drilling in the Middle East and other risky areas had declined. The developing world, which accounts for 50 percent of the total prospective area for oil and gas, accounts for only 20 percent of cumulative world oil production plus reserves. Bilateral and multilateral programs to finance and to guarantee oil development might substantially reduce these risks and add to new oil and gas supplies from oil-rich but unexploited areas.

This second view advocates full decontrol of oil and gas prices with profits going to producers as inducements to further production. Increasing oil and gas supplies will extend the transition period for conversion to other energy sources and will ease further price increases. Though physical constraints may eventually limit world oil and gas supplies, the costs of transition might be considerably lower if oil and gas production were encouraged in the interim. Investments in new sources of energy, as well as in expensive conservation measures, could be reduced, thereby alleviating future capital shortages. Environmental problems could also be minimized because gas in particular is a clean-burning fuel.

From this perspective, Mexican oil and gas supplies acquire greater significance for meeting future U.S. energy needs. Such supplies are to be encouraged, even in the face of temporary oil and gas surpluses. Higher prices might be paid initially for Mexican gas in order to ensure access to Mexican oil. Prices over time will be moderated anyway by increasing supplies. Moreover, under this scenario, U.S. oil and gas imports may be expected to continue, particularly if world production expands in previously neglected areas (for example, in the developing world). Security of supply, therefore, remains an important long-term consideration. Provided that domestic stability in Mexico continues, Mexican oil and gas may be considerably safer than Persian Gulf supplies. Hence, it is important to U.S. interests not only that Mexican oil be exported but also that it be exported to the United States. If it is necessary to pay Mexico an initial premium for its gas as a way of ensuring subsequent and related oil exports to the United States, the benefits may be well worth the price, even the price of indexing Mexican gas exports to future world oil price increases (which was eventually done in the 1979 agreement, but the reference price was based on a basket of crude oil types to ensure that no one crude oil supplier could significantly affect the reference price).

Mexican Supplies

Whatever the perceived value of Mexican oil and gas in the United States, U.S. choices are clearly interwoven with Mexican decisions concerning what, how, and with what consequences Mexican reserves are exploited. The key questions would seem to include:

- How much oil and gas does Mexico have?
- How much can Mexico produce, with and without foreign assistance?
- What products (crude, refined, petrochemicals) and how much of each product will it export and to what markets?
- How will revenues be divided between the nationalized petroleum industry (PEMEX) and other sectors of the economy (industrial, agricultural, and service)?
- Can Mexico manage the social and political disruptions associated with energy and broader economic development?
- What are the implications of Mexican energy development for broader Mexican foreign relations with oil suppliers, OPEC and non-OPEC, and with oil consumers, particularly the United States?

Reserves. Official estimates of Mexican reserves have increased dramatically in recent years. From 5.5 bb at the end of 1973, proven reserves shot up to 60 bb by September 1980. Potential reserves have increased even more to an estimated 150–250 bb including the discovery of another large oil field near Tampico. These figures, particularly the latter, seem to place Mexico in the same league as Saudi Arabia, whose proven oil reserves total 150 bb. It is important to remember, however, that Mexican reserves are hydrocarbon reserves, of which only 70 percent is oil (the rest gas and gas liquids), and that the upper estimates are potential, not proven, reserves. Thus, Mexico is still far from becoming another Saudi Arabia. Nevertheless, Mexican sources (principally PEMEX) have been historically conservative in their estimates of reserves; and if estimates were to continue to increase in the future at even a fraction of the past rate, Mexican reserves could conceivably come to rival those of the major oil producers.

Production. Whether Mexico could produce at the level of Saudi Arabia (in late 1980, about 10 mbd) or Iran under the shah (5–6 mbd) is another matter and unlikely by most estimates without significant assistance from foreign oil companies. Onshore production in the Reforma area seems to be manageable within the limits of PEMEX resources, although foreign firms are involved in joint ventures with Mexican firms for both oil and gas production. Wells are extremely productive, averaging about 5,000 barrels per day (bd) per well. In the newly discovered Chicontepec field near Tampico, wells are considerably less efficient with structures said to be more like Texas oil fields producing at a rate of 200–300 bd per well. Economic factors may limit exploitation of this area to 25–30 percent of the total deposits even with expensive water flooding.

Offshore development is a different question and involves a new environment and challenge for PEMEX capabilities. Foreign assistance is required. U.S. firms are clearly involved in some or all of the ten drilling platforms being constructed in the Gulf of Mexico off Campeche. Because 50 percent or more of recent Mexican hydrocarbon discoveries have been in offshore areas, it is highly unlikely that Mexico could achieve maximum rates of oil and gas development without substantial and highly controversial foreign assistance, particularly from the U.S. oil majors.[8] How will the oil majors react to these opportunities, and what are the foreseeable points of conflict between oil company policies, on the one hand, and Mexican and U.S. government policies, on the other? The political difficulties of inviting major oil company assistance may constitute a significant constraint on Mexican production, particularly after 1982 when a new administration will have to cope with the inevitable social and political dislocations resulting from current development activities.

Exports. What products will Mexico export in what quantities to what markets? Under the current administration, emphasis has been placed on crude oil and gas production and export, with two-thirds to four-fifths of the oil and all of the gas going to the United States. (Refined capacity is also being doubled and petrochemical production tripled.) Following the breakdown of the gas negotiations with the United States in 1977, the Mexican government announced a program to use the gas internally, releasing further oil, especially heating oil, for export. This program has apparently met with success. But how much oil and gas can or will Mexico consume internally in the future? Domestic energy prices are well below world price levels, and Mexico expects to consume about one-half of near-term oil production output. Moreover, leftist groups in Mexico oppose the emphasis on crude oil and gas production and export, arguing that hydrocarbon reserves should be conserved for later domestic use (as Mexico is poor in coal and hydroelectric energy sources), that rapid development risks dependence on foreign, particularly U.S., technology and markets, and that more desirable employment and environmental conditions could be achieved by slower growth and greater reliance on value-added industries.

The emphasis on crude exports, nevertheless, is likely to continue through the present *sexenio* (or six-year presidential term) and perhaps beyond, as world markets for refined and petrochemical products remain saturated and unattractive. Nevertheless, some slowdown in crude production and export is conceivable after 1982, and even before then a determined effort to diversify crude markets may materialize. In 1980 Mexico began to ship oil in sizable amounts to Cuba, Brazil, and Japan. It is also constructing port facilities to handle 5 mbd of oil and to accommodate supertankers required for economic transport of oil to long-distance markets. The question of Mexican natural gas production and export is more uncertain and hinges delicately on how U.S.–Mexican energy and other relations evolve over the next few years.

Revenues. In 1979, PEMEX accounted for 20 percent of total government expenditures, the largest single spender of federal funds in Mexico. In the industrial category alone, PEMEX absorbed 60 percent of all government investments. PEMEX is a strong and semiautonomous actor in the Mexican political system and is supported fully by the current administration. It may be expected to continue to garner the lion's share of future increases in government revenues derived from oil and gas exploitation. Future constraints, however, may emerge in three areas. The need to diversify Mexico's energy resources to prepare for the end of the oil and gas era may lead to increasing expenditures for nuclear power and other nonpetroleum energy development. Second, and probably more important, the private industrial sector in Mexico may increasingly resist the expansion of the nationalized petroleum sector. The industrial communities have more to gain from enhancing the competitiveness and export potential of Mexico's manufacturing sector. Third, the increasing demand for social services to offset and legitimize the inevitable disruptions from oil and gas development and to reduce the huge national disparities in income in Mexico may be expected over time to cut into petroleum as well as other industrial uses of oil and gas revenues.

Social and Political Management. The contest over the revenues or spoils of energy development is but a part of the larger debate over political and social objectives and policies in Mexico. Oil plays a particularly important role in this debate, as it does in the history of Mexican politics. The nationalization of the oil industry in 1938 was one of the first such moves by foreign countries and accordingly holds a special place in the memory and legitimacy of the Mexican Revolution. At one level, hydrocarbon reserves represent the hope of the masses in Mexico, which suffer from severe disparities in income distribution. At another level, hydrocarbon reserves play into the politics of elite conflict and cooperation and add to the potential of corruption in a historically corrupt political system. Given this legacy, can Mexico manage successfully the social and political aspects of energy development?

Answers depend on perceptions of stability in Mexican politics before and since the oil bonanza. In 1976, Mexico appeared to be a society headed for shipwreck on the shoals of inflation and rising foreign debt. To López Portillo at least, oil and gas development was the way out, promising $20 billion worth of new revenues from 1977 to 1982, or almost the equivalent of Mexico's foreign debt.[9] Others contend, however, that energy revenues will only delay the day of reckoning in Mexican society, preempting fiscal and other reforms that are essential to deal with long-term social and political development. Are these reforms preconditions to the successful management of Mexican energy development? Can Mexico avoid the recent fate of other oil suppliers—Iran or, in another sense, Venezuela?

These are but a few of the imponderables of Mexican politics affecting the outcome of all technical and economic projections of Mexican and U.S. oil and gas relations. It would seem to be a safe assumption, in view of the unavoidable social and political costs of economic development and in view of the historical pendulumlike swing of Mexican domestic politics, to anticipate some slowdown of Mexican oil and gas development after 1982, if for no other reason than to consolidate and regroup following the frenetic change that will have characterized energy development in Mexico during the previous six years. While that is a safe assumption, however, it may also be a wrong one, as were similar assumptions in 1976.

Foreign Relations. How will Mexico, as an important oil supplier, relate to other world oil suppliers, both OPEC and non-OPEC? Mexico has shown no interest thus far in joining OPEC while pricing its oil at comparable or slightly above OPEC levels. If Mexican exports should become important enough, however, to have a significant influence on world price levels, would OPEC members increasingly pressure Mexico to observe tacit or explicit production constraints? Even if Mexico remains outside OPEC and free of direct OPEC pressure, how will it line up on issues of future price increases—with the moderates or with the radicals in OPEC, with the so-called Friends of OPEC (Norway, the United Kingdom, etc.) or with certain oil consumers, such as the United States? What are the implications of different pricing strategies for Mexico's broader relations with these countries? On the supplier side, Mexico's relations with Venezuela would seem to be especially critical; and on the consumer side, Mexico's relations with the United States hold special significance, particularly if the latter remains Mexico's principal export market.

Special Relationship

The varying perceptions of U.S. needs and Mexican production and export capabilities combine to yield the central question: How much is Mexican oil and gas worth to the United States, and what price is the United States willing to pay in other areas of U.S. relations with Mexico, as well as in U.S. energy and broader foreign policy relations with other oil suppliers (OPEC, Friends of OPEC) and consumers (Western allies)?

The various outcomes discussed above may be summarized in a two-by-two matrix:

| | | Mexican Production and Export Levels | |
		High	Low
U.S. needs	High	1	2
	Low	3	4

Let us look more closely at the price, volume, security and other issues involved in a special relationship under the varying combinations suggested by each box.

1. High U.S. Need/High Mexican Production. In this case, Mexican oil and gas production is likely to have the greatest significance for volumes and prices of world oil and gas. Various forecasts before the Iranian crisis in 1978–1979 anticipated a growth in world demand by 1985 of 10–35 mbd. OPEC production was expected to meet anywhere from 0–20 mbd of this demand, whereas non-OPEC production was seen to increase from 17.5 mbd in 1976 to 20–40 mbd in 1985. If these forecasts had remained on track, Mexican production of 2–5 mbd by 1985 could have supplied anywhere from 5 (2 mbd/35 mbd) to 50 (5 mbd/10 mbd) percent of new world oil supplies. Except at the lowest end, this amount would have represented a sizable percentage of new world production and, *ceteris paribus,* could have exerted a significant influence on world prices. Since the Iranian crisis of 1978–1979, forecasts have projected a much slower growth of world demand from 0–10 mbd. Of this amount, OPEC is likely to supply 0–5 mbd, with non-OPEC supplies increasing by 4–5 mbd. Under these altered projections, Mexican supplies figure even more importantly in world oil markets and could have a considerable impact on future world oil prices.

The price benefits of Mexican oil supplies would be available to the United States whether or not Mexico exported the oil predominantly to the United States. Security benefits, on the other hand, would depend on the oil coming to the United States. The United States would have to make a judgment of how stable supplies of oil would be from Mexico compared with other suppliers. This judgment in turn would depend upon the stability of domestic and foreign policies in Mexico compared with other suppliers. Foreign policy considerations may favor Mexico because it is not located in a region of massive instabilities, as is the Persian Gulf. On the other hand, all-out oil production in Mexico is likely to place great strain on Mexican domestic stability, making security benefits somewhat less certain. Moreover, to achieve the highest levels of production, Mexico may require foreign oil company assistance, meaning essentially U.S. oil company assistance, although some opportunity might exist for disguising these activities or for diversifying foreign assistance (for example, British companies). This could exacerbate domestic tensions as well as expose Western oil companies and their governments to embarrassing entanglements in future domestic political struggles in Mexico.

The principal value of Mexican oil and gas to the United States under this scenario, therefore, may be in terms of price and volume, rather than security. The United States would refrain from direct forms of assistance to minimize U.S. visibility and resulting unrest in Mexico, while the United States would show its appreciation for indirect energy benefits largely in other areas, such as trade concessions or compromises on the illegal immigration question. A special relationship of this sort would be compatible with U.S. alliance relations, as U.S. concessions would not be bartered directly for oil (the sort of special relationship we have nominally opposed in the case of our European and Japanese allies but, of course, practiced ourselves indirectly with Saudi Arabia and with Iran under the shah). This relationship also would not represent a departure from U.S. policies toward OPEC, especially Saudi Arabia. On the other hand, this scenario would do nothing to reduce U.S. dependence on Middle East oil, as Mexican oil might go to other countries rather than to the United States. It might also lead to increased tension between Mexico and OPEC, as well as the Friends of OPEC, if Mexico increased output to the point where additions to world supplies noticeably depressed prices.

2. High U.S. Need/Low Mexican Production. In this case, the value of Mexican oil and gas to the United States would seem to be just the reverse of the previous scenario. Mexican production and export would be likely to have little impact on the world volume and price of oil, yet continued U.S. need for oil and gas would probably raise somewhat the value of substituting Mexican oil and gas for vulnerable Arab sources. Moreover, lower production volumes in Mexico would be more consistent with the requirements of domestic stability, improving the prospects of security of supply. Security benefits of Mexican oil and gas might nevertheless remain small, reducing U.S. incentives to offer the same range of concessions in other areas such as trade. Energy assistance to Mexico would also continue to be limited, both because it would be less needed and because the economic benefits most important to the oil companies (assuming security is primarily a government interest) would be smaller. Under this scenario, U.S. relations with the allies might benefit from a reduction of U.S. demand on Middle East oil, but such reduction could also leave the allies feeling even more alone in their exposure to Arab OPEC policies. U.S. relations with OPEC might be slightly strained since Saudi Arabia or other friendly Gulf oil producers could interpret a reduction in U.S. oil dependence as a reduction of broader U.S. foreign policy interests in the Middle East (at least to the extent that these interests derive from our oil dependence). Conversely, Mexico's relations with OPEC and the Friends of OPEC might be improved in comparison with the previous scenario, since Mexican production levels would not pose an important threat to OPEC pricing objectives.

3. Low U.S. Need/High Mexican Production. Given this combination, the United States essentially forgoes the price, volume, and security benefits of Mexican oil and gas, unless Mexico voluntarily exports to the United States. Even in this case, Mexican oil and gas will primarily substitute for other, principally Persian Gulf, sources, as U.S. demand in this scenario is presumed not to be growing significantly. And security of supply may not be improved if Mexican production levels threaten internal stability in Mexico. The beneficiaries in this scenario are principally other oil consumers, Japan and European allies, who profit from the higher world oil volumes, moderated prices, and greater security offered by Mexican exports (these benefits being even greater than in the first scenario because U.S. demand on world supplies is now considerably less). The United States benefits from lower world prices for the oil it continues to import, but domestic programs to convert out of oil and gas reduce the amounts to be imported and raise domestic energy prices well above world levels. The United States may benefit politically from the improved circumstances of its allies, but both the United States and Mexico may also experience increasing tensions with OPEC and Friends of OPEC due to the increasing pressures on oil prices brought about by their respective policies (the one cutting demand and the other increasing supply of world oil). A special relationship between the United States and Mexico in this case would have to be justified largely in terms of U.S. relationships with its allies and/or a U.S.–Mexican and probably broader U.S.–non-OPEC producer alignment to break OPEC.

4. Low U.S. Need/Low Mexican Production. This scenario offers few possibilities for change in present circumstances, although it provides greater justification for a costly domestic effort in the United States to convert to nonoil and nongas alternatives. Under these circumstances, the possibility of a special relationship between Mexico and the United States is worked out best in other, nonenergy areas. Concessions to Mexico in energy (high price for gas, etc.) may still be considered desirable, but the reasons would lie in broader economic or political, not energy, relations.

Conclusion

The scenarios in the previous section dichotomize U.S. and Mexican requirements and, as such, do not allow for the most common type of projection of these requirements, which emphasizes moderate outcomes, namely moderately high or low requirements.[10] This is done, however, for a purpose. Moderate scenarios assume continuity and have accordingly fared rather badly in the turbulent times of the 1970s. The 1980s may be more stable; but to anticipate surprises, it may be useful to think in scenarios that frame a problem rather than ones that project a continuous course. In terms of the matrix used in this essay, U.S.–Mexican energy relations have moved rather rapidly from box 4 before 1973 to box 2 in the mid-1970s to box 1 in the early years of the López Portillo and Carter administrations and, perhaps to box 3 in the early 1980s if trends since 1978 persist. For since 1978, U.S. requirements for oil and gas imports have declined and may continue to do so under price decontrols. Meanwhile, Mexico's production and export of oil have steadily increased. These trends, however, may be no more reliable than earlier ones. A widening of the Iranian-Iraqi war may once again intensify U.S. and world import demands, and a change in administrations in Mexico may bring with it, as has happened so often in the past, a reversal or at least leveling off of previous programs. The phenomenon we are watching may not be a trend at all but a ping-pong ball bouncing rather erratically around the four-cornered framework offered by the scenarios considered in this essay.

Notes

I wish to acknowledge the able research assistance of Gabriel Szekely in the preparation of this essay.

[1] On the negotiations in 1977 to export Mexican gas to the United States, see Richard R. Fagen and Henry R. Nau, "Mexican Gas: The Northern Connection," in Richard R. Fagen, ed., *Capitalism and the State in U.S.–Latin American Relations* (Stanford, Cal.: Stanford University Press, 1979), pp. 382–427. After more than two years of protracted and sometimes contentious negotiations, the United States and Mexico finally signed an agreement in September 1979 to ship 300 million cubic feet of natural gas per day from the Reforma fields to the Texas border at a price of $3.625 per thousand cubic feet. The price is tied to quarterly increases in world crude oil prices but is considerably below the price demanded by Mexico in 1977 (which would now equal some $5–6 per thousand cubic feet). The amount of gas, on the other hand, is considerably less than the 2 billion cubic feet per day the U.S. companies initially desired.

[2] For an optimistic view of these possibilities, see Richard B. Mancke, *Mexican Oil and Natural Gas* (New York: Praeger, 1979). For a more skeptical view, see Fagen and Nau, "Mexican Gas."

[3] See Roger D. Hansen, "The Evolution of U.S.–Mexican Relations: A Sociopolitical Perspective."

[4] This assumes, of course, that Mexico continues to export large amounts of oil to the United States. These amounts dropped in 1980 as Mexico began to diversify its customers, and in December 1980, Mexico announced that it was temporarily cutting oil exports to the United States by one-half because of port backlogs caused by hurricane Jeanne in November 1980. See *Washington Post,* December 6, 1980.

[5] For the low estimate, see Congressional Research Service, Library of Congress, *Mexico's Oil and Gas Policy: An Analysis,* prepared for the Committee on Foreign Relations, U.S. Senate, and the Joint Economic Committee, U.S. Congress (December 1978). For the high estimates, see Mancke, *Mexican Oil and Natural Gas.*

[6] The questions are deliberately phrased from a U.S. perspective, since it would be presumptuous for this analyst to pose the issues as they may be perceived in Mexico.

[7] This may have been one of the factors accounting for the failure of the Carter administration to respond favorably to what some believed was a Mexican offer of a special

relationship in energy when López Portillo, the new Mexican president, visited Washington in February 1977. See Richard A. Nuccio, "The Redefinition of U.S.–Mexican Relations, 1977–1980," prepared for the Second International Seminar of the Centro de Investigación y Docencia Económicas, A.C., Guanajuato, Mexico, July 28–August 1, 1980.

[8] The issue of U.S. oil company involvement in Mexico is an explosive one. In 1938, Mexico carried out the first significant expropriation of foreign oil assets. Independence of U.S. oil companies is thus deeply embedded in the psychology of the Mexican Revolution. Moreover, incidents such as the blowout of the Mexican oil well in the Bay of Campeche in June 1979 reveal the potential for added conflict over U.S. oil company involvement. The U.S. firm Sedco supplied some of the equipment and was involved in the operation of this well.

[9] Since 1976, Mexico's foreign debt has continued to increase, totaling about $35 billion in mid-1979. But Mexico's oil revenues have also increased, particularly as a result of the 130% increase in the price of oil in 1979.

[10] See, for example, the projections in D. Ronfeldt, R. Nehring, and A. Gandara, "Mexico's Petroleum and U.S. Policy: Implications for the 1980s," Rand Corporation, 1980.

Water Problems and Issues Affecting U.S.-Mexican Relations: Policy Options and Alternatives

Albert E. Utton

General Context

Catalytic forces that can be anticipated to raise significant water issues affecting Mexican–U.S. relations are population and economic growth. This growth can be expected to place increased demand upon scarce surface and groundwater resources along much of the 3,100-kilometer border separating the two countries.

Briefly, on the U.S. side we find that the entire Southwest is part of the so-called Sunbelt, and population projections are for continued growth in that area.[1] On the Mexican side of the border, Francisco Alba projects a national population growth rate of 3.2 percent per year, which could mean a doubling of the national population every twenty years. His figures show an even faster growth rate for those Mexican states bordering the U.S.–Mexican frontier, with a 3.6 percent per annum growth rate.[2] These figures are put into even more dramatic relief when compared with the growth rate of India, which is 2.4 percent per annum.[3] In addition, in the Colorado River basin large energy resources are found, and the development of these energy resources will place substantial additional demands upon the limited water resources of that basin, which will, in turn, have transboundary impact upon Mexico.

Surface Water: Quantity and Quality

Colorado River. The 1944 Colorado River Treaty with Mexico quantified the respective shares of Mexico and the United States. The share of Mexico was established at 1.5 million acre-feet per year. This amount of water is to be delivered in accordance with annual schedules formulated by the Mexican section of the International Boundary and Water Commission (IBWC) before the beginning of each calendar year.[4] The schedule for the Mexican allotment includes maximum and minimum amounts to be delivered by the United States during particular months.[5] In the event of "extraordinary drought or serious accident"

212

in the United States, however, minimum amounts may be reduced in the same proportion as are consumptive uses in the United States.[6] This "extraordinary drought" provision is the major remaining water quantity issue.

The generality of the language could lead to substantial problems in times of water shortage. César Sepúlveda observes that these questions "could seriously affect the relations between the two countries" and goes on to illustrate the concern of Mexico:

> The Treaty of 1944 failed to specify whether the drought could occur in the total region served by a river system or only in a portion of it, and also did not define the intensity or duration of the drought. Further, no precise measurement is provided. Such imprecisions give rise to many interesting hypothetical questions. For example, if severe drought conditions do indeed exist in the U.S. during one year, the reduction in consumption would not be immediately calculable, and until such calculations would be made, would Mexico not be entitled to receive her full allotment of water?

A respected American commentator adds, "It takes little imagination . . . to foresee conflict if Mexico's deliveries are ever cut" under the "extraordinary drought" provision.[7]

On the other hand, the water quality problem has been a prime irritant to the peaceful relations of the two countries and is one that each will have to watch closely. The two countries have struggled with this problem through a series of interim agreements that culminated in Minute 242, a binational agreement to constitute a "permanent" solution to the salinity problem. Minute 242 was signed on August 30, 1973, by Ambassadors D. Herrera of Mexico and Joseph Friedkin of the United States. Its most important provision is that the salinity of the water at the Morelos Dam shall be no more than 115 parts per million, plus or minus 30 parts per million above that of the salinity at the Imperial Dam. This, in fact, means that the farmers in the Mexicali Valley of Mexico will be irrigating with water that is no more than 115 parts per million plus or minus 30 parts per million higher than the salinity of the water that their American neighbors in the Imperial Valley across the international boundary receive from the Imperial Dam.

In order to reduce the salinity at the Morelos Dam to the 115 plus or minus 30 parts per million above the salinity at the Imperial Dam, a reverse-osmosis desalting plant near Yuma, Arizona, and a canal through the Santa Clara Slough to the Gulf of California in Mexico are required. The canal is to carry the brine produced by the desalting plant. All of the construction cost is to be borne by the United States.

The other principal elements of the agreement are: (1) "that the

U.S. will support efforts by Mexico to obtain appropriate financing on favorable terms for the improvement and rehabilitation of the Mexicali Valley"; (2) that each country "shall limit pumping of groundwaters in its territory within five miles . . . of the Arizona-Sonora boundary near San Luis to 160,000 acre-feet . . . annually"; (3) that "the United States and Mexico shall consult with each other prior to undertaking any new development of either the surface or the groundwater resources, or undertaking substantial modifications of present developments, in its own territory in the border area that might adversely affect the other country"; and (4) that Minute 242 constitutes a "permanent and definitive solution of the salinity problem."[8]

Nonetheless, there still is potential for water quality questions to arise between the two countries. There is a range of potential water quality effects from energy development in the Colorado River basin, but, as A. Bruce Bishop states, "The water quality problem of most concern to both the U.S. and Mexico is salinity."[9]

The water of the Colorado is the lifeblood of the thirsty southwestern United States and the Mexicali Valley of northwestern Mexico. It presently meets the needs of 15 million people by supplying the water for their cities and for the agriculture, mining, and industrial enterprises within the basin and by supporting the recreational, fishing, and wildlife uses of the river. In addition, that basin is being called upon to meet the nation's energy demands. It has been said that the Colorado River basin is one of the richest storehouses of energy resources in the United States. Within the four states of New Mexico, Arizona, Colorado, and Utah, conservative estimates indicate that there are more than 23.5 billion tons of recoverable coal reserves, of which more than half are of the low-sulfur variety that is in demand for electrical generation. In addition, these four states contain nearly 90 percent of the uranium reserves of the United States, and virtually all of the domestic oil shale reserves are located in Colorado, Wyoming, and Utah.

As Professor Lee Brown and associates point out, "It is an inescapable conclusion that the upper Colorado will play an important role in any U.S. effort to achieve even semi-independence from foreign energy sources."[10]

Numerous projections of energy-related water consumption in the Colorado have been made. The July 1974 "Report on Water for Energy in the Upper Colorado River Basin," prepared by the U.S. Department of the Interior, concluded that "under this set of projections, there could be significant shortages occurring in all states on the upper basin except Wyoming by the year 2000." More recent studies have been less pessimistic. The August 1975–1976 assessment of the U.S. Water Resources Council concludes that "the projected future modified flow of the out-

214

flow point of the region when compared with the delivery requirements to the lower Colorado region implies surplus water still available after the year 2000 for upper basin use."[11] The various projections vary as to when a water crunch might arise in the basin.[12] Technological changes in electrical generation techniques, for example, may affect these figures significantly,[13] but whatever the estimate, there is unanimity that significant additional demands for consumptive use will be placed upon the Colorado River for energy developments.

Because Mexico's allocated share of the waters of the Colorado is a prior obligation under the Colorado River Treaty, one would not anticipate water quantity disputes except in the case of an extreme drought, which would affect both nations under the terms of the treaty. Water quality is another matter, however, and the question of salinity on the Colorado has to be the prime continuing water issue between Mexico and the United States.

Bishop, in his study, says that "the impacts of pollutants on stream quality levels in the upper Colorado River basin are potentially significant in areas of intense energy development."[14] And he goes on to state that "the most pervasive and important water quality problem facing the U.S. and Mexico is salinity. Since the two countries have agreed under Minute 242 on a salinity level for water delivered to Mexico, an important water quality concern is the effect of energy development on the future of salinity levels in the river."[15]

Various studies have attempted to assess potential changes in Colorado River salinity as a consequence of future development, and it generally is agreed that increased energy development will lead to increased consumption and that salt concentrations in the river therefore will rise. This increase can be expected because of reduced amounts of water for dilution. Various strategies have been devised to contain salt releases into the Colorado, and under Minute 242 the desalting plant at Yuma has considerable capacity for taking salt from Colorado River waters, but water and salt mass balance model studies have analyzed the effect of future development of compact waters in the Colorado basin for a variety of alternative energy development futures. Bishop concludes that "the total dissolved solid concentrations are seen to increase below Imperial Dam even though the total salt load in the River is reduced via water diversion for energy. Thus salinity concentrations are affected more by taking water that serves for dilution out of the river than by the removal of salt load from the water."[16]

The Yuma desalting plant has substantial capacity for meeting future salinity increases, but because the projections are for increased salinity concentrations and because the quality of water delivered to Mexico is tied to the quality of water delivered to the Imperial Valley in the United States, there has to be a continuing concern about water quality in the Colorado and, as Bishop concludes, "These effects of future development will have to be considered in the planning and implementation of programs to meet water quantity and quality commitments to Mexico."[17]

Rio Grande. The Rio Grande rises in the Rocky Mountains of Colorado. It then quickly descends to the arid lands of New Mexico where it flows past the Jornado del Muerto before passing on to form the boundary between Texas and the Mexican states of Chihuahua, Coahuila, Nuevo León, and Tamaulipas.[18] The area drained by the Rio Grande can be divided into the upper and lower basins. The upper basin lies between the Colorado headwaters and Fort Quitman, Texas; the lower basin extends from Fort Quitman to the Gulf of Mexico. The Rio Grande has, for centuries, been the giver of life to this water-short region. Disputes inevitably arose as population increased along the river valley.

These disputes led to the 1906 Rio Grande Irrigation Convention, which provided an amicable solution by quantifying the Mexican share of the flow of the upper basin. Under the treaty of 1906 the United States is obligated to deliver in perpetuity to Mexico 60,000 acre-feet each year in the bed of the Rio Grande.[19] Deliveries of this water are distributed throughout the year, pursuant to an agreed schedule,[20] without cost to Mexico.[21] The United States pays the cost of storing the water in a dam at Engle, New Mexico, now known as Elephant Butte Dam.[22] There is an escape clause that allows the amount delivered to Mexico to be reduced in the same proportions that deliveries to the United States are reduced, in the event of a serious drought or accidental failure of supply in the United States.[23]

Then, in 1944, the waters of the lower basin were allocated, after nearly a half century of discussions and intermittent negotiations, by the Rio Grande, Colorado, and Tijuana Treaty of 1944.

Some 1,900 kilometers of the boundary between Mexico and the United States are formed by the Rio Grande. All but 160 kilometers of this river boundary is below Fort Quitman and is thus in the lower Rio Grande basin.[24] Drainage from Mexico accounts for 70 percent of the water flowing in the lower Rio Grande, and that from the United States contributes approximately 30 percent.[25] The treaty of 1944 allocates the waters of the lower Rio Grande about equally between the two countries.[26] To the United States is allocated all of the waters contributed to the mainstream by the principal U.S. tributaries below Fort Quitman;[27] one-half of the flow in the main channel of the Rio Grande below the lowest major international storage dam; one-third of the flow into the mainstream from the principal Mexican tributaries above Sal-

216

ineno, Texas,[28] which is guaranteed by Mexico to average at least 350,000 acre-feet per year over a five-year period;[29] and one-half of all other waters flowing into the main channel of the Rio Grande, except for water coming from the San Juan and Alamo rivers and any return flow coming from land irrigated by these two rivers.[30]

Mexico is not guaranteed any of the flow of the principal U.S. tributaries below Fort Quitman. It receives two-thirds of the flow of the principal Mexican tributaries above Salineno, Texas; all of the waters reaching the main channel from the San Juan and Alamo rivers; and one-half of all other flows occurring in the main channel of the Rio Grande.[31] Thus, although the larger portion of the water of the Rio Grande below Fort Quitman comes from Mexican tributaries, the United States receives about one-half of all the water of the river.[32] These allocations and their administration by the International Boundary and Water Commission have been a model of international cooperation.

Quality: Although water quality problems in the Rio Grande have not reached the point that they did on the Colorado prior to the negotiation of Minute 242, there certainly is potential for increasing water quality concern as population and economic development increase along the Rio Grande on both sides of the border. John Hernandez concludes that the "quality of the surface flow of the Rio Grande is of great interest both to the U.S. and Mexico, and it is important that analytical studies on historical water quality records be carried on so as to detect changes in quality before serious adverse effects occur."[33]

Groundwater

The heaviest groundwater users in the United States are the states contiguous to Mexico;[34] and yet, paradoxically, the law and institutions of the border states are woefully inadequate to control the exploitation of their groundwater resources.[35] In addition, international competence over aquifers divided by the frontier is largely undefined; it is fair to say that the legal and institutional situation is chaotic.[36] None of the border states

> has adequate legislation or regulations for the protection and management of diminishing supplies within the state and along the border areas. New Mexico has the only public control system, but regulations under it do not contemplate joint controls in the area of the border. Arizona and Texas have virtually no controls except voluntary ones, and the California law is beholden to similar rules of capture which do little to discourage excessive pumping and waste.[37]

217

In contrast to the legal situation on the U.S. side of the frontier, Mexico does have legal authority to control groundwater withdrawals. The national government, through the Secretariat of Water Resources, can regulate extraction, and the secretary on his own initiative can establish prohibited groundwater zones if existing developments or the aquifer are in danger of being adversely affected,[38] or if it is otherwise in the public interest.

Coincident with the near legal vacuum, significant population increases are projected on both sides of the border, making it reasonable to anticipate that there will be increasing investment in groundwater facilities and accelerating demand placed on groundwater resources bisected by the international boundary between the two countries.[39] The coming together of these two factors could be described as a collision course. With increased demand for a limited resource, combined with a striking absence of institutions for either resolving disputes or managing the resource, the potential for dispute between the two countries has to be something more than imaginary.[40]

The Legal Context. The situation of a near legal vacuum is not unique to the U.S.–Mexican frontier, as it is only recently that much attention has been directed to groundwater resources. Robert D. Hayton observes that "traditionally there has been a failure to focus on the regulation and management of ground water in most legal systems."[41] Robert Emmet Clark adds that "legislative attention to the physical relationship between surface and ground water sources is scarcely older than the concern for pollution."[42] It has been, in fact, a question of being out of sight and out of mind. The primary attention of domestic water law has been focused on surface water, and there is an almost complete lack of groundwater practice at the international level. There are some treaties, such as the agreement between Poland and the U.S.S.R., signed at Warsaw on July 17, 1964,[43] that refer to groundwaters. That treaty came into force on February 16, 1965, by an exchange of the instruments of ratification at Moscow and, in a general way, includes groundwaters "intersected by the state frontier" in frontier waters.[44] There is also Minute 242 between the United States and Mexico, which limits pumping on both sides of the frontier in the Yuma area,[45] and the International Boundary and Water Commission has dealt successfully with groundwater problems on a pragmatic, ad hoc basis; but, by and large, groundwaters have not been a matter of concern at the international level. As in the case of groundwaters generally, "it is more a case of non-management than of mismanagement."[46]

Ludwik Teclaff points out that frequently groundwater has not been included in the established surface-water law regime: "It was thought quite adequate to treat groundwater either as part of the land . . . or as a commodity, susceptible of ownership through the act of capturing it by sinking a well."[47] Under Spanish law, for example, which has influenced the groundwater law in Latin America and the Philippines, "groundwaters had traditionally belonged to the owner of the super-adjacent land."[48] English common law also has given absolute ownership of groundwaters to the superadjacent property owner. Wells Hutchins stated that the English common law doctrine

> in its original form . . . accords exclusive property rights in the water to the land owner; it gives him any quantity, for any legitimate enterprise, either on or off the overlying land; . . . but if the effect of heavy pumping by a land owner, while engaged in any legitimate enterprise, . . . is to exhaust the groundwater supply of his neighbor by drawing all the ground-water from the substratum of the latter's tract into his own heavily pumped well, it cannot become the ground of an ac-tion.[49]

Texas follows the English common law theory, and the Texas law of groundwater has been summarized as "You can steal your neighbor's water, but you can't pollute his well."[50]

It has been suggested that "the problem, then, is to fashion a legal regime and a management machinery"[51] that will be integrated in order to achieve the optimum sustained yield of a nation's or a region's total water resources.

The Economic Context. Under the common law doctrine, each owner's right to the water itself, or the right to use the water, is insecure because other pumpers may take possession of the mobile resource at any time.[52] Accordingly, the individual surface owner is encouraged to exploit the groundwater resource as quickly as possible, so that the fluid and mobile water resource will not be captured by others. S. J. Ciriacy-Wantrup points out: "The definitive property rights belong only to those who are in possession—that is, who gets there 'fustest with the mostest.' Every user tries to protect himself against others by acquiring ownership through capture in the fastest possible way. Deferred use is always subject to great uncertainty; others may capture the resource in the meantime."[53] Terrance S. Veeman adds that "in the absence of effective social institutions to guide resource use, private groundwater use can be predicted eventually to generate excessive investment and extraction costs; induce a pumping rate which is greater than socially optimal, and which may lead to irreversible depletion; dissipate economic rent or producer surplus, and in general create economic waste and resource inefficiency."[54] This situation leads to great insecurity for all existing users of water from an aquifer, although the concepts of "security" and "flexibility" are essential criteria for an adequate water rights system.[55] Underlying the concept of physical security is the premise that holders of groundwater rights must have a reasonable degree of certainty—the supply of water must not be unreasonably uncertain. Ordinarily, the physical supply of groundwater is more secure than surface water, because the aquifer frequently stores water in seasons and years of heavy rain and above-average recharge that can be used in seasons or years of lower rainfall and lower recharge.

In addition, however, there is the factor of tenure security. "Tenure security" refers not to reliability of supply but to the effect of human actions on the reliability of supply, that is, the security of the landowner from the unreasonable use or export of groundwater by his neighbor. The common law rule of absolute ownership obviously increases tenure insecurity because it countenances the unrestrained right of one's neighbor to pump all the water he may need, without restraint or liability to other overlying owners for any adverse effects of his pumping. This has the economic effect of stimulating investment in groundwater development because of the uncertainty of one's property right over this "fugitive resource."[56] There is an incentive to each landowner to protect himself against his neighbor's lawful acts by capturing as much of the resource as quickly as possible. Therefore, there is an economic incentive for overinvestment and for depletion rather than for conservation of the resource.

This conceptual approach has been elaborated on by Maurice Kelso, William Martin, and Lawrence Mack:

> Two aspects of water rights most significant for an understanding of men's behavior relative to water and to one another over water are: (1) . . . that whatever rights they hold to water and its use will be stable and dependable over time, and (2) the flexibility permitted to them to effect changes in use and location of use of the water covered by their rights, and to acquire and transfer water rights from and to others. . . . Security and flexibility are the twin essences of socially efficient property relations."[57]

Veeman points out that "the indefiniteness of property rights associated with a fugitive resource such as groundwater leads to its rapid development and, perhaps, depletion."[58]

Specifically, in regard to the situation along the U.S.–Mexican border, it cannot be said that water users have security in their expectations, nor can it be said that whatever rights they hold to water and its use will be stable and dependable over time. Quite the contrary, there are

(1) projections for growing population along both sides of the border, (2) a situation in which no state north of the border (with the exception of New Mexico) has legal institutions adequate to control pumping, and (3) no international control except at Yuma under the interim arrangement of Resolution 5 of Minute 242,[59] which can prevent either nation from "stealing its neighbor's water."[60] Therefore, a situation exists that encourages each nation to outdo its neighbor by developing its groundwater resources as rapidly as possible, perhaps even to the point of depletion of the groundwater resource. The legal situation encourages overdevelopment; overdevelopment results in overinvestment in developing the resource, and therefore both economic waste and resource waste are likely due to the insecurity arising from inadequate institutional controls.

Alternative Institutional Opportunities. In suggesting possible institutional arrangements for the management of transboundary resources between the United States and Mexico, it is necessary to consider, in addition to the twin criteria of security and flexibility, the goal of avoiding conflict between the two countries and the fundamental goal of the public interest in providing for an orderly development of groundwater supplies, in the interest of the best utilization of this natural resource.

A system should be devised that will reduce the likelihood of water users on one side of the international boundary adversely affecting water users on the other side of the boundary, thereby causing conflict between the two countries.

Management Options. The first option would be to leave the situation largely as it is, following the essentially laissez-faire English common law doctrine allowing each country on each side of the boundary to use and exploit the groundwater resources on its respective side as it sees fit, without regard to its neighbor. This would lead to (1) neither of the water users having security in that resource, (2) uneconomic development of the resource by encouraging overly rapid development, (3) increased marginal cost to all exploiters of the resource, and (4) encouragement of the depletion of the resource. It, therefore, would not provide the security essential to a good groundwater system. Further, at some point it inevitably would lead to conflict between the two countries which, if not settled amicably by agreement, might be taken to the International Court of Justice or an arbitration tribunal. This scenario is not an attractive one. Friction between the two countries and potential for conflict would be raised to undesirable levels, and the economic waste caused by overrapid development already would have occurred, as well as undoubtedly substantial damage to the groundwater resources due to excessive withdrawals. In addition, it always is hard to assess the perils and uncertainties of resort to litigation.

Variation A (equitable apportionment). There is a spectrum of possible variations on the option of establishing institutional mechanisms for managing the resource. One would be to grant the IBWC the following powers: (1) jurisdiction over groundwaters intersected by the international boundary; (2) comprehensive authority to make the engineering studies necessary to determine such information as the area, depth of water, aquifer thickness, volume, quality, quantity, anticipated yields, transmissibility, and recharge rate of an aquifer (IBWC could determine allowable levels of withdrawal in order to maintain a sustained yield from the aquifer or a calculated mining plan; it should be noted that the IBWC already is gathering this type of information); (3) responsibility to identify and declare designated international groundwater areas that have reasonably ascertainable boundaries; and (4) authority to apportion the waters of the aquifer and close the area to withdrawals beyond the allowable as determined by the physical criteria of the aquifer.

This approach would follow roughly the current practice of the state of New Mexico, in which the state engineer has jurisdiction over declared basins that have "reasonably ascertainable boundaries"[61] and has power to close these declared basins to further withdrawals.[62] The IBWC, rather than waiting for developments to reach the point at which a safe yield of the aquifer was threatened, could apportion in advance the groundwaters intersected by the boundary on its own initiative. Alternative methods conceivably could be suggested as guidelines in calculating the division: (1) the amount of water that each nation would receive could be based upon the amount of recoverable water underlying each nation; or (2) the amount of water could be based upon the relative surface areas of each nation overlying the water—each nation would receive the proportionate share of the groundwater that its surface area reflected in proportion to the total surface area overlying the aquifer. Both of these approaches would require much more study.[63] There is, in fact, some international practice in apportioning shared petroleum resources.[64]

Once the division of the groundwater was made, regardless of the method followed in arriving at the division determination, the internal administrative water machinery of each nation would be responsible for allocating that nation's share of the aquifer according to its water laws and administrative procedures. This would have the advantage of providing security for investment in water resources on each side of the border. It would prevent the possibility of pumping wars, because each

222

side would know with certainty the amount of water to which it was entitled. Further, the resource would not be threatened through uncontrolled exploitation, and the potential for conflict between the two countries would be reduced.

Variation B (case-by-case negotiation). Granting the IBWC the power to identify and declare "designated international groundwater areas" and the authority to apportion the waters of such designated aquifers will be controversial and undoubtedly strongly opposed. The difficulty in obtaining such a treaty cannot be overestimated. Therefore, a less far-reaching option would be a case-by-case or aquifer-by-aquifer approach. Individual agreements would be negotiated for each groundwater area as problems arose, using a variety of engineering and legal measures, including the negotiated apportionment of the waters of the aquifer. This approach would very possibly vary from basin to basin, and agreements, therefore, would have to be reached by treaty on a basin-to-basin basis. This could be termed the pragmatic, case-by-case approach—pragmatic both politically and technically. This is in fact a description of the present state of affairs, for example, pumping in the Yuma area was dealt with in Minute 242, which limited pumping within eight kilometers of the border to 160,000 acre-feet per year. The IBWC is carrying on a data exchange program and an aerial surveillance program to identify groundwater developments and potential trouble spots. The IBWC is keenly aware of possible stress points such as in Ciudad Juárez–El Paso, Nogales, and the Colorado delta areas.

The problem with such a basin-to-basin and treaty-to-treaty approach is that problems such as these are so difficult to get on the national agenda that they tend to be shelved until a crisis is reached. If it were politically possible, it would be desirable to give the IBWC continuing authority to designate groundwater areas and, therefore, control withdrawals before the crisis point has been reached.

Variation C (comprehensive management). A third variation of the management option would be to give the IBWC the complete spectrum of administrative powers from investigation and planning to rule making and enforcement. This would put it not only into the investigative, engineering, and planning fucntions but also into the regulatory and enforcement end of the administrative process. This, perhaps, would be the ideal approach, but it is the least likely to be accepted. It would empower the IBWC to control withdrawals and thereby preserve the resource, providing security to water users at the time. It also would allow the IBWC to plan for and carry out policies that would be responsive to changing conditions. Undoubtedly this would be objected to as the creation of a superagency and would expose the IBWC to the criticism and controversy caused by an international agency being placed

223

in the business of enforcement inside the domestic boundaries of a sovereign nation.

International Litigation. Whichever of the above options, or combinations of options, might be chosen, it undoubtedly would be better for the two countries to reach agreement on a binational basis rather than to allow the problem to become so intense as to require litigation before the International Court of Justice or a tribunal of arbitration,[65] with all of the perils, uncertainties, and delay that litigation entails.[66]

The problem, succinctly stated, is that there is a limited supply of groundwater along this international frontier and that both the United States and Mexico are facing the prospect of greater demand because of increased population. It would be highly desirable to anticipate the situation before it reaches crisis proportions. The United States and Mexico should, by agreement, establish the means for managing the resource and avoiding damaging disputes between the two countries. Resolution 5 of Minute 242 contemplates such an agreement.[67]

The courts, too, undoubtedly would prefer that the parties settle the matter between themselves rather than resort to litigation. For an example of judicial attitudes involving interstate disputes, the Court, in *Colorado* v. *Kansas*,[68] reflected that "the reason for judicial caution in adjudicating the relative rights of States in such cases is that . . . they involve the interests of quasi-sovereigns, . . . of interstate differences of a like nature, that such mutual accommodation and agreement should, if possible, be the medium of settlement, instead of the invocation of our adjudicatory power."[69]

Ward Fischer concludes that, in regard to interstate groundwater problems in the United States, there are "two apparently viable alternatives . . . .: the interstate compact, and litigation between the states."[70] He is pessimistic, however, in his assessment of the likelihood that the states can reach agreement before the crisis point is reached and resort has to be made to the courts:

> Our conclusion must be that the interstate compact is by far the most effective, most sound, most flexible, and overall most satisfactory approach that can be recommended. Regrettably, our conclusions must also be that, between these two alternatives, it is also the less likely; that litigation between the states resulting in equitable apportionment of available ground waters can be expected, unless there is an unprecedented awakening to responsibility and to reality among the water users and water administrators of the affected states.[71]

The record of dealing with joint water problems between the United States and Mexico is a good one and leaves some room for hope, perhaps even optimism, that Mexico and the United States may be able to handle the problem in advance by agreement rather than by resort to international litigation. "In any event, we must expect that our international conflicts will not be limited to surface waters, but rather that, sooner or later, we must grapple with the depletion and pollution of international waters."[72]

In the event a groundwater question between Mexico and the United States resulted in litigation, the court undoubtedly would conclude that a nation does not have absolute territorial sovereignty and that it cannot act in disregard of its neighbor.[73]

In the interstate water litigation between Wyoming and Colorado, the U.S. Supreme Court reached an analogous conclusion:

> The contention of Colorado that she, as a State, rightfully may divert and use, as she may choose, the waters flowing within her boundaries in this interstate stream, regardless of any prejudice that this may work to others having rights in the stream below her boundary, cannot be maintained. The river throughout its course in both States is but a single stream, wherein each State has an interest which should be respected by the other.[74]

The International Court, if given the case by agreement of the parties, no doubt also would look with favor upon the language of the Supreme Court[75] in a suit by Kansas against Colorado for equitable apportionment of the Arkansas River:

> Whenever . . . the action of one State reaches through the agency of natural laws into the territory of another State, the question of the extent and the limitations of the rights of the two States becomes a matter of justiciable dispute between them, and this court is called upon to settle that dispute in such a way as will recognize the equal rights of both and at the same time establish justice between them.[76]

The much quoted *International Trail Smelter* case, although dealing with air pollution, also would be relevant, for it states "that, under the principles of international law, . . . no State has the right to use or permit the use of its territory in such a manner as to cause injury by fumes in or to the territory of another . . . when the case is of serious consequence and the injury is established by clear and convincing evidence."[77] Thus, an international tribunal would probably reject the international law equivalent of the common law doctrine—absolute territorial sovereignty. It would, instead, look to the 1966 Helsinki rules for guidance in settling a case on the basis of equitable utilization.[78]

The problem with litigation is that the question is referred to the court as a last resort when the crisis already has been reached. The courts deal in a case-by-case, after-the-fact manner and are not in a position to anticipate the problem and to engage in the long-term planning and management of the resource that is desirable if optimum use is to be achieved. As the Supreme Court said in *Colorado* v. *Kansas*,[79] water cases "present complicated and delicate questions, and due to the possibility of future change of conditions, necessitate expert administration rather than judicial imposition of a hard and fast rule."[80]

Conclusions. Of the various alternatives, perhaps the option most likely to be accepted would be a compromise position between the utopian international commission, with the complete panoply of powers from investigation and planning to regulation and enforcement, and the existing status quo. A relatively objective and, therefore, perhaps acceptable approach would be one that provided the means for an equitable apportionment of transboundary groundwaters, leaving the actual planning, distribution, regulations, and enforcement of each country's share to that country.

Ward Fischer, in discussing interstate compacts, has stated that one of the basic decisions

> required in the development of any particular compact is that between allocation v. management. Should the compact provide that each state is allocated a specific quantity of water? Or, on the other hand, should the states agree that the water resource is one that should be subject to year-to-year to decade-to-decade management, without specific quantities of water allocated to the participating states? Allocation in absolute quantities or in percentages is the simplest solution. Management is no doubt the best, allowing, for example, planned recharging of the undergroundwater resource for the ultimate greater benefit of all of the states.[81]

The allocation option is likely to be the simplest for international groundwaters as well. Specifically, this has been the model followed in the case of surface waters shared by the United States and Mexico where the waters of the Rio Grande and the Colorado have been divided by quantity, leaving the actual administration of each country's amount to each representative country.[82]

Notes

[1] See Carpenter and Blackwood, "The Potential for Population Growth in the Counties that Border Mexico: El Paso to San Diego," *Natural Resources Journal* 17 (1977): 545; and Henry W. Ayer and Paul G. Hoyt, "Industrial Growth in the U.S. Border Communities and Associated Water and Air Problems: An Economic Perspective," ibid., p. 585.

[2] See Francisco Alba, *La Póblacion de México: evolución y dilemas* (El Colegio de México, 1977). It is anticipated that the 1980 census will show a decline in those figures.

[3] Environmental Fund, *1978 World Population Estimates,* August 1978.

[4] Colorado River Treaty, Arts. 10 and 15.

[5] Ibid., Art. 15A, schedule I.

[6] Ibid., Art. 10.

[7] César Sepúlveda, "Instituciones para la solución de problemas de superficie entre México y los Estados Unidos," *Natural Resources Journal* 18 (1978): 131,140. Also see Charles V. Meyers, "The Colorado River," *Stanford Law Review* 19 (1967): 367–411.

[8] See Herbert Brownell and Samuel Eaton, "The Colorado River Salinity Problem with Mexico," *American Journal of International Law* 69 (1975): 255.

[9] A. Bruce Bishop, "Impact of Energy Development on Colorado River Water Quality," *Natural Resources Journal* 17 (1977): 649, 669.

[10] F. Lee Brown et al., "Some Remarks on Energy Related Water Issues in the Upper Colorado River Basin," *Natural Resources Journal* 17 (1977): 635.

[11] U.S. Water Resources Council, "75 Water Resources Assessment, Specific Problem Analysis, Upper Colorado Region," Tech. memo. no. 2, p. 46 (August 1976).

[12] See Gary Weatherford and Gordon Jacoby, "Impact of Energy Development on the Law of the Colorado River," *Natural Resources Journal* 15 (1975): 171.

[13] Brown, "Some Remarks," p. 637.

[14] Bishop, "Impact of Energy Development," p. 655.

[15] Ibid., p. 661.

[16] Ibid.

[17] Ibid.

[18] See National Resources Commitee, *Regional Planning, Part VI: The Rio Grande Joint Investigation in the Upper Rio Grande Basin in Colorado, New Mexico, and Texas,* vols. 1 and 2 (1938). For a vivid and romantic account of the Rio Grande, see Paul Horgan, *Great River: The Rio Grande in North American History,* rev. ed. (New York: Holt, Rinehart, and Winston, 1960).

[19] Rio Grande Irrigation Convention with Mexico, May 21, 1906, 34 Stat. 2953, T.S. 455, Art. I.

[20] Ibid., Art. II.

[21] Ibid., Art. III.

[22] Ibid.

[23] Ibid., Art. II.

[24] Ibid., subsection 152.1.

[25] U.S. Congress, Senate, Committee on Foreign Relations, *Hearings,* 79th Congress, 1st session, 1945. See also Royce Tipton, in Six States Committee, *Engineering Memorandum on Treaty with Mexico Relating to the Utilization of the Waters of Certain Rivers* (1943), 2:74.

[26] Senate Committee on Foreign Relations, *Hearings,* p. 29.

[27] Colorado River Treaty, Art. 4B(a): "All of the waters reaching the main channel of the Rio Grande (Rio Bravo) from the Pecos and Devils Rivers, Goodenough Spring, and Alamito, Terlingua, San Felipe and Pinto Creeks." Also see Senate, Committee on Foreign Relations, *Hearings,* p. 1809.

[28] The primary tributaries are the Conchos, San Diego, San Rodrigo, Escondido, and Salado rivers and Las Vacas Arroyo. Tipton, in Six States, *Engineering Memorandum,* 2: 74, 75.

[29] There is a saving clause that permits Mexico to make up any deficiency in one five-year cycle in the next five-year cycle if the deficiency was caused by "extraordinary drought or serious accident." Colorado River Treaty, Art. 4B(d).

[30] Ibid., Arts. 4A, 4B.

[31] Ibid., Art. 4A.

[32] Senate, Committee on Foreign Relations, *Hearings*, p. 1809.

[33] John Hernandez, "Interrelationship of Ground and Surface Water Quality in the El Paso-Juárez and Mesilla Valleys," *Natural Resources Journal* 18 (1978): 1, 8.

[34] Robert Emmet Clark, "Institutional Alternatives for Managing Groundwater Resources," *Natural Resources Journal* 18 (1978): 153–55.

[35] Barbara Burman and Thomas Cornish, "Needed: A Groundwater Treaty Between the United States and Mexico," *Natural Resources Journal* 15 (1975): 385, 388–91.

[36] It has to be noted, however, that the International Boundary and Water Commission has done a remarkable job of resolving groundwater problems to date with a minimum of treaty mandate or international practice as precedent.

[37] Clark, "Institutional Alternatives," pp. 155–56.

[38] Ludwik Teclaff, "Abstraction and Use of Water: A Comparison of Legal Regimes," U.N. Doc. ST/ECH/152 62 (1972). See *Constitución Política*, Art. 27 (Mexico).

[39] See Francisco Alba, "Condiciones y políticas económicas en la frontera norte de México," *Natural Resources Journal* 17 (1977): 571; Michael Bradley and Kenneth De Cook, "Ground Water Occurrence and Utilization in the Arizona-Sonora Border Regions," *Natural Resources Journal* 18 (1978): 29; J.C. Day, "International Aquifer Management: The Hueco Bolson on the Rio Grande," *Natural Resources Journal* 18 (1978): 163.

[40] The metropolitan area of Ciudad Juárez, Chihuahua, and El Paso, Texas, for example, has nearly 1 million inhabitants. Both cities depend largely upon shared groundwater reservoirs for municipal water supplies. Studies indicate that both sides now are pumping water at a rate faster than the groundwater reservoir is being recharged. See Day, "Aquifer Management," pp. 168–69.

[41] Robert D. Hayton, "The Ground Water Legal Regime as Instrument of Policy Objectives and Management Requirements," in *Annales Juris Aquarum*, Second International Conference on Water Law and Administration, Caracas, Venezuela, February 8–14, 1976, 2: 272, 275.

[42] Clark, "Western Ground Water Law," in *Waters and Water Rights,* ed. R. Clark (Indianapolis: Allen Smith Co., 1972), 5: 411, sec. 440.

[43] Agreement Concerning the Use of Water Resources in Frontier Waters, July 17, 1964, Poland–U.S.S.R., no. 8054, 552 U.N.T.S. 188 (1966).

[44] Ibid., Art. 2, n. 2.

[45] Text of IBWC Minute No. 242, in U.S. Department of State, *Bulletin* 69 (1973): 395, 396, res. 5; reprinted in *Natural Resources Journal* 15 (1975): 2, 6.

[46] Hayton, "Ground Water," p. 284.

[47] Teclaff, "Abstraction," p. 57.

[48] Hayton, "Ground Water," p. 278.

[49] Wells Hutchins, "Reasonable Beneficial Use in the Development of Ground Water Law in the West," in *Ground Water Economics and the Law*, Western Agriculture Economic Research Council Committee on Economics of Water Resources Development, Report no. 5 (1956), p. 24.

[50] Roger Tyler, "Underground Water Regulation in Texas," *Texas Bar Journal* 39 (1976): 532–33.

[51] Hayton, "Ground Water," p. 293.

[52] See S. J. Ciriacy-Wantrup, *Resource Conservation, Economics, and Policies,* 3d ed. (University of California, Division of Agricultural Sciences, Agricultural Experiment Station: Berkeley, 1968), pp. 141–45.

[53] Ibid., p. 142.

[54] Terrance S. Veeman, "Water Policy and Water Institutions in Northern India: The Case of Ground Water Rights," *Natural Resources Journal* 18 (1978): 569.

[55] S. J. Ciriacy-Wantrup, "Concepts Used as Economic Criteria for a System of Water Rights," in *Economics and Public Policy in Water Resource Development*, ed. S. Smith and E. Castle (Ames, Iowa: Iowa State University Press, 1964), pp. 251–71.

[56] Ibid., pp. 258–60.

[57] Maurice Kelso, William Martin, and Lawrence Mack, *Water Supplies and Economic Growth in an Arid Environment: An Arizona Case Study* (Tucson, Arizona: University of Arizona Press, 1973), pp. 52, 54.

[58] Veeman, "Water Policy."

[59] Text of IBWC Minute No. 242, in Department of State, *Bulletin* 69: 396, res. 5.

[60] Tyler, "Underground Water," p. 532.

[61] New Mexico Stat. Ann., sec. 75-11-1 (1968). This proposal is not unlike the 1973 Oklahoma statute, Okla. Stat. Ann. tit. 82, sec. 1020.5 (West Supp. 1977), which proposed to assign each landowner a specific quantity of water based on a percentage of the hydrologically determined yield of the basin. His allocation is to be measured acre for acre by the relationship his ownership bears to the total acreage overlying the basin. Under this system each landowner receives a quota, as it were, which he can retain or dispose of and which will exhaust his interest. Robert Emmet Clark, "The Role of State Legislation in Ground Water Management," *Creighton Law Review* 10 (1977): 469, 482.

[62] For further discussion, see Robert Emmet Clark, "New Mexico Water Law since 1955," *Natural Resources Journal* 2 (1962): 484, 496.

[63] The formula for division might be a variation of the correlative rights prorationing formula: each country would have a share of the underlying water in proportion to the amount of its land supplied by the groundwater source within the designated groundwater area as compared with the total area supplied by the groundwater source. This approach, designed for agricultural uses, does not comfortably suit an urban situation or mixed agricultural-urban context. A corollary formula might be that each country would have a share of the underlying water in proportion to the amount of water presently being beneficially used by it as compared with the water being beneficially used by the other country. This would appear to have serious objections in that it would freeze the future use patterns in conformance to existing patterns. The division also could be based upon the guidelines of the Helsinki rules regarding surface waters.

[64] William T. Onorato, "Apportionment of an International Common Petroleum Deposit," *International & Comparative Law Quarterly* 17 (1968): 97–98.

[65] Inter-American Arbitration Treaty with Other American Republics, January 5, 1929, 49 Stat. 3153, 3158, T.S. no. 886, p. 6 (effective April 16, 1935). For a discussion of the agreement, see Charles Meyers and Richard Noble, "The Colorado River: The Treaty with Mexico," *Stanford Law Review* 19 (1967): 367, 400–402.

[66] For a comprehensive discussion of dispute settlements ranging from "referral to government" to arbitration and the International Court of Justice, see "Management of International Water Resources: Institutional and Legal Aspects," U.N. Doc. ST/ESA/5 144 (1975).

[67] Text of IBWC Minute No. 242, in Department of State, *Bulletin* 69: 396, res. 5.

[68] 320 US 383 (1943).

[69] Ibid., 392.

[70] Ward Fischer, "Management of Interstate Groundwater," *Natural Resources Law* 7 (1974): 546.

[71] Ibid.

[72] Ibid., p. 545.

[73] Albert E. Utton, "International Streams and Lakes," in *Waters and Water Rights*, ed. Clark (1967), 2: 422.

[74] Wyoming v. Colorado, 259 US 419, 466 (1922). See Wyoming v. Colorado, 286 US 494 (1952).

[75] Report of International Arbitral Awards, supra 1964 (1949), reproduced in *American Journal of International Law* 35 (1941): 684, 716.

[76] Kansas v. Colorado, 206 US 46, 97–98 (1907).

[77] Reports of International Arbitral Awards, p. 716.

[78] The Helsinki Rules on the Uses of the Waters of International Rivers, Art. 5, in *Management of International Water Resources: Institutional and Legal Aspects,* U.N. Doc. ST/ESA/5 188–89 (1975).

[79] 320 US 383 (1943).

[80] Ibid., p. 392.

[81] Fischer, "Management," p. 532.

[82] Norris Hundley, *Dividing the Waters* (Berkeley: University of California Press, 1966); César Sepúlveda, *La frontera norte de México* (1976); Charles Meyers, "The Colorado Basin," in *The Law of International Drainage Basins,* ed. Albert Garretson, Robert Hayton, and Cecil Olmstead (Dobbs Ferry, N.Y.: Oceana Publications, 1967), pp. 486–607; "Streams and Lakes," sec. 152.2.

Part
Three

Mexican Development

Economic Development Policy in Mexico: A New Penchant for Planning

Calvin P. Blair

The Present State of Development

Size, Growth, and Structure. By any absolute measure, Mexico is a very large country. Its nearly 2 million-square-kilometer area (one fifth that of the United States) makes it thirteenth in the world in geographic size. Its 67 million people in 1978 made it the eleventh most populous nation (larger than West Germany), and its gross national product (GNP) of $67.6 billion in 1976 ranked it as the world's eighteenth largest economy (see table 1). Mexico's per capita GNP of $1,090 in 1976 placed it well into the upper reaches of the World Bank's "middle-income countries."[1]

The three decades from 1910 to 1940 were a turbulent period of revolution and reform in Mexico, and real output grew slowly; but between 1940 and 1978, real gross domestic product (GDP) increased almost tenfold, an average rate of growth of 6.2 percent per year, well ahead of the population growth rate of 3.3 percent. Total productivity rose at a healthy 3.2 percent annually, reflecting the combined effects of growing productivity in *all* sectors and the shift in *relative* employment from agriculture to industry and services (see table 2).

The economy has undergone major structural transformation. Agriculture has declined in relative importance, from 21 percent of GDP to 9 percent, while industry has grown. Manufacturing has increased from about 19 percent of total output in 1940 to 23 percent in 1978, and its composition has shifted significantly. To modernizing facilities in light manufactures (food, beverages, tobacco, textiles, clothing, shoes, and paper) have been added contemporary technology plants in iron and steel, petroleum refining, petrochemicals, fertilizers, electrical energy, glass, automobile assembly, and transport equipment.

Mexico is one of the world's successful development "models," a creative society that has generated its own relationships between the public and private sectors, managed the politics of a major social revolution, and become a potent moral force in the third world.

As of 1978, Mexico was among the leading ten or twenty countries in size of labor force and in total use of energy, steel, cement, fertilizers,

233

TABLE 1

MEXICO: RANK AMONG THE WORLD'S LARGEST COUNTRIES, 1976

	Area			Population (mid-1976)			Gross National Product (1976)[a]	
Rank	Country	1,000 km²	Rank	Country	Millions	Rank	Country	$ Billions
1	Soviet Union	22,402	1	China (P.R.C.)	835.8	1	United States	1,698.1
2	Canada	9,976	2	India	620.4	2	Soviet Union	708.2
3	China (P.R.C.)	9,597	3	Soviet Union	256.7	3	Japan	553.1
4	United States	9,363	4	United States	215.1	4	Germany (Fed. R.)	457.5
5	Brazil	8,512	5	Indonesia	135.2	5	France	346.7
6	Australia	7,687	6	Japan	112.8	6	China (P.R.C.)	343.1
7	India	3,288	7	Brazil	110.0	7	United Kingdom	225.2
8	Argentina	2,767	8	Bangladesh	80.4	8	Canada	174.1
9	Sudan	2,506	9	Nigeria	77.1	9	Italy	171.2
10	Algeria	2,382	10	Pakistan	71.3	10	Brazil	125.6
11	Zaire	2,345	11	Mexico	62.0	11	Spain	104.1
12	Saudi Arabia	2,150	12	Germany (Fed. R.)	62.0	12	Poland	98.1
13	Mexico	1,973	13	Italy	56.2	13	India	95.9
14	Indonesia	1,904	14	United Kingdom	56.1	14	Netherlands	85.3
15	Libya	1,760	15	France	52.9	15	Australia	83.4
16	Iran	1,648	16	Vietnam	47.6	16	Sweden	71.3
17	Mongolia	1,565	17	Philippines	43.3	17	Germany (Dem. R.)	70.9
18	Peru	1,285	18	Thailand	43.0	18	Mexico	67.6
19	Chad	1,284	19	Turkey	41.2	19	Belgium	66.7
20	Niger	1,267	20	Egypt	38.1	20	Iran	66.2

[a] Preliminary estimates.

SOURCES: World Bank, *World Bank Atlas* (1977), pp. 27–30; and *World Development Report, 1978,* "Annex-World Development Indicators," pp. 76–77.

rail freight, air travel, motor vehicles, telephones, radios, television, movie theaters, and medical doctors.[2] Its recent oil finds secure its energy future for decades, and it has excellent long-run prospects for alternative energy sources. In the aggregate, Mexico exhibits many key features of a large, modern, industrial nation-state.

Inequality and Structural Imbalances. Its thirty-eight years of impressive development have nonetheless left Mexico with profound structural problems: massive underemployment, strong pressures of population on the land and on urban services in major cities, a poorly educated labor force, a slow pace of autonomous scientific and technological development, vast regional inequalities in production and wealth, and a pattern of income distribution with a concentration typical of the world's most backward nations.

The sum of unemployment plus underemployment may easily reach 40 to 50 percent of the labor force,[3] with major variations by economic sector and geographical region. The fastest growing sector, manufacturing, has always had a low elasticity of employment with respect to output, and 800,000 new jobs may be needed yearly just to employ *additions* to the labor force.[4] Regional inequalities are as marked in income, output, and welfare services as they are in underemployment.[5] Agricultural and industrial output are highly concentrated geographically. Five states account for 40 percent of the annual value of crops and livestock, and over half of industrial production originates in Mexico City and Monterrey. There are gross inequalities in Mexico's income distribution on both geographical and personal bases. Average income per capita in the richest zone, the Federal District, is six times that in the poorest state of Oaxaca. The upper fifth of families receives well over half of all income, whereas the poorest half receives less than a fifth, a situation that has changed only slightly in twenty or thirty years. The Gini index for Mexico is above 0.6, indicating one of the world's most unequal income distributions.[6]

External Dependence. Structural imbalances have left the Mexican economy dependent upon the external world, especially the United States, in profound and intricate ways. Persistent and growing deficits in the current account of the balance of payments have been financed by a growing volume of foreign public debt and foreign direct investment. As Mexico has substituted domestic production for imports in one product after another, the structure of production has grown more import-dependent, requiring raw materials, intermediate goods, capital goods, and technical services to keep the industrial process going. Higher rates of growth are typically accompanied by a worsening deficit on current

TABLE 2

Mexico: Population, Product, Employment, and Productivity, Selected Years, 1910–1978

	1910	1921	1930	1940	1950	1960	1970	1978
Population (millions)	15.2	14.3	16.6	19.6	25.8	35.0	50.7[a]	66.8
Gross domestic product (billions of 1975 pesos)								
Total	74	80	85	114	223	386	761	1,105
Agriculture[b]	20	20	17	24	39	61	88	100
Industry	14	18	21	27	60	112	262	401
Services	39	41	47	63	123	211	410	604
GDP/capita (1975 pesos)								
Total	4,870	5,570	5,150	5,820	8,630	11,000	15,000	16,540
Agriculture[b]	1,350	1,430	1,050	1,230	1,530	1,750	1,740	1,500
Industry	920	1,260	1,250	1,400	2,330	3,210	5,170	6,000
Services	2,600	2,880	2,850	3,190	4,770	6,040	8,090	9,040

Employment (thousands)							
Total	5,260	4,880	5,150	5,860	8,270	11,270	13,340	17,100
Agriculture[b]	3,600	3,490	3,630	3,830	4,820	6,100	5,000	5,600
Industry	900	660	770	910	1,320	2,140	3,080	4,300
Services	760	730	750	1,120	2,130	3,030	5,260	7,200
Employment/population ratio (percent)	34.6	34.1	31.0	29.9	32.0	32.2	26.3	25.6
Productivity (GDP/worker, 1975 pesos)							
Total	14,000	16,300	16,600	19,500	26,900	34,200	56,900	64,600
Agriculture[b]	5,700	5,870	4,790	6,280	8,190	10,100	17,700	17,900
Industry	15,400	27,300	26,800	30,200	45,500	52,500	84,800	93,300
Services	51,800	56,100	63,000	56,000	57,800	69,700	77,900	83,900

[a] Population estimates differ in various sources. The high figure shown here leads to a high growth-rate estimate for the 1960–1970 period (and consequently to a somewhat low rate of growth in GDP per capita for the same period).
[b] Includes forestry and fishing.
SOURCES: Nacional Financiera, *Statistics on the Mexican Economy*, 1977, pp. 3–4, 13–15, 38–39. Banco Nacional de México, *Review of the Economic Situation of Mexico* (September 1978), p. 350. *International Financial Statistics*, May 1978, p. 275, and May 1979, p. 258. Banco de México, *Informe anual 1978*, pp. 21–32, 50–64. Figures in 1975 pesos were calculated by the author from data given in the sources cited. Estimates for 1978 were made on the basis of preliminary and partial data. Details may not add to totals because of rounding.

account. Foreign firms, mostly U.S.-owned, are important in the export of manufactures; and Mexico is heavily dependent upon the United States for export markets, import sources, tourism, and bank credit—and as a labor-market refuge for its migrants.

Mexico is heavily dependent upon externally developed science and technology. The country spends only 0.22 percent of its gross domestic product on research and development, a low figure by comparison even with Argentina and India. With notable exceptions in agriculture and petroleum, research efforts are poorly coordinated; and Mexico imports and adapts foreign technology, often in "packages" that discourage the use of Mexican production capacity and know-how.[7]

There is an abiding concern in Mexico that its northern neighbor exercises a sort of cultural or intellectual domination or "colonialism," with Mexicans striving to adopt U.S. symbols and habits of consumption.

Current Trends in Mexican Economic Policy: An Evaluation

A strong national desire to "do something" about the most obvious defects in the economy—massive underemployment, gross inequality, major structural imbalances, and profound external dependence—motivates much of contemporary policy in Mexico. That policy is in a state of ferment, with changes in many directions at once. To appraise selected elements of contemporary Mexican economic policy, with an emphasis on the planning process, is the task of this paper.

An Entrepreneurial State and a New Penchant for "Planning." The Constitution of 1917 established the principle of a "mixed economy," confirmed the state in key roles as property owner and promoter, and made a series of remarkable declarations of intent to make Mexico a progressive, democratic, and modern nation-state. Although those declarations were initially pious hopes, beyond the resources of the society and the power of the political system, each has become, in time, the constitutional basis for progressive change. Every "revolutionary" government has pushed a vigorous entrepreneurial state to intervene in the economy in intricate ways to promote economic development and social justice.

The state distributes land to peasants and subsidizes large commercial farmers. It attempts to protect low-income consumers by controlling the prices of selected "basic" commodities. It tries to protect workers by incorporating organized labor into the political structure, by extending the social security system, by requiring private employers to provide fringe benefits, by negotiating minimum wages, and by making substantial public investments in workers' housing.

238

The Mexican government invests heavily in infrastructure and in direct ownership of key firms in telecommunications, energy, steel, fertilizers, petrochemicals, transport equipment, paper, sugar, and a wide variety of other products. The entrepreneurial state runs 800 or so enterprises, enters into joint ventures with private capital, even foreign investors, and pushes its investments into any key area in which private investment appears to be lagging.

Despite its traditional "guidance" of the economy, the government is not wedded to any socialist ideology. It relies heavily on private initiative, it takes great pains to promote native entrepreneurial talent and periodically to reassure the private sector, and it avoids rigid centralized planning. Taxes on income from capital have always been low by world standards, and no exchange controls have restricted the transfer of capital or earnings. A central objective of policy *has* been to reduce the role of direct foreign investment (and of foreigners in general) in the Mexican economy, leading Mexico to expropriation, "Mexicanization," or "investment screening."

Current trends in Mexican policy are largely extrapolations of the past, but with some major changes that will enhance the role of the entrepreneurial state. Oil revenues promise a growing importance and a high degree of autonomy for public investment, and the proliferation of national "plans," beginning with López Portillo's Alliance for Production, signals the evolution of a sort of Mexican version of French "indicative planning," in which the state will play the key "guiding" role.

Planning, "Mexican Style." Planning, "Mexican style," is a loose system of overlapping studies, programs, targets, models, projections, and scenarios. It is based on a series of laws, presidential decrees, and formal "accords" signed by representatives of various industries and of various government entities. It is to be monitored and to some extent administered and coordinated by key federal secretariats, especially those of Finance (Secretaría de Hacienda y Crédito Público), National Property and Industrial Development (Secretaría de Patrimonio y Fomento Industrial), Commerce (Secretaría de Comercio), Human Settlements and Public Works (Secretaría de Asentamientos Humanos y Obras Públicas), and Programming and Budget (Secretaría de Programación y Presupuesto). The secretariats in turn will deal with a variety of special coordinating commissions and promotion committees.

Scarcely a segment of Mexico's economy and society has been left out. There are "national plans" for urban development, industrial development, agriculture and forestry, fishery development, water resources, education, and even family planning. Within (or without) the various plans, there is a multitude of programs: for the development of a capital goods industry, for "integral assistance" to small and medium-sized industrial firms, for housing finance, for rural development, for the development of border areas and free-trade zones, for the geographical decentralization of federal public administration, and so on. In the lexicon of the federal technocrats, "programming" and "planning" have become synonymous.

The Overall Development Plan (Plan Global de Desarrollo) is thus far only a "first proposal," a general framework or set of guidelines related to President López Portillo's program of administrative reform. The plan calls for much consultation, coordination, and participation by "all sectors." Mexicans are assured that planning is neither an "academic exercise" nor a "unilateral technocratic task."[8] The code word is "participative," Mexico's variation on the French theme, "indicative." The overall plan is meant to set out general quantitative and qualitative objectives, to stimulate the programmatic analysis of specific projects, to cross-check for consistency the various "sectoral plans," and to integrate federal budgeting into the whole process.

It would be easy to pass off the new plans as just so much political rhetoric. What they seem to be is a genuine first step toward a rapid development phase, more coordinated than in the past, and with the role of the entrepreneurial state more important than before.

With or without formal plans, the federal government controls enough key inputs—investment spending, credit, imports, energy, transport, communications, fertilizers and irrigation water, and key industrial materials such as steel, sulphur, copper, and chemicals—to produce a "guided" economy, if not a "planned" one. It also possesses the political power to line up support.

López Portillo's central ideas of "participative planning," of "strengthened federalism," of "decentralization," and of an Alliance for Production all embody politically astute mechanisms for co-opting key state and local politicians and key representatives of the private sector.

The political and economic rewards can be handsome indeed. Governors and mayors get to influence the choice of key members of the Promotional Committees for Socioeconomic Development (Comités Promotores del Desarrollo Socioeconómico, COPRODES), who "function as participative organs of popular consultation for the State Governments"[9] and who help to decide which states and which localities get new or expanded industries, federal investments, and government contracts. The system cannot help but strengthen the Partido Revolucionario Institucional (PRI), the overwhelmingly dominant official party; despite much opportunity for "consultation"—or perhaps because of

240

it—many instances are sure to arise where politics will dominate the decision process. A deliberate policy of decentralizing economic activity through the role of an activist state is as full of regional conflicts and of the need for political compromise in Mexico as is energy policy, let us say, in the United States.

Increased participation seems destined to include only established interest groups and not many effective voices of dissent; it may increase the opportunities for influence peddling, special deals, bribery, and corruption—or at least public suspicion of the same, already something of a national malaise. The practices are not new, and Mexico is not much different from the rest of the world, as daily press accounts readily attest.[10]

For businesses that play the game, increased profits can run to billions of pesos annually, in the aggregate; and to individual firms, they can easily represent order-of-magnitude improvements. Organized business, through its Coordinated Business Council, has publicly announced its support of President López Portillo's policies.[11]

Planning in Mexico today is a far more serious activity than it appears at first blush. It is likely to grow even more serious—and more formal—in the future.

Elements of Mexico's Plans. The key plan from which most of the others seem to spring is the National Plan for Urban Development (Plan Nacional de Desarrollo Urbano), approved by presidential decree in May of 1978[12] and legally grounded in the General Law of Human Settlements (Ley General de Asentamientos Humanos). The law and the plan, though they call for "ample consultation" with state and municipal governments, clearly establish the federal government as a major participant in the planning of population settlements and the regulation of urban development, including such sensitive issues as land use, industrial location, congestion, and environmental pollution.

The purpose of such planning and regulation would be to alter significantly Mexico's current trends of high population growth and overconcentration of both people and production in Mexico City and a few other urban centers.

Adopting national family-planning goals of reducing population growth rates to 2.5 percent per year by 1982 and to 1 percent by the year 2000, the plan envisions for turn-of-the-century Mexico: a national population of 104 million, some 20 million of whom would inhabit the capital city and its metropolitan area; 3 to 5 million each for Guadalajara and Monterrey; another eleven cities of over 1 million inhabitants; some seventeen cities of one-half million to 1 million; and perhaps seventy-four cities in the population range of 100,000 to one-half million. That

241

scenario pictures a nation considerably less populous and less centralized than current trends would produce if unabated and one that would possess numerous potential "poles of growth."

At the other end of the scale, Mexico would promote "systems of rural population centers" in an effort to "consolidate" a very diverse population (now about 38 percent of the national total) who live in more than 95,000 localities of fewer than 2,500 inhabitants.

The urban plan is exceedingly ambitious in its long lists of things to be stimulated, from infrastructure to family planning and cultural activities; and it bristles with proposed "programs": decentralization of federal public administration; decentralization of industry; regional integration of urban services; intercity transport and communication; rural services; natural resource use and conservation; infrastructure for fishing villages, tourist centers, energy-producing areas, and industrial seaports; urban development; community development; new population centers; industrial parks; water and sewerage; housing; streets and roads; land use; and several more.

More important than the urban development plan, though clearly growing out of it, is the National Industrial Development Plan.[13] It incorporates every major feature of Mexico's promotional policies, including the adoption of general quantitative "targets," the designation of sectoral priorities, the emphasis on geographical decentralization, and the specification of fiscal stimuli and input subsidies. The industrial planners have produced a set of projections that are taken as tentative goals for the "medium term" (1979–1982, the remainder of the López Portillo administration) and for the "long term" (1982–1990).

To highlight the stimulus implied in the plan, its projections (the "plan trajectory") are contrasted with a set of projections (the "base trajectory") made on the assumption of continuation of preplan policies. Only the plan trajectory will be considered here.

The plan foresees Mexico's real GDP accelerating in annual growth rate from 7 percent in 1979 to 10 percent by 1982 and continuing at an average rate of growth of 10 percent for the 1982–1990 period. It envisions employment as increasing in accelerating fashion, too, from a 3 percent growth rate in 1979 to 5 percent by 1982 and to 6 percent or so by 1990, an average annual rate of growth of more than 5 percent for the entire twelve-year period. Industrial output should grow at 10 to 12 percent annually, with some high-growth sectors of manufacturing (for example, petroleum equipment, petrochemicals, and transport equipment) increasing at 18 to 20 percent per year. Industry would provide about 30 percent of the increase in employment, with the rest going largely to the service sector. Very little increase in employment can be expected in the agricultural sector, where output is projected in the plan at a minimum rate of growth of 3 percent per year, barely ahead of historical long-run productivity gains (see table 2).

By way of a general appraisal, the plan's macroeconomic goals may be compared with Mexico's historical record of achievement and with the records of other economies.

The target rates of growth for both real GDP and the industrial sector are considerably higher than Mexico has ever sustained, but they are certainly not beyond the economy's possibilities. Nor are they unusual by world standards. Since 1960, eighteen of the developing nations classified by the World Bank as middle-income countries have been able to maintain, for periods of six to sixteen years, average growth rates of 8 percent or more for real GDP. They include Brazil, Iran, Taiwan, South Korea, Romania, Tunisia, and Israel, and also Ecuador and the Dominican Republic. Industrial growth has been sustained for a number of years at average rates of 10 to 22 percent by twenty-three middle-income countries. Japan—in several ways a would-be "model" for Mexico—expanded both total and industrial output at more than 10 percent annually during the 1960–1970 decade.[14]

Still, the target rates of Mexico's industrial development plan contain a large element of aspiration. The plan itself recognizes that the goals are "simple guidelines" and that "the concerted efforts of all the economic agents will barely suffice to meet the targets proposed."[15]

One might make a somewhat more modest set of assumptions about growth rates, recognizing in the process the adverse effects of recessions in the United States and the rest of the industrial world, and still come up with impressive prospects for Mexico over the next decade. Such a "scenario" is expressed in table 3.[16] All projections are alternative visions of the future, and even the assumptions of the industrial plan could prove too modest. The planners are certainly right about one thing, given Mexico's prospects it would make no sense at all to plan for development at a pace no faster than that realized "spontaneously" in the past.

One intractable variable is the rate of inflation. Though the industrial plan makes much issue of developing competitive industries, of promoting small business and diminishing oligopoly power, and of reducing "excessive" protection, it adopts no quantitative target for inflation. That is just as well. Projections of inflation rates (including those in table 3) are but heroic assumptions.

Mexico's National Industrial Development Plan contains three sets of overlapping "priorities": sectoral, regional, and small industry.

Sectoral Priorities. Some seventy "priority sectors" of industry were selected on the basis of multiple criteria: estimates of potential markets;

TABLE 3

Mexico: Product, Population, and Inflation, 1970–1988

	1970	1976	1977	1978	1979	1982	1988
Gross domestic product							
Current pesos (billions)	419	1,228	1,676	2,088	2,580	4,860	15,200
1975 pesos (billions)	761	1,005	1,037	1,105	1,180	1,420	2,250
Per capita (1975 pesos)	15,000	16,130	16,050	16,540	17,100	18,500	24,600
General price level							
GDP deflator (1975 = 100)	55	122	162	189	219	342	675
Population (millions)	50.7	62.3	64.6	66.8	69.1	76.6	91.5
Average annual growth rates (%)	1970–76	1976–77	1977–78	1978–79	1979–82	1982–88	
GDP (current pesos)	9.6	36.5	24.6	23.6	23.5	21.0	
GDP (1975 pesos)	4.8	3.2	6.6	7.0	6.5	8.0	
Per capita (1975 pesos)	1.3	−0.5	3.1	3.4	3.0	4.9	
Prices (GDP deflator)	14.2	32.8	16.5	16.0	16.0	12.0	
Population	3.5	3.6	3.4	3.5	3.5	3.0	

Source: Data for 1970, 1976, and 1977 from *International Financial Statistics*, May 1978 and May 1979. Estimate for 1978 and projections for 1979, 1982, and 1988 were made by the author on the basis of preliminary and partial data and of assumptions about growth rates.

origin of inputs; and macroeconomic impact on income, employment, investment, exports, and technology. This "weighted effects" method allowed Mexican planners to include as priorities their longstanding desires to promote the export of manufactures and the development of a capital goods industry. To the extent possible, Mexican origin of inputs counts heavily in the selection; but even so, the projections of the plan show the ratio of imports to total demand rising for industry as a whole from 10 percent in 1978 to 12 percent in 1982 and to nearly 15 percent by 1990.

First priority (if that really means anything in a list of industries that account for 60 percent of Mexico's gross industrial output) is given to food processing; second priority is given to capital goods. At the top of the capital goods list stand food-processing machinery and food-producing equipment, a symbol of Mexico's desire to feed itself.

Second on the capital goods list are machinery and equipment for the petroleum and petrochemical industries (for example, exploration and drilling equipment, valves, pumps, blowers, compressors, pipes, heat exchangers). Here the commitment is real and immediate; direct purchases to meet expansion plans of PEMEX (the Mexican government petroleum monopoly) will virtually guarantee the growth of this sector at something approaching the projected rates of 18 to 23 percent annually. But imports will grow very fast, too, at first to satisfy demands that cannot be postponed until Mexican production comes on stream, then to meet machine tool, technical services, and other specialty inputs required by the Mexican capital goods sector itself.

Other priority activities include nondurable consumer goods (for example, textiles, shoes, soaps and detergents, containers, school and office supplies, paper), consumer durables (for example, appliances, furniture, auto parts, optical goods, hand tools), and intermediate industrial goods (for example, chemical fibers, resins, acids, alkalis, pharmaceuticals, aluminum, specialty steels, glass, plastics, ceramics). All of these activities are existing industries in Mexico, and they are expected to expand at rates ranging from 7.5 to 20 percent annually.

Expansion of the priority industry sectors and a growing demand for food imports will produce a continuing deficit on current account in the balance of payments, projected in the plan to a cumulative $2 billion over the 1979–1982 period. That projection could easily be too low, but almost any foreseeable deficit can easily be financed.

Regional Priorities. The National Industrial Development Plan makes the regional priorities of the urban development plan concrete, classifying priority zones and specifying federal incentives for decentralization. The target of the plan is to reduce the share of industrial output produced in Mexico City and its environs to about 40 percent by 1982 by slowing down industrialization in the central valley and promoting output in a number of middle-sized cities.

Three zones are established: Zone I, "preferential stimuli"; Zone II, "state priorities"; and Zone III, "ordering and regulation."

Within Zone I, priority IA is given to four industrial seaports and their surrounding areas (twenty-four municipalities in all): Coatzacoalcos, Veracruz; Tampico, Tamaulipas; Salina Cruz, Oaxaca; and Lázaro Cárdenas, Michoacán. Priority IB, "for urban industrial development," is designated for ninety-nine municipalities located in coastal zones, border areas, and interior states already singled out by the urban development plan. Many of these are located along the natural gas distribution network or in areas judged to have abundant raw materials of the kind that require processing near the source.

Zone II is a movable feast consisting of any municipalities selected by state governors for the location of industry as part of a state plan duly coordinated with the national plan. The governors and their political teams at local levels will have much room for initiative and maneuver, but the federal bureaucracy and its political mentors will make the technical planning decisions that count.

Zone III is designated to control growth in Mexico City and other congested centers. It is subdivided into two areas: IIIA, "Area of Controlled Growth," consisting of the Federal District (that is, Mexico City) and 53 surrounding municipalities; and IIIB, "Area of Consolidation," consisting of 144 municipalities close to Mexico City and very much subject to its influence. In the jargon of Mexican planning, "consolidation" is a code word meant to reassure; it implies continued growth without the negative effects of concentration.

Conspicious by their absence from Zone III are Monterrey and Guadalajara, the two largest poles of growth outside of Mexico City. The omission was deliberate. Federal subsidies are available to all priority industries *except* in Zone III. By remaining off the list, Monterrey and Guadalajara retain their considerable locational advantages.

Small-Industry Priority. Small industry, because of its role in generating employment, and because of its consistency with decentralization objectives, is given a separate priority. A "small enterprise" is defined as one whose investment in fixed assets is less than 200 times the annual minimum wage for the Federal District, currently about 10 million pesos ($439,000 at recent exchange rates). Use of the minimum-wage definition will allow for inflation or for improvements in wages; and "small" becomes, as it rightly should, a relative rather than an absolute measure.

The accent on small enterprise may contain a dollop of salve for the political conscience. Despite the plan's stated objective of "balancing Mexico's market structures" (meaning, presumably, reducing oligopoly power), large businesses are best able to make the investments that qualify for the subsidies.

Subsidies and Other Incentives. Mexico's industrial development priorities are to be pursued through a combination of federal subsidies, public-sector expenditures, government loans, technical assistance, and tariff and other protection from import competition.

The key element of subsidy is a federal tax credit. It may be granted to any business firm of Mexican nationality for (1) investing in fixed assets, (2) increasing employment, (3) purchasing machinery and equipment made in Mexico. A tax credit is equivalent, in the year used, to a net addition to after-tax profits. The amount of the tax credit for investment varies in two dimensions, reflecting sectoral and regional priorities.[17]

Small business is favored with the highest rate, 25 percent of the value of new investment in fixed assets. Regional priorities are brought into play by offering the tax credit for both expansion and diversification in Priority Zones I and II, and for expansion only in the rest of the country—with none available at all for Zone IIIA. For industrial firms that are not small, the tax credit is scaled at 20 or 15 or 10 percent, to express sectoral and regional priorities, with the same constraints on expansion versus new product lines.

To keep the beneficiary firm from getting a "double credit" for income tax purposes, depreciation must value assets at original investment cost less tax credit. Thus, the present value of the subsidy to the beneficiary firm will vary directly with the rate of tax credit, the length in years of the depreciation schedule, and the rate of discount; but any investment is more profitable with it than without it.

Because it lowers the cost of capital, this subsidy should stimulate investment, thus achieving one of the objectives of the plan; but it will also stimulate the substitution of capital for labor and thus run counter to the employment objective.

To offset the latter effect, a tax credit is also given for any increase in employment; it is a uniform 20 percent of the annual payroll cost of the additional employment, calculated at the equivalent of the minimum annual wage for the economic zone in which the beneficiary firm is located. Any small firm has the option of choosing *either* the small-industry priority, with its higher investment tax credit, *or* the appropriate sectoral priority with combined investment and employment tax credits. To spur more intensive use of existing plant and equipment, additional work shifts qualify for the tax credit, without regard to sectoral priorities.

247

There is an additional tax credit for any industrial firm that purchases new machinery and equipment made in Mexico; it is 5 percent of the purchase price.

A second major stimulus to Mexican industry is offered in the form of subsidized prices for energy and petrochemicals produced by the public-sector firms, PEMEX and the Federal Electricity Commission. In Priority Zone IA, industrial firms get a 30 percent discount on natural gas, residual fuel oil, and electricity. Petrochemical firms also get a 30 percent discount on basic petrochemical inputs, provided they export at least 25 percent of their production for a minimum period of three years. In Priority Zone IB, price discounts vary to reflect both a regional scaling and supply availabilities within the zone. For petrochemicals, the subsidy may last for a period of ten years, for energy, from six to nine years. Future decrees and accords can easily modify the periods or extend the deadlines.

These price discounts are not available to firms outside of preferential Zone I, nor are they available to firms in the northern border townships that are included in Zone IB. Mexico's border areas and free zones are ruled by a special incentive scheme of their own, though they may be incorporated into the general scheme within a few years.

Some Implications of the Subsidies. The federal government subsidies adopted by Mexico to promote industrial development are at once simple in concept, familiar in precedent, and complex in possible results. Investment tax credits and subsidized inputs are well-known, if controversial, stimuli in industrial market economies. Employment tax credits are less widely used, but their principle is analogous to that of the investment credit. A great deal of careful thought and argument have gone into scaling the subsidy types and levels to reflect competing priorities and into regulating the process so as to reduce opportunities for abuse.

There is nothing in the scheme of subsidies, however, to protect labor's share of the national income. Indeed, the net effect of the various subsidies—all of which go to profits—is to raise the ratio of property income to labor income in *every* beneficiary firm. The degree of the shift varies with the ratio of fixed assets to total wages paid per year, with the length of the depreciation period, with the share of Mexican capital goods in new fixed assets, and with the proportion of costs represented by energy and petrochemical inputs. Questions of equity plague subsidy programs everywhere; but this adverse effect on income distribution is a major flaw. It is also a potential source of much national conflict. How can labor, for example, abide a program that will cause one of the world's worst income distribution patterns to become worse yet?

There are policy measures that could correct the distribution effects: business profits could be taxed at higher rates, the share of profits distributed to workers could be raised, fringe benefits could be increased, or wages could be raised to increase labor's share in the national product. Any of these measures, however, might deter some of the investment and employment that the subsidy program is designed to stimulate.

There is an alternative subsidy scheme that would be free of the deterrent effect and also consistent with output, productivity, and income distribution objectives. That is a direct subsidy payment for *output* to be shared by the beneficiary firm and its employees in proportions that would raise the ratio of labor income to profits. Such payments would offer incentives to labor and capital alike to increase the real product. The subsidy would have the added social and political advantage of distributing widely a part of the patrimony of the whole nation— namely, the petroleum revenues that are to finance whatever subsidy scheme is adopted—instead of transferring them, as the present subsidy scheme does, wholly to the industrial propertied class.

Several lesser issues surround the subsidy program. First, there is the questionable effect of the employment subsidy, designed to slow down, as it were, the substitution of capital for labor. The general drive to increase productivity leads to a progressive increase in investment per worker—a desirable economic and social result, necessary for higher incomes per capita over the long run. Managers may also "prefer" more capital-intensive methods, where choice is feasible, both for the modernity and precision of the process and for the preservation of managerial "prerogative." Moreover, many of Mexico's high-priority industries (for example, petroleum refining, petrochemicals, fertilizers, natural gas transmission, electrical energy, iron and steel) have limited technological choices with high capital/labor ratios, making it nearly impossible to give "employment" priority over "investment."

On the equity front, a new subsidy always discriminates implicitly against existing business firms by subsidizing new entrants; but in Mexico's case, existing firms can defend themselves through "expansion," with access to the same subsidies as the new entrants.

A requirement that expansion, to qualify for subsidies, must represent more than 40 percent of existing capacity, could lead existing firms into either temporary overinvestment, not justified by near-term markets, or temporary underinvestment, while they wait for market potential to justify the "lumpy" increase of 40 percent.

249

Despite the denial of subsidies to firms that locate or expand in Mexico City and its environs, the attractions of nearness to markets and of enormous external economies may frustrate to some extent the decentralization objectives of the industrial plan.

The 5 percent subsidy for the purchase of capital goods made in Mexico may not be sufficient to make them attractive, though that will depend very much on the degree of effective protection afforded from competitive imports.

The export requirement may cause petrochemical firms to develop differentiated markets, with price discrimination in favor of foreign buyers, a practice that could lead to antidumping or countervailing duties. Indeed, any of Mexico's exports that can be shown to benefit from any subsidy may be subject to countervailing duties.

Regional rivalries in Mexico may be heightened by the differential subsidy provisions of the industrial development plan. In particular, businessmen and politicians in Zone II and in the northern border cities of Zone IB may object to the special competitive advantage conferred on other areas through subsidized energy and petrochemical prices.

There is an abiding question of administrative efficiency surrounding such a complex subsidy program. Anyone familiar with government-business relations can predict that the government's *técnicos* will develop considerable technical competence and business understanding but will preserve an intimate sense of "dealing" with private enterprise—conditions long familiar to Mexican businessmen and to which they have adapted with finesse. The tentative and experimental nature of Mexican planning, with its flexible instruments of presidential "decrees" and ministerial "accords," allows the subsidy program to be modified substantially, even in the short run.

Finally, there is the question of the quantitative effects. Mexico's industrial development plan contains numerous projections, but nowhere does it offer any estimate of the amount of subsidies to be paid. The difficulties of making even order-of-magnitude estimates may be illustrated using selected data and projections from the industrial plan itself. Over the three years 1980–1982, for example, the plan projects an aggregate fixed investment in *private* industrial enterprises of some 200 billion pesos (at 1975 prices). About 60 percent of that amount is in the priority sectors of the plan. If one assumes the subsidies to average 15 percent, their gross value will aggregate 18 billion pesos (at 1975 prices), equivalent to four-tenths of 1 percent of the total gross domestic product over the three years.

If Mexico creates 600,000 new jobs per year, about 43,000 of those will be in industries eligible for the employment subsidy. At the minimum wage prevailing in Mexico City in 1979, that would call for subsidies totaling some 600 million pesos (at 1975 prices) over the 1980–1982 period.

The subsidy issue is complicated. Public-sector enterprises are also eligible; energy and petrochemical inputs are highly variable; and ultimately the amounts paid will be determined by the degree of response of the industrial sector to the subsidy incentives themselves.

Whatever their precise amounts, they have been characterized aptly by President López Portillo as *subsidios monstruosos*.[18]

Public-Sector Expenditures and Other Measures. The role of the entrepreneurial state will clearly be strengthened. The state can pursue the objectives of the plan, within limits, by a judicious direction of the current and capital expenditures of general government and of state enterprises; by the use of fiscal stimuli and subsidized prices, as explained above; by channeling credit to favored firms; by offering technical assistance, import protection, or export subsidy; and by controlling the licenses, permits, and dispensations needed to do business in Mexico.

The industrial plan envisions a growing participation of the public sector in capital formation. Over the long run (to 1990), it is general government whose fixed investment grows spectacularly, due to heavy investments in infrastructure needed to attend the needs of agriculture, transportation, communication, public health, social security, housing, tourism, science, education, and local government. Over the shorter period (1977–1982), fixed investment by public enterprises would grow fastest, due mainly to growth in petroleum and petrochemicals, electricity, fertilizers, and iron and steel—industries in which public enterprises are already dominant.

Despite rapid growth of investment by government and state enterprises, the plan projects a dynamic private sector whose fixed capital formation grows at annual rates in excess of 10 percent for the entire period 1977–1990 and whose annual amounts, in real terms, greatly exceed the total fixed investment of the public sector. By the target year 1990, however, the entrepreneurial state would be virtually an equal partner with private enterprise in Mexico's annual capital formation, this time as a "programmed" result of planning and not, as occasionally in the past, as a circumstantial result of cyclical declines in private investment. Purchases of machinery and equipment by the public sector will be used to promote the capital goods industry; additional stimuli are provided by tax credits and by preferential financing through public-sector credit institutions.

Preferential financing is also available for small and medium industrial firms through a maze of special federal government trust funds, now being "coordinated" through a program of integral support for medium and small industry.

On the technical assistance front, the Mexican government aids industry in two quite different ways. First, it offers a variety of services at subsidized prices, often accompanied by public credits or equity investments. The effectiveness of these efforts is limited by the small financial resources available, the large number and overlapping functions of the agencies involved, the heterogeneity of requests, and the tendency of the public authorities to expect too much from "inventories" of needs, "studies" of opportunities, and "profiles" of projects. Second, the government intervenes directly in the technology transfer process between Mexican business firms and their foreign suppliers, trying to improve the economic benefits that Mexico obtains in licensing foreign technology.

Import controls and export promotion are also used as instruments of industrial development policy. The traditional mechanism for restricting imports has been the license, whose highly discretionary use and "negotiability" appeal to the interventionist policy orientation of the state. In 1977, Mexico began a gradual substitution of tariffs for licenses, and the industrial plan urges a continuation of the process, but the emphasis is really on "gradual."

Whether Mexico should join the General Agreement on Tariffs and Trade (GATT) has been a highly controversial issue. No overriding advantage to the country is apparent, and many features of the industrial development plan would contravene the articles of agreement. Mexico has negotiated terms of its "eventual" joining to include the indefinite retention of prior import permits where "necessary" and the use of import quotas to protect national production.

Export promotion by the Mexican government has included a variety of elements. The foreign trade bank (Banco Nacional de Comercio Exterior) offers financing; the foreign trade institute (Instituto Mexicano de Comercio Exterior) offers information, marketing, and promotion services; and the fiscal authorities offer tax rebates.

What is relatively new is the growing contribution of state enterprises to Mexico's merchandise exports. That fact is certain to generate friction with trading partners and competitors over the issue of "state trading."

Petroleum and the Development Push. Whatever priorities prevail, the key to development finance is petroleum, characterized by President López Portillo as Mexico's "potential for self-determination."[19] Mexico is well into an oil-led boom. Its proved reserves of about 46 billion barrels in late 1979 made it the world's sixth largest oil state; and estimates of proved reserves could rise quickly—even spectacularly. Exploration and development have been rapid. Mexico will easily meet a 1980 production target of 2.25 million barrels a day, with 1.5 million available for export; and pressures are building for faster rates of exploitation.

In 1979, PEMEX, the government oil monopoly, began a policy of quarterly adjustments of its export price for crude oil, raising it from $14.10 per barrel in January of that year to $32.00 per barrel in January 1980.[20] At an average price of $30.00 per barrel, Mexico would earn $16.4 billion from oil exports in 1980, an amount three times the value of *all* merchandise exports in 1978. Such export revenues will dramatically reduce any foreign exchange constraint on development, greatly increase Mexico's capacity for servicing foreign debt, and propel PEMEX into the ranks of the world's largest multinational corporations. At home, Mexico will have abundant energy supplies; and the federal government's revenues from petroleum royalties, profits, and taxes will finance much of the development program.

The central questions of Mexico's economic policy have thus become how much oil and gas to produce and how to manage their sale in ways that will promote rapid development and avoid both flagrant waste and strong inflationary pressures. The key phrase, in the jargon of Mexican planning, is the use of surplus oil revenues, *el excedente petrolero*.

Because the petroleum sector itself requires large expenditures with major import content, and because Mexico began its industrial planning phase with very large commitments to external debt service, no "petroleum surplus" was foreseen before 1982; but recent increases in oil prices assure the appearance of such surpluses in 1980.[21]

The industrial plan defines the petroleum surplus in a very peculiar way, as "the additional capacity for expenditure as compared with the base projection, given the constraints imposed by the balance of payments." The "additional capacity for expenditure" means "increase in real gross domestic product," whereas the "base projection," it will be recalled, was made assuming the continuation of preplan policies. Projections of the petroleum surplus, as defined, are for 185 billion pesos (at 1975 prices) accumulated over the period 1979–1982; and 4.5 trillion accumulated over the period 1983–1990. The surplus may be considerably larger than projected, due to modest price and volume assumptions in the industrial plan.

Mexico is making very large additional investments in petroleum-related activities and will soon become a reliable source of gasoline, fuel oils, and petrochemicals. The country is certain to find it in its interest

253

to make downstream investments in tanker fleets and in production and marketing facilities in foreign countries.

Mexico's independence in petroleum has led to a real improvement in its bargaining power. Mexican decisions, however, must still be made with careful considerations of access to industrial markets, of uncertainties in world petroleum supplies, and of its own balance-of-payments pressures.

Other Economic Policy Issues. A new emphasis on planning is but one manifestation of the many ways in which Mexico's economic policies are changing. Brief mention will be made here of some other key elements.

Fiscal reform has been postponed, and the abundance of petroleum revenues is likely to postpone it indefinitely. Two fiscal changes have occurred, one for the better, perhaps, and the other for the worse.

As of 1980, Mexico substituted a value-added tax (VAT) for its old tax on gross business receipts (*impuesto sobre ingresos mercantiles*) and for seventeen other indirect taxes on specific commodities and services. That is an improvement of sorts. The VAT avoids the "cascade effect" of the gross receipts tax, and it may be rebated to exporters under the rules of the GATT. But it has created considerable confusion, and it hurts in the same way that the gross receipts tax hurts; it must be paid whether the firm sustains profit or loss. Small businesses oppose the VAT because it is not based on ability to pay; they prefer a tax on business profits.[22] The VAT hurts most—as did the gross receipts tax— those very sectors of the economy that the Mexican government says it wants to help: labor-intensive small firms. Whatever its name, it is still a sales tax with regressive impact.

The second major fiscal change, that of subsidies under the industrial development plan, was discussed above. Both the subsidies and the VAT work in the "wrong direction" on the distribution of income in Mexico.

Despite the Mexican government's commitment to capital formation, its current expenditures have grown faster than its investments. Given its emphasis on employment, the government has little choice but to maintain aggregate demand, with the frequent results of deficit finance, rapid expansion in the money supply, and inflationary pressures. The social costs of slower growth or of recession would include an increase in political unrest, more violence, increased illegal migration to the United States, and more land invasions by *campesinos* without employment alternatives.

Monetary policy measures in Mexico have largely reflected the need for financing the federal deficit. The Mexican authorities have allowed rapid growth in the money supply—perhaps by as much as 37 percent in 1979. Mexican money markets have grown more integrated with world money markets, and the authorities may move slowly toward the use of general quantitative credit controls, gradually giving up their elaborate qualitative system of "directed credit" and "managed interest rates." Growing exports of petroleum could create future inflationary pressures, as foreign exchange is sold for pesos to commercial banks and the Central Bank.

The "managed float" of the peso practiced since late 1976 amounts to a de facto peg to the dollar. Mexico is "trapped" by its exchange rate policy—so important a corollary to monetary policy—into severe repercussions from measures originating in the United States.

On trade policy, Mexico wrestles with the question of GATT membership while simultaneously designing intricate measures to protect domestic industry from import competition and to promote exports. In a related set of policy issues, it struggles to develop its northern border zone and integrate it more closely into the national economy.

Agriculture is surely the weak link in any chain of development policies in Mexico—but that is another story for another time. Suffice it here to note that the industrial development plan points out that a doubling of public investment in the sector between 1977 and 1982 will barely arrest the decline in agricultural output; and if that output grows no faster than the 3 percent minimum rate projected in the plan, food imports will require 21 percent of petroleum export revenues in 1982 and 54 percent in 1990.

At a more general level lies the problem of education and technology. Will Mexico be able to educate and train the technical and managerial personnel required by its own ambitious plans, or will the flood of enrollments and a decline in the quality of higher education become the ultimate "bottleneck" to development?

There are, of course, dozens of other economic policy issues scarcely hinted at in this essay.

Conclusion: Sifting through the Priority Matrix

What meaning can be attached to "priority" in such a complex matrix as that represented by Mexico's development plans, scaled as they are in many directions at once? What effects can one forecast from the great variety of subsidies and stimuli available, each theoretically translatable into equivalent economic benefits but with relevant "supply functions" unknown and unknowable (in Mexico or anywhere else)?

The answers can be given in terms of direction only. The seaports in Zone IA get all of the positive stimuli at their maximum amounts, and there can be little doubt of their prospects for attracting major

255

industry. The central valley of Mexico City gets no stimulus at all, but its accumulated advantages of dense markets and abundant "external economies" may outpull the centripetal forces of decentralization, subsidies included. For all other areas of Mexico, the answers are unclear; but the battle is joined, and regional rivalries are on the upswing. Under such conditions, the terms "tentative" and "participative" should become not mere code words but real descriptive terms for the planning process—with an already dominant Partido Revolucionario Institucional, the official party, strengthened further by its mediating role among competing interests and with the entrepreneurial state strengthened in its economic role.

There *are* clouds on the development horizon. Even projected increases in employment will leave millions of Mexicans without jobs. And, despite the rhetorical commitment to an improved pattern of income distribution as a "priority," the "planned" phase of rapid growth may make it worse.

Notes

[1] World Bank, *World Development Report, 1978,* "Annex-World Development Indicators," pp. 76–77.

[2] See Nacional Financiera, *Statistics on the Mexican Economy* (Mexico, 1977), pp. 429–52; and Consejo Nacional de Ciencia y Technología, Dirección de Programación, "Prontuario estadístico," 1976 (mimeographed), pp. 153–75. Mexico's rank varies with year and with specific measure and is derived from data found mostly in the U.N. *Statistical Yearbook* for recent years.

[3] There are no regular official data on unemployment. A thorough treatment of the problem appears in Grupo de Estudio del Problema del Empleo, *El problema ocupacional en México: magnitud y recomendaciones,* versión preliminar para discusión (n.d.); see pp. 35–39.

[4] William P. Glade, "Prospects for Mexico's Socioeconomic Growth," *Texas Business Review,* March-April 1979, p. 48.

[5] Sidney Weintraub et al., "Growth and Equity in Mexico," final report to the Agency for International Development, Lyndon B. Johnson School of Public Affairs, University of Texas at Austin, 1978 (mimeographed).

[6] The Gini index can range from 0.0 (complete equality) to 1.0 (absolute inequality). Recent measures for advanced economies range from 0.25 to 0.4, and for underdeveloped economies from 0.2 to 0.7. See David Felix, "Income Inequality in Mexico," *Current History,* March 1977, p. 111.

[7] National Council for Science and Technology, *National Indicative Plan for Science and Technology* (Mexico, 1976), esp. pp. 12–17.

[8] "Plan Global de Desarrollo," *El mercado de valores,* April 2, 1979, pp. 265–66.

[9] Ricardo García Sáinz, "Instrumentos de desarrollo regional," *El mercado de valores,* February 20, 1978, p. 130.

[10] See Lester A. Sobel, ed., *Corruption in Business* (New York: Facts on File, 1977).

[11] Félix Arciniega, "Businessmen Make 180° Turnabout," *The News* (Mexico City), April 26, 1979, p. 2.

[12] *Diario Oficial,* May 19, 1978. An abbreviated version of the urban plan appears in *El mercado de valores,* June 19, 1978, pp. 477 ff.

256

[13] Secretaría de Patrimonio y Fomento Industrial, *Plan nacional de desarrollo industrial, 1979–82* (Mexico, March 1979). There are two "volumes," but vol. 2 is a loose-leaf collection of pamphlets, to be updated from time to time. An abridged version of the plan is available in Spanish, "Plan nacional de desarrollo industrial en forma abreviada," *Diario Oficial,* May 17, 1979, reprinted in *El mercado de valores* (Supp. to no. 30, July 23, 1979), pp. 3–34; and also in English, *Industrial Development Plan, 1979–1982–1990 (Abridged version)* (Mexico: Secretaría de Patrimonio y Fomento Industrial, 1979).

[14] World Bank, *World Development Report, 1978,* pp. 69–120.

[15] *Industrial Development Plan (Abridged Version),* pp. 11, 16.

[16] The projections in table 3 were made before the author had access to the industrial plan. They correspond deliberately to presidential periods (ending in 1982 and 1988).

[17] See the table in *Plan nacional de desarrollo industrial,* p. 181.

[18] "Tercer informe de gobierno," *El mercado de valores,* September 10, 1979, p. 767.

[19] "Tercer informe de gobierno," p. 767.

[20] See *Wall Street Journal,* July 6, 1979, p. 3; October 9, 1979, p. 2; and December 31, 1979, p. 2.

[21] "Tercer informe de gobierno," p. 767.

[22] See Advisory Commission on Intergovernmental Relations, *The Michigan Single Business Tax* (Washington, D.C., March 1978), pp. 10–15, 20–31.

Mexican Industrialization: Past Developments and a Near-Term Plan

Redvers Opie

After several months of expectant waiting, in March 1979 the Mexican government published its National Plan for Industrial Development (Plan Nacional de Desarrollo Industrial). Its period of gestation was long, for a first outline was given to the president in February 1977, barely three months after he assumed office. It was issued by the Secretaría de Patrimonio y Fomento Industrial in two volumes under the title "National Plan for Industrial Development, 1979–82." In fact, however, the plan contains a vision of industrial development up to 1990, two years after the next administration will have ended.

A shortened version of volume 1, which contains the essential features of the plan, was published in the *Diario oficial* on May 17, 1979. Most of the contents of volume 2 had already been published in the *Diario oficial* between June 20, 1977, and March 9, 1979, for it consists of eighteen decrees, agreements, regulations, and laws, which constitute the legal foundation of national industrial policy. The rest of volume 2 consists of a list of machinery and equipment that will be purchased by four large state enterprises, Petróleos Mexicanos (PEMEX), Comisión Federal de Electricidad (CFE), the steel companies (SIDERMEX), and Fertilizantes Mexicanos (FERTIMEX). The list will be kept up to date in order that the private sector may be in a position to make bids on the contents.

Description of the Plan

As described in volume 1, the plan does not lend itself to a short, succinct summary, although it contains only fifty-nine pages of text. It is divided into four chapters entitled "Strategy" (eighteen pages of text), "Goals and Predictions" (twenty-eight pages of text and seventy pages of tables), "Priorities" (five pages), and "Instruments" (eight pages). The chapters were preceded by a "Presentation" (six pages) by Secretary José Andrés Oteyza of Patrimonio y Fomento Industrial, and an introduction (three pages). The whole of the former, and all except three paragraphs of the latter, were omitted from the shortened version published in the *Diario oficial.*

The account of the plan in this paper will summarize and appraise the contents of the four chapters, but first it is necessary to explain the general nature of the two sets of projections that are made in the study. They are called "trajectories" (*trayectorias*), rather than the more usual "projections" (*proyecciones*). Perhaps consciously or unconsciously a metaphorical analogy with the trajectory of an artillery shell is being drawn, in which the alignment of the gun must be adjusted after successive firings, in the light of observations of error, in order finally to get on target.

First, the basic trajectory (*trayectoria base*) is calculated. This estimates what would have happened "under the existing framework of economic policy," if it were to continue unchanged in the future. Then, on the assumption that the policy framework will be different from what it was, the plan trajectory (*trayectoria del plan*) is calculated, which means predicting the actual future.

The calculations are made by a computerized model of the economy, the publication of which, although promised, has not yet been forthcoming. Presumably there are two models for the two trajectories—which will henceforth here simply be called "projections."

The Nature of the Basic Projection. The task of calculating historical might-have-beens (which is what the base projection attempts) is more hazardous than predicting the future. This is especially so when the hypothetical events lie not in the past but in the future. And the results are of course never capable of verification. The effort suffers from two inherent weaknesses: it depends on the observer's interpretation of the past and present in describing the existing framework of economic organization and policy; and it makes the arbitrary assumption that the framework could and would remain substantially unchanged during the future period under study.

As for the interpretation of the past, the report lists four defects, said to be not in economic policy but in the "economic structure." (1) Industry depended excessively on the domestic market, which resulted in plants being small in scale and noncompetitive for export. (2) Industry was geographically overconcentrated in three centers, the Valley of Mexico, Guadalajara, and Monterrey. (3) Industry was oriented to import substitution of consumer goods, and basic materials were exported in too raw a form. (4) The market structure was characterized by the coexistence of large oligopolists and a multitude of small enterprises "existing in a precarious state." It is a moot question whether these defects (if they are defects) are justifiably characterized as inherent in the economic "structure" rather than as manifestations of government policy.

As regards the first and third defects, the fundamental error was the government policy of encouraging import substitution of *consumer goods*, a policy that was also widely adopted throughout Latin America. By closing the border to imports of consumer goods, while freely admitting capital equipment for the new consumer industries, domestic production of capital goods was penalized, and Mexico lagged far behind Brazil, for example, in starting such industries. To increase the rate of industrial development, more capital goods had to be bought with foreign borrowings. The report states: "Paradoxically, the search for less dependence on other countries resulted, in the long run, in a more acute dependence"—but there is no paradox. The aim of import substitution was not to increase national independence; it was to develop home production of consumer goods, with the knowledge that capital goods would have to be imported. Domestic industries were given a degree of protection that guaranteed built-in inefficiency and high cost. This was what precluded exports—not the small scale of production for the domestic market only, as stated in the report. As time went on, the neglect of agriculture and the extractive industries (partly the result of overenthusiasm for industrializing) resulted in less exports of nonprocessed materials, which made more foreign loans necessary to buy more capital goods in order to achieve a higher rate of growth. This borrowing was referred to as using foreign "savings," and it was deliberately planned.

If these actions distorted the economic structure, the cause at work was an extraneous force destroying the structure, to wit, erroneous government policies. From time to time, lip service was paid to the intention of changing these protectionist policies, but for more than ten years nothing was done. Yet the report states that the structural defects became evident only with the 1976 devaluation.

As for the second defect, geographic overconcentration certainly exists, and it was the result of the lack of a government policy over the location of industry and of ten years of inadequate incentives to decentralize. Mexico shared this absence of policy with virtually all market economies. Urban planning in general and control over the location of industry in particular are still in an embryonic state, if present at all, for two very good reasons: they are difficult to achieve in a free society; and most countries consider that the loss of economic freedom involved in moving far enough toward a collectivist state to achieve them is far too high a price to pay. On the other hand, with full recognition of the difficulties that have been encountered elsewhere, Mexico is justified in trying to devise incentives that will succeed in improving the location of industry. Heavy penalties on, or even actual prohibition of the location of, new enterprises in Zone I may be necessary to succeed, however.

The fourth feature, even if big firms *are* oligopolies, still may not be a defect. Certainly the condition is not peculiar to Mexico; it is a universal and enduring characteristic of market economies, which suggests that a complex of relatively few large with numerous small firms is inherent in efficient industrial organization. Insofar as large firms possess monopolistic or oligopolistic power, that raises the separate question of controlling the abusive exercise of it.

The report not only errs in dating the detection of the alleged structural defects at the time of the 1976 devaluation but also is remiss in its failure to recognize that devaluation was forced upon the country by the inflation of 1972 onward, an inflation that is still continuing. It refers to "a framework of growth that had been increasingly conditioning all economic sectors to depend financially on the outside world." It describes what happened during the inflation as follows:

> The progressive subjection of monetary policy to international financial discipline was associated with inflexible management of the rate of exchange. Its maintenance was converted into an end in itself. The government responded to the pressures on the external sector by supporting the parity. Thus, the debt generated by the whole economy, necessary to cover the deficit on current account in the balance of payments and the speculative outflow of capital, was gradually converted into public debt.

This reads like a travesty of history. It shows no recognition of the facts that the initiating cause of inflation was excessive government spending, financed by the central bank and reflected in an increase in the money supply; and that the government refused to admit that the peso was overvalued, as evidenced by the excessive rate of increase in imports and the declining rate of increase in exports of goods and services, which made an early devaluation not only inevitable but also desirable. An earlier devaluation, which it was in the power of the government to make, was certainly preferable to one forced upon the country later. When the devaluation was already imminent, some elements in the private sector were so misled by the government's obdurate refusal to devalue that they even argued that an overvalued currency was a clever device that enabled Mexico to buy imported capital goods more cheaply! In these matters, it is important to set the record straight, lest the same policy errors be committed again.

Another curious (and, I think, erroneous) interpretation of the

261

past, which may affect future action, is the explanation of cyclical fluctuations in the economy. It is not clear whether the text refers only to post-1965 or to a longer period, but the economy is said to have "fluctuated between two limits: that imposed by the capacity to borrow abroad and that derived from internal pressures such as unemployment, which accentuated the depression."

The inevitability of a limit on foreign borrowing is obvious; but why this limit on the national rate of growth should lead to depression is not explained. And, of course, unemployment is a manifestation of depression rather than a cause of it, although spiraling unemployment, resulting from the failure to use available policy instruments to arrest it, will most surely also manifest itself in a still deeper depression. But the text does not cite, much less condemn, specific acts of government policy as being responsible for the "sequence of stagnation and moderate boom" (*auge*). Instead, it condemns the whole economic process, which is without justification pejoratively called "development with stability" (*desarrollo estabilizador*). It blames development with stability for causing the great national social objectives to be gradually pushed out of sight. It also blames that process, instead of the government-imposed inflation, for deepening Mexican dependence abroad, for creating uncertainty, for leading to a slower growth in effective demand, for limiting investment in productive projects, and for encouraging speculative types of investment.

Two further general charges seem to be made against the process of stable development: that the need to reduce imports encouraged indiscriminately *any* action to avoid them, "without taking into account . . . whether it would have long-term negative effects on the trade balance"; and that basic industries were left to the public sector, which had to operate unprofitably, "owing above all to the price ceilings which were imposed for the very purpose of decreasing inflationary pressures."

Surely these last two charges are a powerful indictment of government policies. They do not discredit the economic "model" of stable development. The correction of the erroneous government policies that were responsible for the economic—and especially monetary—destabilization preceding the devaluation will bring Mexico more into line with orthodox and soundly based economic policy.

Insofar as this report on the Plan Nacional attributes the poor performance of the economy in the past to defects in the "model" of the mixed economic system instead of to the errors in government policy, and especially to the destruction of financial stability by inflation, the base projection is a considerable understatement of potential achievement by comparison with what could be expected to happen with sound government policies, including the stopping of inflation. This doubt about the magnitude and even the composition of the future might-have-beens destroys the base projection as "a framework of reference in order subsequently to examine the viability of the Plan goals." The undefined concept of "a framework of reference" seems to include making the base projection a means both of judging the "viability" or the feasibility of the goals and of measuring the magnitude of the plan's achievement above the nonplan alternative. But if the "base" is highly uncertain, the instrument for judging and measuring is shattered.

This report on the planning of industrial development has very little to say about the problem of inflation. It merely asserts that the goal of 8–10 percent annual growth in real gross domestic product (GDP), although higher than any in Mexican history, "is compatible with reducing inflation" ("Presentation"). It gives no estimate of the rate of inflation that will occur in implementing the plan. It is therefore all the more important to point out that the brief analysis of the problem of inflation in the report exhibits confusion, especially in respect to the time element in the processes of stopping it. Discussing "financial self-determination" (a hazy concept that conveys the impression that Mexico is to become less dependent on the outside world, whereas in fact it is becoming more *interdependent* with it), the report condemns the idea of diminishing public spending or of restricting credit to overcome a "crisis," on the ground that such a "policy attacks only the symptoms and not the causes." It claims that although this policy restores equilibrium in the balance of payments and also *"lowers inflation in the long run"* (italics mine), it reduces still more the growth of production and employment. The report concludes that in "the best of cases it is a policy that has to be pursued for a long time," which conduces to social unrest.

The process so described is the opposite of what actually happens. Once decided upon, the stopping of inflation has in the past taken, and almost certainly will take in the future, only a short period of time, a period too short to cause serious social unrest. It is the long-postponed effort to stop it, the continuing inflation, that causes long-lasting suffering and thus engenders serious social disorder. The nature of the process of stopping inflation is illustrated by the experience in 1973–1974 of members of the Organization for Economic Cooperation and Development (OECD), a group of twenty-four industrial countries. Those countries in the group that decided to stop inflation had to endure only from three to five quarters of decline in output (negative growth). By restoring monetary stability, they have in succeeding years been in far better economic shape than the United States, which now faces much graver problems than if it had acted with the other industrial countries to stop inflation. The degree of slowdown in the OECD countries caused neither a massive increase in unemployment nor social unrest. Nor would similar anti-inflationary action, if it were taken in Mexico, bring either of these misfortunes.

In Mexico the problem of inflation may prove to be more stubborn to resolve than in the OECD countries, because it is more intense and of longer duration. No adequate action is likely to be taken against it, however, until the Mexican government becomes convinced that long-lasting inflation distorts, impedes, and destroys economic activities; that it imposes suffering on all the people, except perhaps the very richest. It especially injures people with fixed or very low incomes, including the "majority" that it is the declared policy of the present administration to help. The sum total of this suffering from inflation exceeds by far that resulting from the short-term marginal increase in unemployment involved in stopping it. Unless the government can be so convinced, Mexico is faced with the prospect of double-digit inflation through 1990, with no hope that the problem will be given the absolute priority that is necessary to restore financial stability. According to the Wharton econometric model of the Mexican economy, which projects GDP real growth rates much lower than in the plan, cumulative inflation measured by the most general index (the implicit price deflator of total GDP) would be 92 percent from 1978 to 1982. It is painful to contemplate the loss of nearly 50 percent of the purchasing power of the peso in four short years and the suffering by the people and destructive effects on the economy that it entails.

Strategy of the Plan. The chapter on strategy, after again giving an interpretation of past policy, briefly summarizes the ground covered by the following three chapters (2 to 4), thereby giving an overall view of the plan projection. In most general terms, the plan aims to use the oil surplus to restructure the economy to achieve a high rate of growth on a sustainable basis "with the central objective of finishing with nonemployment and unemployment [*desocupación y desempleo*] by the end of the century." This is basic to achieving the other fundamental objective—minimum welfare for everybody.

Five more specific requirements underlie these two general objectives. (1) Production must be reoriented to basic consumption goods. (2) The high-productivity branches of industry must develop the capacity to export and provide efficient substitutes for imports. (3) The industrial structure must be more integrated in order to make better use of our natural resources and to develop the capital goods industries. (4) Industry must be decentralized in the direction of the coastal areas, the land frontiers, and other "viable" localities. (5) A more balanced market structure must be achieved by attacking the tendency to oligopolistic concentration in the more dynamic industries and by "articulating" large enterprises with small and medium-sized firms.

The report states that the specific objectives and the methods of achieving them must be congruent with one another. Hence the need for programming. It is noted that although programming is not a novelty in Mexico, heretofore it has been used ad hoc or even improvised. And it is concluded that *permanent* instruments are needed to direct and regulate economic activities.

Up to now, the state is said to have encountered resistance from vested interests when it has attempted to strengthen the public finances, which it did not have sufficient resources to overcome. The nationally owned oil surplus has changed all that. It gives the state the directing capacity that it previously lacked. Now, as never before, it can "play a prominent role in economic programming." In the first instance, the goals established for the private and the "social" sectors are indicative only, but once an agreement for action has been reached, they become obligatory. This is the essence of the Alliance for Production.

The report lists the most important "actions of industrial programming." (1) Goals are established within a coherent macroeconomic and sectoral framework for 1979, for the medium term 1979–1982, and for the longer term 1982–1990. (2) Priorities are set for some branches of industry. (3) Regional priorities are established in the interest of decentralization. (4) Preferential treatment is given to small and medium-sized firms to counteract oligopolistic tendencies. (5) Instruments to implement the plan are created; outstanding among these are the incentives in connection with the sectoral, regional, and small-business priorities. (6) An organization is established "in the bosom [*seno*] of the public sector" to carry out an industrial policy based on general standards in order to eliminate "bureaucratic confusion and case by case treatment [*casuismo*]." (7) Mechanisms are established for negotiating contractual commitments from the private sector and for monitoring them.

The foundation (*fundamento*) of these seven actions are then briefly summarized in the rest of chapter 1.

Objectives and Priorities of the Plan. In pursuit of the ultimate objective of abolishing unemployment, the planned target is to increase employment by 5 percent a year (in contrast to the forecast of 3 percent in the base projection). To achieve this goal, the rate of growth in GDP must reach 10 percent a year by 1982 and stay there for the next decade. It is stated that experience elsewhere (no examples are given) shows this to be feasible. It is also said to be compatible with domestic and external

265

financial equilibrium, but no estimate is given of the magnitude of the rise in the price level that will occur. Industry will contribute about 30 percent of this annual increase in employment or 1.5 percent a year. The remainder will be contributed by agriculture and, "above all," by the service industries.

Three types of priority are established: the sectoral, the regional, and that for small and medium-sized companies. Within the sectoral category, two kinds of priority are to be given to industry. In the first kind, maximum priority goes to agroindustry and the manufacture of capital goods: the former because it promotes rural development; the latter because of its importance in providing the "industrial structure" with a solid base of fixed capital and technology. In the second kind, priority is given to "the existing nucleus of industrial structure," which produces more than 50 percent of total industrial production. Because it produces essential consumer goods for the workers and is also an important source of exports, it must be strengthened.

The industrial priorities are given in considerable detail in chapter 3, which is entitled "Priorities." An elaborate classification extending over eight pages (147–54) divides them into two categories. Category 1 contains three groups—agroindustry, capital goods, and strategic industrial inputs. Each group contains first-degree and second-degree subgroups, and this category contains forty-seven individual items in the fourth numeral of the classification (that is, the second-degree subgroups). The items are not, in general, individual products but groups. Category 2 contains three groups—nondurable consumer goods, durable consumer goods, and intermediate goods. They contain thirty-six individual items, making the total eighty-three in the two categories.

The taxonomic scheme is complex, and it presents some difficulties in assigning annual rates of growth in total demand, which are attached to the classification. They are predominantly given for the first-degree subgroup (third numeral)—twenty-four out of the twenty-eight cases— no doubt for some technical reasons in the breakdown in the statistical data available.

Regional priorities are given by establishing three "zones." But these are not zones in the accepted sense, for they consist of widely scattered places and areas throughout the country, with none of the contiguity that characterizes a zonal area. In Zone I, new economic activities receive preferential incentives. It comprises four ports, two on the Gulf and two on the Pacific, and their adjacent municipalities, and another eleven towns that have potential for urban industrial development. Zone II includes all the areas that have been designated industrial centers by the states in their agreements with the federal government. Zone III, which is subject to "ordinance [ordenamiento] and regulation," is subdivided into an "area of controlled growth" comprising the Federal District and its adjacent municipalities and an "area of consolidation" comprising population centers to which the influence of the Federal District radiates. With a few exceptions, new enterprises established in this zone receive no incentives, in order to discourage industry from locating in the Valley of Mexico.

The municipalities that are to receive regional priority are set out in the National Plan for Urban Development (Plan Nacional de Desarrollo Urbano). The geographical selection of priority areas was based on such criteria as facilitating exports, which put ports and land frontiers in the forefront; or easy access to energy, as in the case of towns in the interior that are situated along the pipelines; or abundant raw materials. The government would prefer to see the foreign owned assembly companies (*maquiladoras*) located in the interior, as a measure of decentralization and to diminish the attraction of migrant workers to the northern border.

Details are given of places and areas receiving regional priority and of those in Zone III that are denied it or are subject to control. These are contained in seventeen pages (156–72) of lists and maps. They do not lend themselves to summarizing.

The purposes of the priorities to small and medium-sized businesses are to encourage labor-intensive enterprises and to improve the market structure by strengthening the system of subcontracting to smaller firms. The report also relates these priorities to the problem of diminishing the monopolistic strength of larger firms, but it is not clear how this can be done through encouraging smaller enterprises. The four paragraphs in chapter 3 on this third type of priority call for no comment in addition to what has already been said in this paper.

The complexity and magnitude of this vast system of priorities call for comments. The fact that priority is to be given to the existing nucleus of industry, which represents 52 percent of total industrial production, raises the question whether the very concept of priority is not being emasculated by so broadening its coverage. Selective encouragement of industrial development ceases to be the leading characteristic of the plan and is replaced by a scheme of subsidies to, and control over, almost the whole of industry.

Furthermore, the incentives to small and medium-sized firms are different in kind from those to the sectoral and regional. In his "Presentation," José Andrés Oteyza stated that the "field of priorities" determines "what," and geographically "where," to produce. The incentive to small businesses, however, deals not with the *what* or *where* but rather with the *how* to produce. This priority touches on much thornier problems than the other two, as can be seen by the experience of other countries in trying to provide small businesses with more ample credit facilities or in taking other measures to improve their efficiency as a part of the market organization.

One of the myths that has had to be exploded at intervals during the last fifty or more years is that large corporations (whether monopolistic or oligopolistic or operating more competitively under antimonopoly laws) are driving small companies out of business. Recently, this myth has again had to be exposed by producing empirical evidence to the contrary in both the United States and the United Kingdom; but the myth is still affecting government policy in many countries. This report, for example, refers to the contrast between large and small businesses as a "polarization," which is not an apt metaphor to describe the intricate relationships and innumerable gradations of size that exist within the apparatus of production and distribution. The report recognizes that we cannot rid ourselves of polarization by diminishing the number of large firms; on the contrary, we need more of them in sectors where there are too few. The logical conclusion would seem to be that what we need is antimonopoly action, through statute and/or an administrative body of the kind that some countries have had for all of this century or longer. There are in the report signs of official preoccupation with this problem.

The position of foreign-owned companies within the plan's incentive system is not dealt with systematically, but the subject is brought into this discussion of polarization. Foreign companies are said to be operating preponderantly in the most dynamic branches of industry, which are those that have the highest degree of concentration. During 1970–1975, however, the degree of concentration became "especially dense in industries in which domestic enterprises predominated." The change in the situation is attributed by the report, at least in part, to the control over foreign enterprises in the 1973 foreign investment law, which gave the large Mexican private-sector groups greater facilities for participating in Mexicanization. It seems that the authors of the plan are uneasy about the situation, and they express the belief that the transfers of ownership to Mexican-owned companies "should be evaluated in detail when they are mere formalities, that is to say when there is no effective transfer of the control and management of these companies to national businessmen. Similarly, it is necessary to examine the cases in which productive activity is concentrated in large financial or industrial consortia, even though the Mexican participation may be in the majority." Evidently, the authorities are showing some concern with the problem of monopoly, whether the power is exercised by Mexican or by foreign companies.

In further discussion of the part to be played by foreign-owned

268

companies, the report states that they can, within the framework of the plan, provide Mexico with access to external markets and to the sources of technical change through their parent companies. In defining priorities, the plan will indicate the activities and methods by which foreign participation may make a significant contribution. Under existing law, complete packages of measures may be negotiated, including the transfer of technology, especially in branches of industry in which national investment is insufficient.

It is impossible to judge whether the above discussion foreshadows the liberalization of the criteria for the entry into Mexico of foreign-owned companies and for their access to the incentives in the plan. The indications are, however, that the subject is under consideration.

The Instruments of the Plan

The federal government has two types of instruments at its disposal to guide and direct the processes of industrialization: those for direct action by investing in infrastructure and through the operations of the state enterprises; and those for indirect action by giving incentives in the form of financial assistance and of protection against foreign competition. With the greater resources at its disposal from the oil surplus, the government can increase all forms of assistance, including health and education, the nonmaterial part of the infrastructure, and the alleviation of extreme poverty.

The whole of the energetics industry will be given priority, not just petroleum, for abundant energy is a prerequisite to sustained development. The report points out that Mexico is the only market economy in which the oil resources are in their entirety the property of the nation; and also it is one of the few developing countries with an existing broad technical base, as well as a stable but flexible political structure that is capable of producing rapid socioeconomic change.

Emphasis is placed on the view that industrialization is a means of transforming perishable raw materials (including oil) into a permanent source of wealth. This is of course true of industrialization anywhere, and it has no particular significance in Mexico. Probably the intention is to emphasize that oil exports should not be used solely to raise the standard of living of this generation of Mexicans. The authors of the report surely would not deny, however, that investment in health and education creates a permanent source of wealth insofar as it improves the quality of the work force. And using the oil surplus to abolish extreme poverty, which is a declared objective of the plan, besides being a necessity on humanitarian grounds, also increases the permanent sources of wealth by raising the quality of the work force.

269

In granting incentives to the private sector, an effort is being made to do so under general rules, "to eliminate bureaucratic confusion and arbitrariness." The most general incentive is the policy of keeping the prices of energetics to industrial users below international prices, as a means of giving an impetus to exports. More specific grants of assistance are to be combined in a single fiscal credit, based on two criteria only—new investments and an increase in the number employed. For maximum effect, the investment credit is conceded at the time the investment is made, when it is likely to have the greatest influence on the decisions of the investor. Its amount is 25 or 20 percent of the value of the fixed assets acquired, according to the priority of the activity. An additional 5 percent incentive credit is given on all purchases of machinery and equipment produced in Mexico. The incentive to increase employment may be as high as 20 percent of the area minimum wage for each extra employee, payable for a maximum of two years. The border zones and the free ports do not come under the general scheme of incentives, because they have a special incentive system of their own.

The protection of Mexican industry against foreign competition is now being made a part of the incentives complex within the system of priorities, because the productive system has passed the stage in which it should be protected indiscriminately. Protection is to be given through tariffs, the level of which will be established with due regard to "integrated chains of production," in order to avoid distorting the cost relationships among different branches of industry through higher prices of imported inputs. The substitution of general tariffs for prior import permits is to be gradual in order to leave ample time for making the necessary adjustments in domestic industries and to minimize injury to existing producers.

Notwithstanding this move toward selectivity, however, the policy of general subsidies to industry through low prices of energetics and of some raw materials will continue to be, of course, an indiscriminate form of protection, and it is a subsidy to exports. The policy suffers from the same defects as indiscriminate protection in regard to efficiency of home industry. In addition, under the rules of the General Agreement on Tariffs and Trade, the subsidy to exports is subject to surveillance. The government may find it desirable to scrutinize its policy from the point of view of the effect on both domestic industrial efficiency and the integrating of the economy more fully into the world trading system.

Other instruments used by the government include the preferential discounting of export credits in accordance with specific criteria, such as the time taken for an investment to mature. The possibilities are also being studied of facilitating the financing of medium-sized firms through the issue of common shares, and of the state enterprises through preference shares, using a suitable fiscal device to reduce the taxable income of purchasers, in order to persuade individuals to buy these shares.

The Alliance for Production in the Plan. The agreements for concerting action between the government and the private sector provide the mechanism for implementing the scheme of incentives. They are to be granted through two kinds of programs: those of development (*programas de fomento*) and those of manufacturing (*programas de fabricación*). Development programs specify the incentives and the protection that are to be applied uniformly to all participants in a given activity. Each firm commits itself to achieve certain goals as regards investment, production, prices, exports, and the use of domestic inputs. Foreign-owned companies will also commit themselves to a method of Mexicanizing within a stated period of time. By granting the incentives to an activity rather than to the firm, the intention is to avoid the danger of giving different treatment to essentially identical cases. The manufacturing programs, on the other hand, apply to individual firms.

The government recognizes the need for quick action in coordinating the programs, and it therefore will set up an Interministerial Commission (Comisión Intersecretarial), which will decide on the whole complex of incentives to be granted, after which the various government departments will apply them automatically. It is thought that this will prevent the commission from becoming just another bureaucracy. No explanation is given, however, of how the granting of incentives through the existing departments will avoid the risk of enlarging the existing bureaucracy.

Implementing the plan requires consultation between the government and the private sector on a *continuing* basis. The development programs must provide for the entry of new producers, for coordination among small establishments, and for the financing of subcontracting to the latter by large firms. They must anticipate bottlenecks and take action to prevent them. In all these program activities, private-sector chambers and associations must play a leading role.

The report asserts that zeal (*afán*) for defining what areas are the prerogatives (*privativos*) of the public or the private sector must be "relegated to second place," because this kind of discussion is sterile in the light of the high rate of growth offered by the plan. The hope may be expressed here that relegating this vital subject to second place does not mean putting it in limbo, because it is highly important that the debate should be kept alive regarding the functions and economic operating activities that the state can efficiently undertake. The debate is essential, even though a "mixed economy" is universally accepted as a necessary and desirable fact of life. To drop or stifle the debate would

271

run the risk that encroachments on, and strangling controls over, the private sector will multiply—perhaps by inadvertence rather than by design—with incalculable harm to industrial efficiency.

The issue is highly relevant to the concept and practice of planning. It raises the question of who does the planning. The more faith the government has in the organizational virtues of the system of private enterprise, as the best means of decentralizing the decision-making process and of harnessing the energies of individuals to it in the interest of efficiency, the greater the amount of planning that it will consent to leave to the private sector. By parity of reasoning, the less will the government feel the urge to undertake the kinds of decision making—which is what planning means—that are best left widely distributed throughout the private sector. The decisions can then be made under the guidance of the detailed practical knowledge of the relevant facts that only freely operating markets can provide.

The plan is regarded as the first step toward providing industry with a new set of charts with which to navigate and toward the establishment of a "normative framework that institutionalizes the instruments of indicative planning." It implies a "permanent dialogue" between the private-sector organizations and the federal government, and this will require the organization of a National Forum of Industrial Development (Foro Nacional de Desarrollo Industrial).

Goals and Forecasts of the Plan

The encouragement of exports of nonpetroleum industrial products is one of the foremost objectives if not the kernel of the plan of industrialization. Manufactured products were selected for export promotion in accordance with five criteria: (1) cases in which the limiting factor on exports is a shortage of domestic supply, because the international market for them is established—for example, mining; (2) cases in which a large processing value could be added to abundant domestic raw materials and industrial inputs—for example, secondary petrochemicals; (3) cases of recent contraction in traditional exports for lack of investment or competitiveness—for example, textiles; (4) products that need economies of scale to be export-competitive—for example, capital goods; (5) manufacturing sectors with large trade deficits, although they are dominated by foreign companies that "have easy access to international markets," such as automobiles, rubber, pharmaceuticals, and chemicals.

The first criterion is unexceptionable, for it implies that the product is internationally competitive. In the second, however, this condition should be expressly stated, because many such nonprocessed materials might for a considerable time be exported in their raw or semiraw state with advantage to the nation. In the third criterion, if the cause of contraction is "lack of competitiveness," the implication is that additional investment will restore competitiveness. Similarly, in the fourth criterion, though economies of scale may be a necessary condition to attain competitiveness, they are not a sufficient condition. Nor is it by any means certain that the requisite scale of output can be achieved with efficiency merely by crowding on the investment.

The last criterion, however, is more difficult to accept. It exhibits a disturbing lapse into mercantilism, a reversion to the "balance of bargains," the speciousness of which was exposed 200 years ago. The idea that an individual firm or branch of industry should balance its foreign exchange expenditure and earnings is the negation of the declared policy of President López Portillo to make the Mexican economy more open, in order that Mexico may occupy the prominent place in the international trading and financial system that its human and material resources justify. If foreign companies really had easy access to international markets with *Mexican* products, experience shows that they would be only too eager to enter them. To extend to other industries the narrow precept of balancing the foreign exchange account that is now being applied to the automotive industry would spell disaster for domestic efficiency in the allocation of productive resources, and therefore for the national objective of becoming more competitive internationally.

A list is given of twenty-five groups of products that have been selected for export promotion. Estimates were made of the rates of increase in the total, domestic, and export demands for each group of products and for industrial production as a whole (excluding petroleum, gold, and silver) in two periods, 1978–1982 and 1982–1990. The percentages of total demand supplied by imports for the years 1978, 1982, and 1990 were also estimated.

For industrial production as a whole, the estimated rate of growth is higher in 1982–1990 than in 1978–1982 for all three categories of demand. The respective average annual increases are: in total demand, 10 and 12 percent; in domestic demand, 10.1 and 11.9 percent; and in exports, 7.9 and 16.2 percent; import dependency is estimated to grow in each of the three years, the rates being 10.2 percent in 1978, 12.2 percent in 1982, and 14.9 percent in 1990.

The following are the most noteworthy features among the changes in the groups. The highest estimated rates of growth in both periods are in secondary petrochemicals, but the rate of increase in both total and domestic demand declines in each period from 19.6 to 18.3 percent. At the same time, exports increase (13.6 to 15.7 percent) and import dependency declines from 6.7 percent in 1978 to 1.8 percent in 1990. The next biggest increase in demand is in rubber products (12.8 and 16.7 percent), but exports decrease (-0.9 and -2.2 percent) and import dependency rises from 5.1 to 8.8 percent. In the electric machinery group, the increase is from about 4.7 to 16.6 percent in both total and domestic demand and from 9.5 to 18.4 percent in exports; but import dependency rises from 36.9 to 40.5 percent. This increase in the import ratio is exceeded only by that in metal/mechanical, from 41.1 to 56.5 percent, a group in which demand declines from a rate of 16.3 to 13 percent, although exports show an increasing rate from 12.7 to 17.6 percent in the two periods. Apart from the secondary petrochemical and the metal/mechanical groups, the only declines in rates of growth are in flours and nixtamal (a corn-based mixture for baking), from 3.6 to 2.6 percent; metal products, from 13.4 to 12.7 percent; and a miscellaneous group of nonclassified manufactures.

As regards foreign trade, exports are estimated to decline in both periods in three product groups: meats and milks (-10.8 and -1.8 percent), nonclassified foods (-22.1 and -20.8 percent), and rubber products (-0.9 and -2.2 percent). In the period 1978–1982, exports of two other products decline, nonmetallic mining products by -0.1 percent and pharmaceuticals by -4.2 percent; whereas those of transport equipment rise from 18.4 to 27.5 percent, and those of automotive products decline from 15.4 to 7.4 percent. In summary, exports of fourteen product groups show either an increasing rate of growth or a declining rate of increase; five show a declining rate of growth or an increasing rate of decline; and the rest are constant or zero. Import dependency increases in twelve product groups and declines in eight product groups, while five are constant or zero.

The report also gives a complementary list of nineteen product groups in which it is necessary to make a major additional investment (table, p. 61). This list includes seventeen product groups from the export-promotion list, the eight missing being shoes and clothing, paper, rubber, basic chemicals, fertilizers, soaps and detergents, automobile products, and nonclassified manufactures. The two added to the investment list are transport and printing and publishing. The biggest percentage additions to investment over that "autonomously programmed" are in electrical machinery (148.0 percent), milk products (118.1 percent), and the metal/mechanical group (104.5 percent). The biggest absolute increases are in electricity (12.0 billion 1975 pesos), transport (6.6 billion pesos), cement and glass (7.9 billion pesos), and soft-fiber textiles (5.3 billion pesos).

The total additional investment (excluding that in agriculture) required for 1978–1982 is estimated to be 66.1 billion 1975 pesos (130 billion pesos of December 1978, which implies an increase in prices of 97 percent over the three years). What percentage increase over the "autonomous" for the nineteen product groups this investment represents is not given. Instead, the additional investment is said to represent an increase of 12.4 percent over the whole of "productive investment" (excluding that in residential construction, in hydrocarbons, and in agricultural activities by the general government).

Integral Development

Leopoldo Solís

Have We Followed the Wrong Path?

Until now, economic development has been pursued in two predominant patterns: that of dual or unbalanced growth and that of balanced growth. The first is the classical process of modernization based on capital formation—as in the case of the U.S.S.R. or Great Britain—in which one sector of the economy prospers at the expense of others. The high-production sector—usually the industrial sector—is developed by extracting the producers' surplus from the other sectors, in most cases from the agricultural sector. This surplus, along with other productive resources, is transferred from a traditional activity to the modern economy. Thus, the latter grows more rapidly, gaining absolute and relative importance while the traditional economy loses relative weight and becomes less and less significant. In a balanced development, of which China is an example, society's savings are generated and invested in the entire society in such a way that the effort to generate economic development as well as the fruits of progress are attained and shared by the entire population.

Let us study the dual development model. The similarity between Victorian frugality and socialist austerity is no coincidence. Both lead to patterns of development that are radically different in a political sense, yet similar in that they support an investment process with high rates of global savings. If the main thrust is aimed at basic industries and capital goods, the pattern is said to be similar to the Stalinist process; if it is oriented toward the production of consumer goods, it is more of a consumerist process. In spite of sustaining Soviet bureaucracy and the Red Army or the English aristocracy and colonial adventures, the social attitude in both schemes was that of work and austerity expressed in attitudes of self-resignation.

All economic systems are linked to a moral attitude. The best-known relationship of this type is that of Protestantism and capitalism. The anxiety produced by the Calvinist doctrine of predestination became a mundane asceticism, according to Max Weber, a relationship between goals, means, and limited resources that determined capitalist rationality.[1] Victorian morality started its decline with World War I and was dealt the final blow by the Great Depression of the 1930s. Keynes and the Bloomsbury group carried out a frontal attack on Victorian puritanism and, instead, justified an aesthetic ideal, rendering tribute to personal relationships and to beauty. Keynes's philosophy, "In the long run we are going to be as dead as the mutton," was an invitation to enjoy the present and even to engage in conspicuous consumption. In the words of Leonard Woolf, pleasure came to be thought of as "a very considerable good in itself." Keynes's antidepression policy was born of this antipuritan environment, and from it emerged the contemporary theory of economic development: from Keynes to Harrod; from Cambridge to the rest of the world. Escape from the Depression through public spending allowed the growth of national income without any abstinence at all, by using unused productive capacity, a process that is possible only in a mature industrial society. Unfortunately, this instilled hope for development in poor nations that did not fully understand the sacrifices involved in following a capital formation model, yet fully understood consumer habits legitimized by advances of the models to be emulated. The scenario had been set for development based on capital formation with elitist consumerism. The Keynesian mirage turned out to be too attractive to be rejected by underdeveloped nations, who were the passive receptors of economic doctrines and ideas applicable only in contexts radically different from their own. Growth based on import substitution, beginning with consumer goods, a postwar phenomenon, is a form that is unique to the dual model of capital formation. Growth without abstinence became a fallacy that would cost society dearly in terms of inflation and other forms of economic and social instability.

Given the current disorder in the world economy, is development based on capital formation really viable? Certainly, Japan, Korea, Taiwan, Greece, and Spain have attained it recently, and apparently Colombia and Brazil are about to attain it. Nonetheless, I believe this type of development is foreign to the struggles and aspirations of Mexicans, who may be naive but are not wicked. We must bear in mind that an orientation of that nature disregards distributive aspects and contributions to noneconomic sectors. If income distribution worsens and the subsistence sector does not disappear, those who are forced to wait to join the development process will be left staring at a banquet to which they are not invited but for which they must purchase a ticket, whether they want to or not. They will do this at least as witnesses of the depletion of natural resources that were of common domain, from which they could partially feed themselves, and whose access is now blocked to them. And if the demographic response is strong enough, or the capital formation does not occur fast enough, the modernization process can stretch out indefinitely, deteriorating distribution even more and adding stress to the entire social structure.

For historical and cultural reasons, Mexican efforts must be geared in another direction: that of global development, more akin to the philosophy of the Chinese model.

Whether successful or not with a classical capital formation model, a growth effort directed toward inherited cultural patterns and concerned with providing better creative opportunities for all citizens implies a smaller social cost. Individual initiative must be motivated and combined with the advantages of collective activity where those with fewer possibilities and resources can also receive attention and stimulus. We need to achieve conditions in which native dialects will receive as much respect as the national language, where housing and urban development projects are undertaken with global welfare in mind, not just that of automobile owners; where clothing, cuisine, folklore, and crafts receive more attention than the Bee Gees, *Vogue,* or *McCall's.*

Generalized development seems to respond much better to long-time Mexican ideals and to true idiosyncrasy. It is ethically imperative, given the scarcity of resources, to design systems that distribute the benefit to everyone. It is ridiculous to think that all can receive medical care in Houston, yet it is no less extravagant to think of generalizing the medical care provided by IMSS or ISSTE.[2] In Mexico it is impossible to provide Western-tradition medical services for the entire population. After all, the medical problems of countries like Mexico stem mainly from malnutrition and poor sanitation, not peptic ulcers, myocardial infarctions, and other "diseases of modern man." Better nutrition, preventive medicine, and mass inoculation coupled with large programs of supportive research are feasible solutions and would have direct beneficial effects for a majority of Mexicans. Just as vaccination has a very high economic yield, so will almost any type of applied research in support of modern and traditional productive activities and basic research in support of the latter. The same can be said of the dissemination and expansion of the results of these types of research.

A program conceived and oriented in this manner cannot be a romantic abdication of the fruits of contemporary civilization. On the contrary, it is its most judicious use, subject to a scheme of priorities linked to the technological and cultural change of the entire social body, attentive to its less dynamic components, more watchful of its reach and dissemination than of the cost-benefit coefficients. One can begin by redefining the indicators of economic development that are related to the availability and accessibility of basic products, the development of the biological potential of human beings, the potential for evolution of all its components—a development concept with greater upward mobility, where measures of nutrition, shelter, education, and health determine the priorities of resource allocation and in which microplanning is the rule and macroplanning the exception.

Until now, the Mexican development model has followed the dual model, or capital formation based on substitution of consumer goods, with the consumerist accent of post-Keynesian influence. We have retained the utopian illusion of achieving what is possible and reasonable in a mature society but is unattainable in an underdeveloped nation which alters its traditional values.

Designs for a New Style of Development

The intensity of natural resource utilization necessary to achieve the quality of life of industrialized nations cannot be sustained on a worldwide scale. This proves that Mexico will never be like the United States, Germany, or Switzerland. The availability of natural resources, even assuming very favorable changes in their conservation, would not suffice to support current levels of consumption in industrialized nations if they were to be extended equally to the world population. Natural resources and technological possibilities are limited. I say this without intending to be fatalistic but with the conviction that we have the opportunity to establish a life style free of extravagances, less costly in social terms, and with a reasonable and relative isolation from foreign influence. I am aware that it may seem unreal to present arguments for the protection of Mexican economic, social, and cultural values while a cable television set, broadcasting American television programs in English, sits in the living room surrounded by all sorts of similar gadgets; in spite of this, conscious effort must be made to assert the system of values that gives us a national identity. The road to follow is that of strengthening our cultural heritage, examining roots, developing culture, and advancing in genuine assimilation of the sources of civilization from which we have evolved.

Even if Mexico had a larger stock of natural resources, following a pattern of development like that of the United States would blind the creativity characteristic of Mexican people that represents our contribution to universal civilization. Our sense of justice and self-determination has formed a nationalism, which is the link that gives cohesiveness and makes us resistant and malleable. Otherwise, located as we are next to the most powerful nation on earth, all identity would have been lost long ago. Mexicans are not threatened by separatist factions; we have a rich and varied cultural heritage that can become the essence of a

279

genuine process of economic development. The latter, in its fullest concept, can be understood as the advancement of society as a whole—economically, socially, politically, and culturally. The focus of integral development recognizes that society must change as a whole and that evolution originates from all of its parts, as opposed to the traditional economic focus that ignores existing culture and its intimate relationship with the prevailing productive and distributive models.

The development pattern should arise from the evolution of the cultural structure and assertion of existing values, correcting distortions that impair the proper functioning of the system that produces them. Until now, Mexicans have borrowed a multitude of ideas and institutions from advanced Western nations; we have docilely accepted examples and extravagances or made indiscriminate purchases. The result has been that the benefits of progress have not reached the entire society; islands of prosperity have been created in the midst of misery that make it impossible to attain the ideals that were dreamed of long ago and even translated into law. The elite that has been created adopts the scale value of its peers in advanced nations—just as it adopts the fashion of skiing in the mountains of Colorado or Austria, it divorces itself even more from the rest of its fellow citizens. I must vigorously insist that, even though we may long to follow the example of advanced nations and a false pride may drive us to imitate them, we will never be like them. The depletion of our natural resources is in sight and should guide us down the road of austerity and encourage us to adopt a style of our own to preserve and improve what we have. When judging imitative patterns, we should consider ourselves not better or worse but different; with this comes being true to oneself.

Economic development makes no sense if it does not increase the real income of everyone, men and women; if it does not offer better alternatives to one and the other; if it is not accompanied by the flourishing of music, visual arts, and literature; if it does not preserve the cultural heritage; if it remains indifferent to the crumbling of our architectural jewels and their replacement by somber boxes of reinforced concrete.

Though I have a broader purpose in mind, this essay would not be complete without an indication, brief though it may be, of the aspects of economic policy that, regardless of political orientation, we must put into practice in order to grow quickly and achieve a blueprint for integral development. This implies mobilization of all of society's resources. I also must present it in order to compare it with the models that have been followed in the past. Reading this part of the essay is not essential, however, for a full understanding of its general intention, which is that of suggesting a new form of national development. The reader who does not wish to spend time on technicalities may omit it without missing the essence of what I intend to say.

Features of Economic Policy

I would like to present the hypothesis that an economy, regardless of its particular economic system—the degree of centralization of economic decisions or ownership concentration of capital—must perform certain actions in order to achieve growth and efficiency. Moreover, from a logical point of view, any type of economic system can perform these actions, though the type of instruments at hand may and should be, of course, very different in each case.

In the following charts I have synthesized the main areas of economic policy in an attempt to offer elements of judgment about what the country must do, regardless of the policy option it may choose. Among other things, one can perceive conditions to maximize consumer welfare, minimize social costs, achieve intersectoral, intertemporal, and intergenerational equity, achieve efficiency in the utilization of scarce natural resources, achieve an efficient operation that does not overindulge in technological or natural monopolies—those in which technology or large-scale economies are dominant—and choose a rate of growth; in other words, choose the best combination of present and future consumption. The topics chosen here are illustrative in character. The equivalent decision tree is applicable to any sector or area of activity. It would be easy to elaborate in greater detail, but this would transcend the limits of this work.

It has been noted that the task of the social sciences is to discover indirect or secondary unforeseen effects. Economists call them externalities, as they are external to the original purpose of the agent that produces them. Externalities are decisive factors in social efficiency and harmony; they also have an inescapable moral dimension. If, in the process of consumption, someone is contaminated or hurt, he must be compensated, as this generates a negative or damaging externality. If a car were driven on the expressway, one would need to pay the additional cost of operation to other drivers as a result of the congestion generated. There are also positive externalities. A cultural radio station can gain more and more listeners without significant additional costs; in this case, free access to all potential listeners should be guaranteed. Externalities are particularly important in the exploitation of natural resources: the depletion of natural water deposits, the extinction of flora and fauna and above-ground pasturage are examples of this concept. A figure for gross national product (GNP) has little meaning if it does not incorporate externalities in the measure in which they involve social

281

costs or national wealth destruction. The economic policy should be able to solve these problems if the economy is to survive and be reasonably efficient, and the social sciences will not accomplish their mission as long as these complications exist.

A few examples may serve to illustrate our preoccupation. Suppose we are facing a monopoly situation. Monopolies, if they have full price-setting power, obtain monopoly rents. General policy tells us that, in these cases, prices should be fixed not to exceed the costs of operations and replacement, plus a projection of the cost of invested capital or interest rate. If we are to act in defense of society, it is imperative to avoid the existence of prices that involve monopoly rents. Different recipes for economic policy depend on the political framework. In a liberal economy, once costs of production have been determined, tariffs and import facilities would be established that would force the fixing of internal competitive prices free from monopoly rents. In a mixed economy, price controls would set quotations of the same order. Prices of this nature would originate directly from the rules established by the planning or control office of a fully planned economy.

Let us change our analytical perspective and consider the rate of growth or, expressed in different terms, the optimum rate of investment. In a market economy, the level of investment is roughly equivalent to the time preference rate—in other words, the rate that rewards abstinence in present consumption and encourages postponing it for conversion to future consumption. In a socialist economy, this rate could consist of the maximum investment to be applied productively in the sense of increased production per unit of additional investment, according to some theorists of this type of system. The rate of investment in a socialist economy will be higher, under the same conditions, than that of a market economy, although it is always possible that subsidies to the interest-rate cost or fiscal credits on investment—tax exemptions that would increase the yield of the project—can make them coincide. A mixed economy would achieve a combination of both types of decisions until an equivalent level of investment could be reached. The Mexican economy now invests approximately 22 percent of its national economic aggregate. This aspect greatly improved during the period of stabilizing development (1959–1970). Consumption, as a factor of gross domestic product (GDP), decreased from .894 in 1950 to .718 in 1970 whereas capital per working person rose, after eliminating the effects of inflation, from 31,000 pesos in 1950 to 66,000 pesos in 1970.

In regard to "externalities," if the entirety of social action is to evolve in a direction that prevents—internalizes, in the technical sense—undesirable effects from damaging more than benefiting the original actions, it will be necessary to create corrective mechanisms. Any economic system should attend to and resolve those secondary effects. In tables 1 and 2 these effects have been classified according to their area of economic action (consumption, production, intertemporal, as in the case of exploitation of nonrenewable natural resources). Here, economic logic tells us that oil is the property of the nation, of its present and future generations, not an exclusive asset of the present one. Its exploitation thus should only change the form of wealth: oil for productive, reproducible, and permanent capital, for factories and machinery in constant renovation. Oil surpluses should not be dissipated in present consumption, although this is exactly what the industry is fostering when it uses its oil surpluses to maintain excessively low internal prices. This may be comfortable from a political point of view, but it is unfair to future generations.

It would be desirable to correct the current imbalance between physical investment and that realized in human capital, which is still very limited; investment in research is even more shamefully limited. Poverty is mainly a result of lack of education. The viability of integral development depends on correcting this imbalance. As far as integral development is concerned, we must think of four instruments and four objectives: the instruments are level of oil exports, level of exchange rate, public savings, and composition of public expenditure; and the objectives are balance-of-payments stability, employment level, rate of growth of GDP, and advancement of minorities.

Integral Development

Though the focus of development suggested here is biased by my scale of values and thus should be taken in that context, I hope it still has a broad appeal in spite of leading to propositions that, in many cases, are very different from those that Mexico has followed in the past. If poverty is mainly a phenomenon of rural life and lack of education, then these must be the priorities of the economic policy. It is not stimulating to hear of the thousands of millions that have been spent at Las Truchas and to hear our songs of pride in our steel self-sufficiency when, at the same time, we are importing more corn.[3] If urban poverty is largely associated with families headed by women (widows, abandoned women, single women, etc.), they should be provided with better access to the job market. Eliminating the discrimination to which they are subjected should lead us to develop preschool education, with nurseries and child care centers that would allow mothers to participate in the organized job market, instead of trying so hard to achieve a poor imitation of the French education system. To the extent that poverty is a rural problem, we can think that farmers with small landholdings should concentrate

TABLE 1

INFORMATION NECESSARY FOR ACTIONS OF ECONOMIC POLICY

Sectors and Objectives	Private Enterprise Economy	Mixed Economy	Socialist Economy
Cases in which social cost differs from private cost			
(1) In consumption: public goods (defense, education, etc.) *Objective:* to maximize the positive difference between what we are willing to pay and what is paid for consumption of the good; produce additional units of that good, while the social gain obtained defrays the cost of producing them	Determination of optimum levels of present and future activity	Determination of optimum levels of present and future activity	Determination of optimum levels of present and future activity
(2) In production: *Objective:* to manage to have economic agents absorb or receive all the costs or benefits of their operation	Determination of differences between private and social costs of production. Knowledge of transgressors' levels, costs, and techniques of operation	Determination of social costs and production techniques	Determination of operating levels and corresponding techniques
(3) Intertemporal: exploitation of limited natural resources *Objective:* maximization of	Determination of optimum technique and economics for the resource-exploited	Knowledge of costs of production and profitability of operations	Determination of operating levels and corresponding prices and techniques

the difference between the benefits and costs of their exploitation through time

(4) Technological and economic monopolies: *Objective*: maximization of consumer welfare; prices equal to cost of replacement	Determination of the power of monopoly and of discriminatory and collusive practices; determination of present and future market size; information on the costs and techniques of production; knowledge of international prices and levels of production	Control of industrial property and its technological contracts; determination of industries' costs of operation	Knowledge of sectoral industrial demand and of production techniques
(5) Perfect competitive production: *Objective*: maximization of consumer welfare, competitive prices in factors and products	Determination of possible distortions in the markets of suppliers and buyers	Knowledge of financing and marketing practices; costs and scales of operation	Determination of consolidation advantages
(6) Economy as a whole: *Objective*: stability, growth, efficiency, foreign independence, and equal distribution	Complete national accounts; macroeconomic indicators necessary to avoid economic fluctuations and unemployment; alternative use of resources; data on income distribution	Complete national accounts; macroeconomic indicators necessary to avoid economic fluctuations and unemployment; alternative use of factors; data on income and wealth distribution	Complete national accounts; knowledge of technological requirements of raw materials and other materials brought in for the production of goods; financing functions; data on income distribution

SOURCE: Author.

TABLE 2

STRATEGIES AND POLICY ACTIONS

Sectors and Objectives	Private Enterprise Economy	Mixed Economy	Socialist Economy
(1) Public goods (defense, education, etc.): *Objective*: to maximize the difference between the price the consumer is willing to pay and the price he actually pays	Subsidies to production until optimum level is reached (zero distribution cost)	Subsidies to production (private or public property, as the case may be)	Centralized control of production level (public property)
(2) Technological and economic monopolies: *Objective*: maximization of consumer welfare, limited to having the price marginally equal to the cost of production	Price controls, bilateral negotiations in labor market, and government arbitration; antimonopoly laws (Sherman Act), import of products and factors to compete with national products and factors	Price controls at a level that would cover costs of least efficient industries (citizens' property or public property, in some cases); restrictions on foreign investment; competitive imports limited by substitution processes	Centralized control of production level, its prices and reinvestment rates
(3) Productive processes in which the costs or benefits	Unilateral taxation of production and exchange market for	Regulation of conditions of production, taxes, and fines,	Direct accounting of costs and benefits in the originating

incurred are not fully reflected in the market prices (differences between private and social cost): *Objective*: maximization of consumer welfare; manage to have economic agents absorb or receive all the costs or benefits of their operation	property and production rights	in certain cases	industries
(4) Perfect competitive production: *Objective*: maximization of consumer welfare, price-setting freedom	Decentralized production and marketing decisions	Decentralized production and marketing decisions; public intervention in marketing	Decentralized production decisions (preferably cooperative or communal property)
(5) Exploitation of limited natural resources: *Objective*: long-term maximization of the difference between the costs and benefits of their exploitation	Taxes or subsidies to achieve optimum exploitation; private property	Taxes on production and subsidies to national producers; production concessions to specific social groups; public or private property	Centralized control of production; public property

SOURCE: Author.

on crops of greater economic density, backed by storage and refrigeration facilities, or on the development of agroindustry that would normalize the demand for their products and, more importantly, multiply their sales options. It should be noted that greater participation by women in the urban labor force should increase the demand for processed foods that originate from agroindustries. The process of integral development has many self-supporting elements, or elements that are mutually stimulating, to further its viability.

In order to direct development under conditions of social harmony, our efforts must be centered on the production of basic products that satisfy the vital needs of the population in general and elicit everyone's best effort on behalf of the present and future welfare of all. The Soviet Union and Japan proved that evolution without innovation is possible by applying well-known technology to production processes; improving, not substituting, current practices, based on their own resources; protecting their inherited economic, social, and cultural values.

Will Mexican cultural history be rich enough for us to stop imitating blindly and develop our own ideas? It might be appropriate at this point to quote a reflection by Luis Villoro, which, though stated in a different context, serves to illustrate our purpose:

> The new tendencies will not necessarily lead to a new phase of imitative and dependent culture. The discovery of our own peculiarity was legitimate enough to allow us to confront world culture with a personality of our own and without losing our unique perspective. This was the Revolution's greatest legacy to Intelligence: to allow the assimilation of universal culture without losing authenticity . . . . Maybe the next step in our spiritual history will consist of raising our cultural nationalism to the level of the problems and worries which are common to science and modern man. To raise, in the Hegelian double sense of transforming, while keeping that which is transformed at a higher level.[4]

In yet another sphere, but with the same pointedness, Octavio Paz has outlined the road to follow:

> Development and underdevelopment are exclusively socioeconomic concepts with which we pretend to measure societies as if they were quantitative realities. That way, all those aspects that defy statistics and give shape to society are not accounted for: its culture, its history, its sensibility, its art, its goals, its cuisine, everything that used to be called the soul or spirit of the people, its own way of being.[5]

It would be hard to find a better description of integral development by applying those concepts to the economic, political, and social spheres.

But how do we transfer these concepts to other areas of national life? By being attentive to what has been built over a long period of time, which has become better adapted with increasing age and is more worthy of respect. An example may help clarify this. If, instead of developing hybrid varieties of Iowa corn, we had genetically improved native seeds through open pollination, then we would have not only seeds better adapted to the microclimates of mountainous valleys but also better hybrid varieties developed from our own native ones.

In short, the formula is to reinforce our own linguistic, architectural, culinary, artistic, and communications traditions—in summary, an interaction evolving from the fusion of traditional values. Our starting point should be the environment around us, with the characteristics of a modern society that molds and determines its style of development, instead of allowing the style of development to define our way of life.

Final Considerations

Imitative development has been explained in various ways; I shall not elaborate on this. I think, however, that the imitative dependence with which I am here concerned pertains to conceptual dependence. As dependent as the popcorn consumer is the user of Marxist slogans or of pretended Friedmanite paradigms. Be it Keynesianism, monetarism, or whatever is in vogue, a distinction must be made between the application of a method of analysis and the adoption of a scale of values. These come as a package, and one must learn to dissociate them. Until now, we have seen a transfer of ideas motivated by the desire to achieve an industrial society that, like those in developed nations, is based on permanent innovation of production techniques and introduction of new consumer goods. Rules, though not always useful, can certainly be applied to societies where the important thing is the correction of deficiencies in aggregate demand to maintain full employment, but they are of doubtful legitimacy in societies with generalized underemployment and underqualified, overabundant work forces in depressing proportions.

We well know that a society has its origin deeply rooted in its history, culture, and tradition. Culture is an ambiguous and difficult concept to handle: it is produced by men of science and artists, people who are difficult to handle, as Ionesco tells us, complex, and often impossible to understand. Nonetheless, it should be synthesized, understood, and stimulated. We must find something to maintain its cohesiveness and introduce, respectfully, only those elements of change that can be assimilated. Culture is creation, change, evolution, revolution: only through it can we conceive progress.

Economic research has shown that the imitative pattern of development does not bring the fruits of progress to the lower-income groups, does not generalize well-being. The real income of the poor does not increase as a result of the impulse from the modernizing sector. This is achieved only in cases where there is a shortage of qualified manpower and a restructuring of the work force.

Clearly, consumerism and the need for innovation do not always strengthen society as a whole, but social demands can also operate in an inappropriate manner. To think of the working class as a class formed by members with common interests is valid as an analytical instrument only in a country where all manpower is scarce and is fully occupied, where the main problem is the share of the pie: capital versus labor. When the labor force is considerably underemployed, however, are the interests of the underemployed the same as those of the fully employed and organized? When the latter raise the price of their work, do they not decrease the possibility of access for the underemployed? Thus, it is difficult to overlook the thought that one application of integral development, in this respect, would imply a line of action that would protect the long-run rights and opportunities of the entire working force. That line of action should at least be geared to the defense of the rights of the work force in view of the abuses of property owners, but not at the expense of increased productivity or of the possibility of access for others.

I do not pretend—and I want to be clear about this—to suggest a philanthropic system with unilateral support. We should eliminate nepotism, develop a system of compensations, of nonmonetary rewards for personal effort that would help defray the social costs of integral development, instead of granting rewards only on the basis of personal consumption, material compensations, acquisition of property and control of the means of production—a system of rewards that would underline the importance of increasing productivity and extol creative ability. To demand more leisure is to adopt a form of consumerism similar to drinking more Coca-Cola. This same anachronism results when student groups pretend to block imperialism by hindering academic work and intellectual production. I am not asking for an abdication of ideology, only a sense of functionalism. What is the purpose of the federal highway patrol, and for what was it created? To guard highway safety and decrease the cost of operation for motorists and teamsters, or to be a system of bribes and increase those costs? An encyclopedia could be filled with the skewed intentions of bureaucracy. Their obligation is to facilitate citizens' activities, and we must see to it that bureaucrats regain consciousness of their function instead of dedicating themselves to the extraction of monetary or nonmonetary rents from their position. It is necessary to convince all citizens that development, along with all the sacrifices and benefits it implies, is everyone's business.

This means a change, full of obstacles and conflicts, in social conduct because production is not enough to satisfy the extravagant consumption of some and the basic requirements of others. As the real income of the elite or of the organized work force increases, without the support of productivity gains, the possibility of providing basic products to the lower-income groups decreases. Less and less remains of the communal background in which the fruits of production were shared in ways that preserved social harmony and cohesiveness. Thus, the general focus should find a balance among social groups, properly defined, in order to provide basic products to everyone and establish a system of incentives to stimulate behavior that will lead to success in the different aspects of life, that will propitiate social harmony and cohesiveness and elicit everyone's best effort, without allowing the benefit to some to act as a loss to others. This change should stimulate an intergenerational consciousness that would accept present sacrifices on behalf of future generations. If our efforts are geared in support of those who are less fortunate, if everyone does the best he can, if present decisions are made with future welfare in mind, we will be acting on behalf of a present and intergenerational balance that should be the main purpose of integral development. Finally, I would like to add that the style of social conduct I have attempted to outline in this essay is not a plan or even a strategy or a political economic recipe. It is simply a way of thinking.

Notes

Translated from the Spanish by Esther Bailey and republished with the permission of the author and the editors of *Vuelta*. The essay appeared originally in the September 1979 (Number 34) issue of *Vuelta*, pp. 21–28.

[1] Robert Skidelesky, "The Revolt against the Victorians," in *The End of the Keynesian Era*, ed., Robert Skidelesky (London: Macmillan, 1972), pp. 1–10.

[2] IMSS: Instituto Mexicano del Seguro Social. ISSTE: Instituto para la Seguridad Social de los Trabajadores del Estado. These are the two main social security institutions in Mexico.

[3] Las Truchas is a huge steel mill on the south coast of Mexico. When it started ten years ago, there was nothing there except coconut plantations.

[4] Luis Villoro, "La cultura mexicana de 1910 a 1960," *Historia Mexicana* (El Colegio de México, 1960), vol. 10.

[5] Octavio Paz, *El ogro filantrópico* (Mexico: Joaquin Mortiz, 1979), p. 126